Survival Strategies For Parenting Your ADD Child:

Dealing With Obsessions, Compulsions, Depression, Explosive Behavior and Rage

George T. Lynn, M.A., C.M.H.C.

Children with ADD can have severe and very challenging behavioral problems. Research has shown that some children are *born* difficult to parent. These kids may be unmanageable, have no friends, be full of rage, or take dangerous or destructive risks. They may carry any number of psychiatric labels: "ADD," "ADHD," "Tourette Syndrome," "Obsessive Compulsive," or "Depressed" and their extremely stressful behavior can destroy family unity.

In our society these children are frequently medicated or placed in mental hospitals. But this doesn't have to happen. Author and therapist George Lynn works with "difficult" kids in his practice and he has addressed these problems on *National Public Radio.* Writing from his experience as both a parent and a counselor, he provides parents with methods which can heal the fractures and pain that occur in families with these problems. He believes these "troubled" children are invariably gifted in unusual ways.

Lynn describes six essential strategies parents can use to deal with their own distress and rage as a result of a child's provocation. He also addresses the problems confronting single parents with ADD children.

$12.95, Trade paper, 284pp, ISBN 1-887424-19-9

Available at bookstores everywhere
Bulk discounts for ADD groups are available at (800) 788-3123

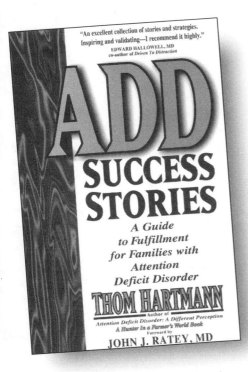

On the book cover:

"An excellent collection of stories and strategies. Inspiring and validating—I recommend it highly."
EDWARD HALLOWELL, MD
co-author of *Driven To Distraction*

ADD SUCCESS STORIES
A Guide to Fulfillment for Families with Attention Deficit Disorder

THOM HARTMANN
Author of *Attention Deficit Disorder: A Different Perception*
A *Hunter In a Farmer's World* Book
Foreword by JOHN J. RATEY, MD

ADD Success Stories

A Guide to Fulfillment for Families with Attention Deficit Disorder

Thom Hartmann

Foreword by John J. Ratey, M.D.

The first specific guidebook on how to be "successful in the world" as a teenager or adult with ADD.

ADD Success Stories is filled with real-life stories of people with Attention Deficit Disorder (ADD) who achieved success in school, at work, and in relationships. This book shows children and adults from all walks of life how to reach the "next step" — a fulfilling, successful life with ADD.

Read this book and discover

- which occupations are best for people with ADD
- how parents of ADD kids successfully juggle work and parenting
- how ADD students are thriving - from kindergarten to medical school
- how ADDers and their spouses can find happiness in their relationships

$11.95, Trade paper, 272pp, ISBN 1-887424-03-2

Available at bookstores everywhere or call (800) 233-9273 to order

Bulk discounts for ADD groups are available at (800) 788-3123

WOMEN WITH ATTENTION DEFICIT DISORDER

WOMEN WITH ATTENTION DEFICIT DISORDER

Embracing Disorganization at Home
and in the Workplace

by Sari Solden MS, MFCC

Introduction by
Kate Kelly and Peggy Ramundo

Foreword by
John J. Ratey, MD

Underwood Books
Grass Valley, California

I dedicate this book with gratitude and love to my husband, Dean, who ventures boldly each day into the eye of the hurricane, where together we find calm and peace in the center of the storm.

A Note to the Reader

I wanted to write this book ... because it became clear to me through my work as a therapist that there are many women who have been struggling with serious unexplained and often mysterious difficulties their entire lives. These women are leading lives filled with secrecy, shame, and a quiet desperation, unable to describe their difficulties to close friends, family or even mental health professionals in a way that could lead to self-understanding. Many of these women have been going through life confused and foggy, unable to access their considerable strengths. They experience their lives as a continuous treadmill, and express feelings of being trapped, unable to make sense of their lives.

I wrote this book because I've watched these women cross a line at some point and see their lives begin to shift. I want to let other women know that I've seen women with these kinds of difficulties learn how to move ahead and begin to take back their lives.

I know that other women also can embark on this same emotional journey, learning to embrace their lives in a new and powerful way.

CONTENTS

FOREWORD

by John J. Ratey, M.D.

Current developments in cognitive science are enabling researchers to uncover the many secrets of the brain. Techniques such as neuroimaging allow us to observe, measure and analyze brain activity as it occurs, leading us closer and closer to an understanding of the brain's tremendous complexity. For many individuals, however, the excitement of this progress is accompanied by the threat that ultimately everything will be defined in terms of matter, and the more ethereal category of the human spirit will no longer be acceptable.

Most recently, neurological discoveries have been complemented by advances in genetics. Yet this advancement is met with resistance as well as by those who oppose the idea that we may be controlled by the past or defined in any way by our genetic destiny. To many, this idea seems to invalidate the core of our very existence, namely, the quest to achieve our own individuality. If even our most subtle characteristics were determined by our genetic history, this achievement would be impossible. What we are beginning to learn, however, is that genetic guidance is exceedingly sensitive to the environment. In fact, neuroscientists, along with others who are delving into the mysteries of human consciousness, emphasize that individuality is apparent throughout the brain. This variation is, for the most part, due to each individual's unique experience of the world. We are learning that everything counts, that everything we experience impacts brain development. While the brain remains susceptible to environmental influences throughout life, the greatest impact occurs in utero, during the first stages of existence.

11

Of particular interest is the role of hormones in the development of the brain, especially in regard to gender differences.

It is now a commonly accepted fact that men's and women's brains differ as a result of exposure to different hormonal environments in the womb. This difference does not imply that one environment is preferable to the other, but simply that they each produce unique effects. After birth, the brain continues to develop and is constantly reorganized through the experience of the environment, especially that of the interpersonal and social milieu. Thus, along with the furious pace at which we are gaining knowledge about the brain and genetics, we are also reconfirming scientifically the belief that the social environment contributes a great deal to the development of the brain and the mind.

For example, these social influences may cause a genetic condition such as Attention Deficit Disorder to be expressed quite differently even among members of the same family. By examining this interplay between genetics and environment, Sari Solden has broken new ground in *Women With Attention Deficit Disorder: Embracing Disorganization at Home and in the Workplace*, a book that follows the dictate of Dr. William Osler, who stated: "Ask not what disease the person has, but rather what person has the disease." On both a personal and professional level, Solden explores just how women deal with the neurologic difference that is ADD. She at once narrows our perspective and broadens our understanding by revealing how the genetic composition of this disorder is manifested in women. Until recently, most disorders had been considered only from a limited perspective, one that explained how the condition was expressed in men. When data was presented regarding both sexes, gender differences at the level of genetics and development were rarely, if ever, reported. In examining the gender differences of ADD, not only hormonal but social influences are important as well, especially as this disorder is often subtle and hidden from view.

For a woman, the ADD traits of impulsivity, carelessness, forgetfulness, changeability and procrastination extend far beyond the environment of work or school to include every aspect of her life. They exist at the very core of a woman's expectations of herself and of society's expectations of her as well. The expectation that she will be the rock, the dependable, steady force in every situation causes her to be much more susceptible to the confining and crippling emotion of shame. This dynamic acts subtly, yet is extremely persuasive and often inhibits the growth from every direction of a woman who has ADD. *In Women With Attention Deficit Disorder*, Sari presents us with a number of meaningful anecdotes and a wealth of invaluable clinical lore. Her work represents one of the first attempts to broaden our perspective by focusing the experience of this genetic disorder on that of women alone. She provides us with a crucial understanding of a woman's experience of ADD within a complicated social matrix.

John J. Ratey, M.D. is the co-author (with Ned Hallowell, M.D.) of the best-selling books on ADD-*Driven to Distraction* and *Answers to Distraction.* He is assistant professor of psychiatry at Harvard Medical School and is a psychiatrist in private practice in Cambridge, Massachusetts where he treats adults with ADHD. He has published numerous scientific papers on aggression and psychopharmacology and ADHD in adults.

INTRODUCTION

by Peggy Ramundo and Kate Kelly

Dear Readers,

When Sari sent us her completed manuscript for review, we were honored and delighted that she had asked us to write an introduction to this important new book.

When we began writing *You Mean I'm Not Lazy, Stupid or Crazy?!*, there were no books available written specifically for ADD adults. Because there was so little written information out there, we felt compelled to attempt the impossible—to create an encyclopedia of ADD!

With such a huge task in front of us, the writing process seemed to go on endlessly. But we did manage to complete the book after more than two years of effort. The book was not finished as quickly as Kate would have liked, nor did it fit Peggy's idea of perfection.

However, we managed to produce a fairly comprehensive self-help guide for ADD adults. Still, we knew that there was so much we had yet to learn about ADD and so much that we didn't have time or space to address.

Although we are women with ADD, we did not address women's issues in any depth in our book.

Sari has used her personal and professional experience to shine some light into the dark closet inhabited by far too many ADD women. A closet of shame and despair and invisibility.

Women's voices have not been heard loudly enough in the world of ADD, reflecting women's situation in society at large.

We do not intend to dishonor the valuable contributions made by men to the field of Attention Deficit Disorder. But we feel that understanding of ADD has been hampered and dominated by a tendency to rely too heavily on objective means of viewing it.

As Belenky et. al (1986) found in their massive study of women's intellectual development, experiential and subjective learning is an important step in women's developmental process. In comparable studies with male subjects, the subjective piece was noticeably lacking.

ADD is a complicated disorder that does not fit neatly into the usual diagnostic boxes. Trying to describe it in terms of the three classic symptoms of hyperactivity, impulsivity and inattention gives us a one-sided and overly simplistic view of the problems faced by persons with ADD.

Too much of the available literature is written from the standpoint of the ADD expert looking at the disorder from the outside.

And the view from the outside tells only part of the story. ADD is a subtle handicap that can impact in ways we are just beginning to understand.

When we were first exploring the impact of ADD on our own lives, there was almost nothing known about ADD in adults. We had to read the child literature and extrapolate mainly from accounts of hyperactive boys. It was a starting point, but it did little in terms of helping us to make sense of our experience as ADD women.

We found that the personal stories of other ADD adults provided the missing puzzle piece that made a more complete picture of our own lives and struggles.

Sari has taken this perspective a step further in her book. She empowers ADD women by validating their experience as worthwhile human beings who struggle with serious organizational problems in many areas of their lives. She illuminates the heavy burden placed on the shoulders of ADD women, who face additional demands for organizational skills by gender role expectations imposed by our culture.

Girls and women with ADD have been socialized to suffer their problems in silence. Or at least in a quieter version than that of the classic picture presented by ADHD boys and men. Hyperactive girls learn to either inhibit their behavior to an unnatural degree or suffer the consequences of being labeled as unfeminine. And those who have ADD without hyperactivity fade into the background.

The problems of ADD women are often trivialized or dismissed. Because they are hidden, locked up in a closet of shame.

Do not be misled by the title of this book. It is not merely another self-help book on how to get organized. There are practical suggestions for dealing with the concrete messes of women's lives, but the heart of the book deals with the much larger issue of the impact of chronic disorganization of all facets of life.

The "messy closet" is a metaphor for a brain that is locked up and hidden because its owner is overwhelmed by the chaos of too many expectations and the inability to sort and prioritize them.

By sharing her personal experiences and those of her clients, Sari will help countless women begin to acknowledge and wrestle with the crippling shame that prevents their emergence from that dark closet.

Peggy Ramundo and Kate Kelly

Kate Kelly and Peggy Ramundo are the co-authors of the comprehensive book about ADD in adults, *You Mean I'm Not Lazy, Stupid, or Crazy?!* Kate is a masters level prepared clinical specialist in psychiatric nursing and is on the board of directors of ADDA, the National Attention Deficit Disorder Association. Peggy, whose post graduate work is in learning disabilities and behavior disorders, is a member of the ADDA board and the founder of the National Institute for ADD.

Reference: Belenky, M.F., Clinchy, B.M., Goldberger, N.R. & Tarule, J.M. (1986) Women's ways of knowing. New York: Basic Books

Introductory Section

AUTHOR'S PREFACE

Why a Book About ADD and Women?

There are many women who have an extremely difficult time organizing themselves in their daily lives. They feel overwhelmed, perhaps depressed, anxious, and may have been struggling with relationships and underachievement all their lives. Some of these women have ADHD, Attention Deficit Disorder *with* hyperactivity. They fit the stereotyped notion of what most people (even mental health professionals) think that ADD is: fast-talking, hyperactive, non-attentive, bouncing-off-the-wall people. Many more women, however, have ADD *without* hyperactivity. Because they don't fit the more common notion of what ADD is, they have never considered ADD as a way to explain their difficulties.

Until recently, the standard quoted ratio varied from six-to-one to ten-to-one of ADD boys to girls. Most experts today, however, say that this is because these studies do not include the quiet, non-hyperactive child. Kate Kelly and Peggy Ramundo say in *You Mean I'm Not Lazy, Stupid or Crazy?!* that if you count girls without hyperactivity, the corresponding ratios approach one to one. Dr. Daniel Amen says in *Windows into the ADD Mind* that "girls are overlooked, and that this huge underdiagnosis would, if corrected, even out the statistics that regularly report so much larger an occurrence in boys." Dr. Larry Silver, author of *The Misunderstood Child*, also agrees that the ratio of girls to boys with ADD is probably much closer to equal because girls who are doing poorly in school are more likely to be withdrawn and quiet, thus appearing disinterested or depressed instead of ADD.

Four reasons why I focus on ADD *without* hyperactivity in girls:

1. ADD *without* is the least talked about form of ADD.

2. ADD *without* is the most common form of ADD in girls.

3. People who have ADD *without* go undiagnosed the longest.

4. Those who have gone undiagnosed the longest often have the most serious consequences.

Much of what I say about girls' ADD *without hyperactivity* applies to girls with hyperactivity as well. Although there is much overlap between girls and even boys in the childhood characteristics of ADD without hyperactivity, the struggles they face in adulthood are much different. We will explore these in depth throughout the book.

Perspective

The perspective from which I write this book is threefold: First, as a psychotherapist trained especially in the impact of life experiences on relationships, interpersonal difficulties, and self-concept. The book is based on six years of clinical observation and work with ADD adults, with a focus on the special challenges facing women. Secondly, as a woman with ADD, I observed my own *personal* process as I began to understand what it means to live successfully in this culture. Thirdly, the book drew from all the talks and meetings I've had with women across the country who have shared their feelings about ADD, disorganization, and how it affects their lives. Integrated with all this are the wonderful writings of many experts as well as the currently available literature on ADD diagnosis and treatment.

The Scope and Focus of This Book

There is great diversity in this thing we call ADD, from those hyperactive to hypo-active, from obviously impulsive individuals to those more shy and withdrawn. There are men with ADD, women with ADD, those who have been diagnosed since childhood, and those just diagnosed in mid-life. There are those with ADD who are well-educated, who have work and relationships they enjoy, and those less fortunate, who are struggling just to get by. I do not attempt to speak to all the faces of ADD or all the elements in ADD, especially the medical and neuro-psychological aspects. While I will touch on the biological issues that impact women, such as PMS, pregnancy and menopause, my perspective as a psychotherapist is to trace the emotional journey that women with ADD embark on as they try to understand their experience.

There have been many fine books written, virtual textbooks, which address a wide and diverse ADD population, their subject matter covering diagnosis, testing, medication, and treatment for both children and adults. These are listed in the resource section at the back of the book. Although much of what I address *will* be helpful to all adults with ADD, the focus will be on three areas that have been previously under-emphasized: *Women with ADD, ADD without hyperactivity, and Disorganization.*

This book should also be very helpful to partners of adults with ADD, both in terms of understanding their partner, as well as exploring their own struggles in dealing with an ADD partner. Finally, this material should also be of assistance to mental health professionals, coaches and counselors who want to intervene in helpful ways with women who struggle to live successfully with ADD.

A Disorder of Dis-Order

Besides the women who already suspect they might have ADD, there are countless women who struggle with serious organizational problems, having no idea that something neurobiological could be at the root of their difficulties. A few years ago I read an article about women who formed a self-help group for "disorganized women." They meet in private to protect their anonymity and describe themselves as "self-confessed slobs." Ever since then, it became very important to me to try to reach these kinds of women, to help them understand that, in the absence of any serious mental disorders, there may be another explanation for severe disorganization.

Because this has been under-addressed issue, I felt there was a need for a book on ADD that focused on disorganization as a major source of difficulty of ADD individuals. The whole experience of living with ADD is one of disorganization—both internally as well as externally. It includes not only environmental disorganization, such as a messy house, office, or stacks of unpaid bills, but also an inner experience of disorganization. The cognitive and emotional experience of not being able to "hold things together" is disorganization on another level.

Disorganization is especially significant for women, who are often expected to "hold things together." Therefore, my primary emphasis in this book is to show that: *the symptom of disorganization is a major reason women cannot meet the cultural expectations of society. Not meeting these expectations is a leading cause of the secondary effects of ADD, such as underachievement, depression, and interpersonal difficulties.*

To illustrate my points, I've used material drawn from my clients as well as interviews with other women with ADD. Most of the examples are in the form of composites, which are representative of actual stories that many women with ADD have shared with me. Other examples are true stories from specific clients who have given me permission to share their experience with the reader. Of course, I have changed the names and other identifiable information for the purpose of protecting their privacy.

In addition, I've created two fictional characters named Jodi and

Lucy. I use this technique in order to provide certain information in a more narrative and interesting form.

Overview

Women with Attention Deficit Disorder includes a "Pocket Guide to ADD," which lays out the basic concepts for those not familiar with ADD, and also for easy reference throughout the book. PART I: *SURVIVING* starts out with my personal and professional ADD story, explaining the beliefs I have come to hold regarding living successfully with ADD as a woman. I then trace the development of a little girl, in order to examine the effects of being undiagnosed at various stages of her life. I'll help the reader understand the challenges and struggles she will face as adult before diagnosis. In PART II: *HIDING* we go beyond the primary ADD symptoms and explore the collision between these symptoms and the cultural expectations placed on women. We will then begin to understand the emotional legacy of "shame" that often results from this life experience. We will also examine the complex and painful "secondary effects" an ADD woman may experience, such as underachievement, depression, and relationship difficulties.

In PART III: *EMERGING* I present an overview of diagnosis and treatment issues especially for women. We'll explore the ease with which women are overpathologized and misdiagnosed. We will travel the variety of roads one might take on the way to understanding their ADD and/or disorganization, and we'll discuss the tools they will need to start this journey, such as moving through the ADD grief cycle. I will outline the MESST model of treatment I have devised, plus a new screening tool designed especially for women.

Finally, PART IV: *EMBRACING* focuses on the essential "three R's" required for anyone to live successfully with ADD, but specifically for a woman: restructuring her life, renegotiating her relationships, and redefining her self-image. Doing these things allows a woman at some point to embrace her ADD. She crosses a certain line where she is able to become pro-active, in order to access the help that she needs. This in turn leads then to a new "cycle of success" where she can begin to thrive instead of just survive.

A Pocket Guide to ADD

This section can be used for important information about ADD before reading the rest of the book. It is useful for people who are not familiar with ADD and can also be consulted as a handy reference throughout the book.

ADD is not ...
Most people start out by telling you what ADD is. I'd like to start out by telling you what ADD is not. Because so many people who don't fit the common picture of ADD rule themselves out prematurely, it is important to clear up the misconceptions and stereotypes that surround ADD.

ADD is:
not just for kids
not just for boys
not just about being hyperactive
not about a "deficit of attention"
not about being irresponsible or having a character flaw

ADD is ...
a neurochemical disorder (not a psychological one) that affects three areas of people's behavior in various ways—their **attention** level, their **activity** level, and their **impulsivity** level. You can only be diagnosed with ADD if these behaviors are **chronic** (meaning you have had them a long time) and **severe** (impacting your life negatively in serious ways, more so than other people).

It is extremely important to understand that while ADD is a serious disorder, it is not characterological or psychological, but neurobiological. **Neurobiological or neurochemical means it's not your fault**, and it means it's the way your individual brain works. It does not mean you have brain damage.

While no one knows *exactly* what causes ADD, it is commonly thought of as being genetically transmitted. You are born this way and there are probably others in your family who either have or have had these difficulties. There also is the possibility that one could have ADD

24

symptoms as a result of or as part of an injury, illness, or a learning disability.

The Information Highway in Your Head

Most people agree that ADD is a result of the inefficiency and inconsistency of the *chemical information transmission system* in the brain. The brain itself is fine. There is no damage, and actually ADD people can be (and usually are) quite bright. It is just that these chemical messengers, called neurotransmitters, sending information to and from the different parts of your brain, are for some reason not firing consistently or efficiently. This causes the kind of inconsistent and unregulated behaviors mentioned previously. It's logical that if the regulators weren't firing properly in the part of your brain that regulates **attention, activity level, and impulsivity**, these areas of behavior would also be inconsistent.

I liken this neurotransmitter inconsistency to problems you may experience with your computer. Even if you have the most expensive, well-built computer, with the ability to process and store great amounts of information, your desktop can get too full, or something can go wrong with the operating system. Or your computer could have great long-term information storage capability but very little or inadequate operating capability to match. Those of us who use computers have all experienced the frustration when an error message suddenly appears without warning: the screen freezes, and the system crashes. In a sense, this is what ADD is like, not being able to use the potential of the fine tool that is there.

The inefficient and irregular transmission of information in the brain causes a host of unique difficulties in each person affected. The huge number of variations and limitless possibilities of combinations that exist in these chemical connections makes what we now call ADD so confusing to understand. It is a difficult definition for many to accept, especially because the symptoms manifest so differently in each person. ADD even looks different in the same person at various times.

Promising new technologies are beginning to allow us to actually see the brain processes, and we are getting closer to a true understanding. One of the leading scientific discoveries has been made by Dr. Alan Zametkin, at the National Institute of Mental Health. Through the use of PET (Positron Emission Tomography) scans, special brain-imaging techniques, he has been able to measure and document the glucose metabolic process in individuals. These tests show fairly conclusively that during tasks that require concentration, the brains of individuals with ADD have a markedly lower level of brain activity in these areas as compared with those without ADD.

There is no clear agreement on the exact process by which ADD symptoms are produced in the brain. However, because the medications that we know affect specific processes in the brain work so well in the reduction of ADD symptoms, researchers surmise that the brain chemicals these medications affect are the ones involved in the creation of ADD symptoms. With the promise of these new brain imaging techniques, in the future we will better understand the great variations in human brains.

For a more in-depth discussion of the neurobiology of ADD I refer you to, in addition to the resources listed in the back of the book, the following excellent materials. Chapter nine in *Driven to Distraction*, (Hallowell and Ratey) is an excellent source as is Chapter two by Patricia Quinn in Dr. Kathleen Nadeau's *A Comprehensive Guide to Attention Deficit Disorder in Adults*. For a layman's discussion that provides a good overview, look at pages 17-20 of Kate Kelly and Peggy Ramundo's book *You Mean I'm Not Lazy, Stupid or Crazy?!*

The Many Faces of ADD

For many years, when people thought of ADD, the picture that came to mind was of a hyperactive, troublemaking little boy, running around causing a lot of problems. In reality ADD is much more diverse than this and has many more dimensions than this common stereotyped picture.

The stereotype described above developed when ADD became synonymous with these overt behaviors: not being able to pay attention, having an overactive activity level, and impulsively acting out. These disruptive behaviors were impossible to miss.

We used to believe that children with these behaviors outgrew their ADD when they became adults. What we eventually learned was that a large percentage of them continued to struggle as adults. What really diminished for many adults, was not their ADD, but their hyperactivity. Even though their difficulties were often less visible as adults, their disregulated attentional system caused them just as many perplexing and frustrating problems. In addition, only recently has the public started to become aware that there is another entire group of adults with ADD who never were hyperactive. These people, largely consisting of women, continue to be underidentified in childhood, and often remain undiagnosed as adults.

There are two main types of ADD.

1. *ADD with hyperactivity* (ADHD). Those with ADHD are the speedy, hyper, bounce-off-the-wall people.

2. *ADD without hyperactivity*, (ADD w/o). This is more the focus of this book. These individuals can be dreamy, work slowly, move slowly, and be underactive. To confuse matters further, when we refer to both groups, since they share many similar symptoms and experiences, it is common to call them both ADD.

Here is a more detailed version of what ADD is and what ADD is not.

ADD does not = a Deficit of *Attention*
instead it means
Attention Irregularity and Inconsistency.
This includes difficulties with:
distractibility, excessive shifting of attention,
activating, deploying, and directing one's attention,
containing and maintaining one's attention,
screening out unimportant matters from one's attention,
and
contrary to the meaning of deficit, ...

There are many positives with ADD, including a surplus of ideas, creativity, excitement, and interest which accompany this kind of mind.

ADD does not = *Hyperactivity*
Instead it means a Dis-regulation of activity and arousal levels,
extremes of activity levels from high to low,
from hyperactive to "hypoactive," or what I call
overly underactive.

ADD does not = *Impulsive Troublemaking*
instead it can be
a quieter, less obvious kind of impulsivity,
with excessive shifting of tasks or life directions.

What we call ADD is often confusing because ADD looks and feels so different for each person. ADD *without* appears differently on the outside from the more commonly understood and more easily seen ADHD. It also feels very different on the inside. It is not a mild case of ADD, however. Both forms of ADD share the same core difficulties but are experienced and expressed in various ways, with different effects in one's life. They are just as extreme, but at opposite ends of the ADD spectrum. The important thing to remember is that none of us has perfect control of our attention, regulation of our activity, or impulses. However, as you can see from the following spectrum, ADD is defined by symptoms that are extreme, chronic, and severe.

ADD SPECTRUM
Average Range

ADD w/o	ADHD
(ADD without hyperactivity)	(ADD with hyperactivity)

ATTENTION

Daydreamy	Highly distracted
Lost in inner world	by outer stimulation
Does one thing at time	Does many things at once

ACTIVITY LEVEL

Hypo-active	Hyperactive
Works, thinks slowly	Rushes through work
Can't start moving	Can't stop moving

IMPULSIVITY

Quiet excessive impulsive shifting	Acting out impulses
of activities, life directions	without pre-thinking

Can you have these symptoms and not have ADD? Yes.

Not everyone who has these symptoms we have been talking about has ADD. There can be other reasons some of these symptoms occur.

1. You can look like this _some of the time_ and _not_ have ADD.

If you have just experienced a major change in your life such as a divorce, a move, or loss of a job, or you are under great deal of stress, you may become very disorganized, depressed, or feel bad about yourself *for a while*. To have ADD these symptoms must be there *most of the time* and *must have been there for a long time.*

2. You can have all these difficulties all the time, a little without much of an impact in your life and _not_ have ADD.

"I lose my keys too. You should see my closets, I procrastinate." This may be somewhat of a problem, but if it's not severe enough to be the problem causing tremendous difficulty in all important areas of life, then it isn't ADD.

3. Okay, let's say you have these problems to a _severe_ level and you have had them as long as you can remember (_chronic_) and even if they weren't very visible they had great impact. Does this mean you have ADD? Not necessarily!

These are necessary conditions we've talked about but these alone are not sufficient for a diagnosis of ADD. There are other elements that must be ruled out. First, other kinds of neurological, psychological, and physical disorders that can account for the same kinds of symptoms we have mentioned must be ruled out or considered. In addition, the individual's difficulties must not have been caused solely by family or environmental reasons, such as growing up with a chaotic family life, for example, in an abusive home, with a mentally ill parent, or in an alcoholic family. Sometimes, these situations can account for these ADD-like symptoms. You can have severe ADD symptoms since child-hood and still not be ADD if they can be accounted for fully and better by something that happened growing up. What takes expert diagnosis is that a person can have had these family backgrounds *and also have ADD*; or that your parent's difficulties could have been a result of *their undiagnosed ADD*.

Because of this possibility and the above reasons it is especially important to get a diagnosis by a mental health professional who understands ADD (with and without), as well as other conditions that look like ADD.

The Impact On Lives

What we have just looked at are the three core symptoms of ADD and the many variations in which they present themselves. The conditions you might actually see as a result of these symptoms in the lives of adults with ADD are:
- Disorganization
- Emotional Reactivity
- Under-Achievement
- Low Self-Esteem
- Impaired Relationships
- Depression

People with ADD have difficulty screening out unneeded information. Individuals without this problem block out internal and external distractions naturally when they are not relevant, without effort or thought. ADD individuals, though, operate with their gates wide open. They can't filter out distractions easily, therefore becoming flooded, bombarded, assaulted and overwhelmed.

It is easy to see how an individual living like this would be *emotionally reactive*. It is also easy to see how this kind of shifting attention could lead to severe *disorganization,* and contribute to feelings of being out of control, and an inner sense of feeling that things are beginning to fall apart. This can easily affect *relationships,* choice of partners, and deeply affect *self-esteem.* These feelings can lead to a growing sense of desperation, hopelessness and *depression,* making it difficult to stay on track or pursue meaningful goals. This then could lead to the *underachievement* of the individual, causing a person to be emotionally reactive once more, and begin this negative cycle over again.

Basic Treatment

The cornerstone of treatment for ADD is medication, usually stimulant medication, most often Ritalin. Medication is thought to improve the transmission of messages in the brain through the neurotransmitters. While medication has proven very effective in reducing many of the primary symptoms of ADD, it is just the first step. Education, support, strategies, and coaching should be added. Counseling can also be extremely helpful in addressing how people think about their ADD, and what they think about themselves.

The Buried Treasure

Millions of people have this neurobiological condition. When undiagnosed it can be devastating and debilitating, silently robbing the individual of their dreams, their hopes, their self-esteem. These people spend their lives trying to solve a riddle— the mystery of their lives must lay somewhere out there, just around the next turn in the road. They remember that they have glimpsed it, that special something once felt or envisioned, before things got so overwhelming and they became trapped and lost—wandering aimlessly in a forest looking for clues as if from an old treasure map. They know the treasure is there somewhere, but perhaps deeply buried or locked behind a fortress. They have incredible perseverance and determination to keep going, often pulling an enormous weight. The remembrance of that special feeling, the knowledge, deep inside, that they have something important of value to do, to create, to contribute, keeps them searching. They continue on, though the memory, that belief, grows more faint each year as despair begins to replace hope. Hope that they will ever find the treasure, that they will even find their way out of the forest and back to the road.

Still, they trudge on, clutching that old, crumpled, faded map, holding on to the hope they will find that buried treasure chest and reclaim their abandoned hopes and lost dreams.

PART I

SURVIVING

CHAPTER ONE

Coming Out of the (Messy) Closet

Introduction to My Personal and Professional Story

It wasn't until I went to my first Adult ADD Conference where I spent three days under the same roof with hundreds of other adults with ADD, that I developed the concept of "being in the closet" as applied to individuals with invisible disorders. It wasn't until I saw hundreds of people not in the closet, being themselves in front of others for the first time, that I realized how much time and energy is spent hiding, pretending, and carefully monitoring one's behavior. I especially enjoyed seeing women tearing through oversized, over-stuffed purses, hunting furiously for something they needed and couldn't find, but without the usual embarrassment or self-consciousness. I stood in delighted wonder as I watched them throw things on the floor in search of that certain piece of paper or phone number they couldn't find, scribbling on their hands when they couldn't find a piece of paper, talking fast, interrupting, laughing—finally finding people who could keep up with them. Sure, there were angry feelings and frustration when things didn't go smoothly, but the picture of adults with ADD being themselves, obviously bright and interested but often confused or disoriented, warm, exciting, even though struggling, brought home to me in a vivid way the extent to which these invisible disorders are hidden in everyday life. How much time these folks spend hiding, pretending, or just plain controlling their symptoms to present themselves well, to pass as "normal."

Even though *I* had been diagnosed and was on medication at the time, not many of my family, friends, or people at work were aware of my "secret." I knew I was living in two worlds—my ADD world and my so-called "straight" world. Although for years I had been talking to other women and clients about the concept of shame, I didn't even realize the extent of *my own* shame until the following incident. I was scheduled to deliver a speech about women and ADD, when a flyer announcing the speech (prepared by the sponsoring organization) was sent out all over town, including to my colleagues, associates and friends. In describing the speech, the flyer announced that I would discuss my *personal* experiences with this condition, and that my husband would comment on life with an ADD woman. There it was. I was "outed." I was mortified and ashamed. I felt as if it had been just announced to the world that I was some kind of awful criminal. I wasn't aware until that moment that I, too, was still so affected by these deeply embedded feelings of shame.

I'd like now to take you back to before that pivotal moment in my life, and trace my personal and professional ADD story, which led to the writing of this book.

I was working at a large counseling agency as a therapist, seeing adult clients in the general population for issues such as relationships, depression, anxiety, and self-esteem. At the same time, I was fortunate to be part of an unusual project within this agency that also served adults with "invisible" disorders, such as learning disabilities and Attention Deficit Disorder. It soon became clear to me that there was a major difference between these two groups of clients.

The very thing that caused the most pain and severely impacted the lives of the adults with hidden disorders, the core of what was discussed week after week during the therapy hour, was very different from my other group of clients without these invisible disorders.

What ADD individuals talked about in therapy was the confusion and frustration of ordinary daily life. This is what their pain was centered directly on. The difficulty they had in organizing themselves in life was monumental compared to people without these kinds of disorders. By the time they reached mid-life, they described it as a kind of desperation born of not being able to achieve what they had originally planned to do. The double whammy seemed to be that coupled with this severe disorganization, they often felt they had "thousands" of exciting ideas started, but laying in rubble, unfinished in their rooms, taunting and haunting them. And even when the ADD clients were struggling with relationships and depression, these difficulties were often the *result* of the underlying disorder.

These people were not alike in their behavior. Some were impulsive—getting in trouble, blurting out words, interrupting others, reacting too quickly, getting angry at the wrong times. Others were withdrawn, very shy, not causing problems at all. Some couldn't get off the couch, couldn't direct their energy from an idea to take action, couldn't mobilize themselves. At the other extreme, some people couldn't *stop* moving, they were driven, and needed to do ten things at once to stay alert and focused. There were those who sought out very high stimulation, while others conversely felt bombarded by any stimulation, and could only do one thing at a time in a very controlled, quiet environment.

From the outside, the personalities of these individuals didn't resemble each other. In many cases, no one could tell them apart from people without these particular kinds of problems. But during the therapy hour, they all described the same kind of pain and told the same story in one form or another. They told tales of unusual twists and turns in their career paths and life directions. They talked about the difficulty of working for large organizations with their inherent paperwork and details; many wanted to be independent and on their own, but were vulnerable to falling into an abyss of emptiness without any structure at all. Most of them felt trapped, and blamed themselves. Most of them, by the time they were adults (especially if not diagnosed early on), had some deeply-embedded notion that a character defect or fatal flaw was at the source of their problems. And even *after* they were diagnosed and treated, they still often berated themselves with words like "irresponsible, lazy, unmotivated, slob, failure." Even *after* they were on medication, and had some idea that a neurobiological condition was at the root of these difficulties, they still were unable to automatically wipe away the years of low self-esteem and feelings of failure.

In the same way that I could clearly see the difference between the ADD and non-ADD groups, I also started to notice in my clinical work significant differences between men with ADD, and women with ADD. This was in terms of both the special challenges they faced in living successfully after diagnosis, and in accessing the help they needed to rebuild and restructure their lives. The patterns that women reported were similar to each other, especially regarding their level of difficulty in taking certain kinds of actions to help them restructure their lives. I began to look at these attitudes as somehow being culturally transmitted. The struggles around cultural expectations seemed to go beyond individual psychology. There seemed to be some unique vulnerability that these women face, that make learning to live with these kinds of difficulties a very special challenge.

Men with ADD certainly face their own painful difficulties in this culture, such as expectations to be a stable provider, the successful "breadwinner," and a strong solid force in the family. But it seemed women faced a whole host of other problems. Observing and understanding these other difficulties became very important in my learning how to help women move through a successful course of treatment. I was able to see that on one hand, the women were very motivated to help themselves. On the other hand, at the moment of trying to ask for an accommodation, at school, or at home, these women froze. They couldn't go any further. At school, they might want to ask for more time on an assignment, or at work, want to request to move to a quieter area, or at home, desire help with the piles and clutter.

But they hit a wall of shame, guilt or embarrassment so strong that this needed to be understood and worked through first, before going on to employ the strategies so often suggested for organizational difficulties.

These internal barriers, as much as the ADD symptoms, impacted the women in a different way from the men, keeping them locked on a treadmill until they were depleted and overwhelmed, continuing to feel like failures even after diagnosis. I watched as these women struggled to overcome these barriers, becoming pro-active, and begin to take control of their lives. It was an exciting process to witness these women slowly come to life. It was as if they had opened a door and started to walk into life again, in quiet but dramatic ways. They didn't begin to live stress-free; they didn't turn into perfectly organized or different kinds of women; but they began to be able to access help, to repair feelings of low self-esteem and to get their lives back on track.

Personal Discovery

At the same time I was engaged in counseling these clients—reading, attending conferences, digging in the literature to understand all I could about ADD, I began to see references to adults with severe organizational problems and that Ritalin was suggested for them just as it was for children. I began to wonder more and more if some of the difficulties I had experienced my entire life could have something to do with ADD. I certainly had done well in school and certainly never had any behavior problems, yet still ...

I had at that time (and all my life) a little room in one part of the house in which I spent each night and weekend, trying in vain to "get organized." I had no idea that other people weren't spending each weekend as a bridge between Friday and Monday, trying frantically to dig their way out of the "rubble" before Monday arrived again. As I began to understand ADD, I began to notice small things; for example, I heard other people making plans to go to the park on the weekend, or to a concert. To me, it was like hearing people from another planet. Each Friday at the agency where I was working, my friend and colleague, Lisa, would ask me, "What are you doing this weekend?" I would say, "I'm getting organized." After a few months of hearing this response, Lisa finally said to me, "Oh, you must be working on a major project!" And I said, "No, I'm just getting organized."

It started to dawn on me that others weren't living the same way, but I had no idea how they did it. I started watching Lisa as she went through her work day. She had a very large loose-leaf notebook, with multi-colored, labeled dividers. What seemed to me thousands of pieces of paper put in our boxes each day at the agency would wind up perfectly divided into their proper sections of Lisa's notebook. What amazed me even more was that she seemed to accomplish this effort-lessly, with very little extra thought or energy expended. She had virtu-ally nothing to bring home with her each day. I watched as she sat every day in the busy, noisy staffroom, writing her notes as she chatted with the other women. This was absolutely unfathomable to me, as the many distractions in the room made it impossible for me to concentrate on even the simplest tasks, let alone my work.

I, on the other hand, behind closed doors, locked in a little office, spent a great deal of time trying to organize all those pieces of informa-tion. But first I had to move the ticking clock in the room, and stuff it into a drawer to muffle the sound. Then I had to close the windows and turn up the fan, to block out any extraneous sounds.

Invariably, at the end of each day, still unorganized, I would stuff all my papers into my briefcase and take them home. I would put them with the other accumulated *stuff* in that little room downstairs, and spend the evening, trying again in vain to organize them. It's not hard to see that I was rapidly becoming buried. At the same time, no one at the agency had any idea what I was coping with, and I certainly wasn't about to risk their favorable opinion of me by letting them in on my embarrass-ing lack of organizational ability.

It seemed that the dilemma I faced up to that point in my life was that I could either *not* achieve up to my potential, thereby staying somewhat organized, or I could continue to achieve but get overloaded and buried, eventually hitting an organizational wall so hard that I would have to change course. As I looked back over the years, I realized that every major decision up until then, every move I had made in my career, relationships or geography, were based not on my true interests or abilities, but on my inability to cope with organizational demands after they increased to a certain level.

Through more research and my growing understanding, I was eventually able to get diagnosed and treated. Since that point, I've carefully observed my life and my process as I've continued to learn to live successfully as a woman with Attention Deficit Disorder.

Living Successfully as a Woman with ADD

I said I've learned to live *successfully* with ADD as a woman. The definition of the word successful is very important, because women very often get locked into a fruitless search for an unachievable goal. When I say I'm living successfully, it doesn't mean that I'm living stress-free. It doesn't mean that I'm perfectly organized. It doesn't mean that I don't have to constantly strategize and struggle. And it doesn't mean I'm never overwhelmed or that I don't sometimes still hide.

What it does mean, for me, to live successfully with ADD, is that I've found a way to move the focus of my life onto my strengths, my talents and my abilities, to increase my choices and options. It means that through medication I am awake, alert, and able to maintain my energy and attention throughout most of the day. It means I can sort out my neurology from my psychology, and figure out what things in my life I can change and what I just need to control or live with. It means that I've learned to separate out my strengths from my weaknesses and to embrace both of those as part of myself, even though it's a long stretch. I've come to accept the fact that I do have deficits out of proportion with the rest of my abilities, and that these do severely impact my life. I've learned to separate out the shame, embarrassment, and guilt surrounding these difficulties from my core sense of self. Now, when my ADD symptoms do appear, I don't add to them a negative self-barrage that creates a downhill cycle.

What I have learned is that to be successful with ADD, you must eventually restructure your life. You move through Shame and Guilt and must ultimately redefine your sense of what it means to be a mature, confident, competent, woman, even if after treatment you are still somewhat messy, disorganized or forgetful. For me, it means I have learned to value myself as a creative woman who will never match some culturally sanctioned image I may have internalized a long time ago about what a woman should be or be able to do.

CHAPTER TWO

Girls and ADD:
An Equal Opportunity Disorder

Mrs. Collins' fourth grade class is sitting quietly doing their math problems. Billy's pencil breaks for the fourth time today; he jumps out of his seat and runs to the pencil sharpener on the other side of the room. On the way he notices a cool picture of Michael Jordan on the cover of a friend's notebook, and stops to pick it up admiringly. His friend yanks it out of his hand, and without thinking of the consequences, Billy blurts out, "You stupid jerk," interrupting the whole class. Since this is the twenty-fifth incident in the last two weeks, Mrs. Collins has finally had enough and banishes him to the Principal's office. He gets upset and starts arguing with her, not knowing why he's in trouble again. He just wanted to sharpen his pencil to get his work done.

Jodi, sitting quietly in the back of the classroom, hasn't noticed any of this commotion. She is looking at a bird outside the window, wondering where it was for the winter, and where the rest of its family is. She is startled back into reality by the sound of Mrs. Collin's voice calling out her name and asking her the answer to problem number seven. She panics because she has barely gotten through problem two. She smiles sweetly and says softly, "I'm sorry Mrs. Collins, I haven't finished yet." Mrs. Collins says, "That's OK honey, try to work on it now," thinking to herself that Jodi is "such a nice little girl" but is a bit slow in math. Thinking of Billy, she wishes she had a whole classroom full of Jodis.

By the end of the month, Billy has been tested by the school psychologist, and been diagnosed with Attention Deficit/Hyperactivity Disorder (ADHD).

41

He has seen his family doctor, who started him on the medication, Ritalin. Mrs. Collins and Billy's parents all see a big difference in Billy's behavior and schoolwork.

By the end of the school year, Jodi barely made it through Math with a C minus average, but she received an A in Citizenship, and got a great report from Mrs. Collins about what a sweet little girl she was. Over the next few years, Jodi's parents continue to get similar reports from her teachers, with her grades continuing to go down in many subjects, even though her parents think Jodi is a bright girl. The teachers keep telling them that nothing is wrong and not to worry, that Jodi is just an average student, implying that they, like most parents, have an inflated view of their daughter's intelligence. At home, they see Jodi becoming more and more overwhelmed by the amount of schoolwork, unable to organize her work or her personal belongings, and becoming more withdrawn and unhappy.

Up until now, when most of us have heard the phrase "ADD," what came to mind was the picture of hyperactive little boys, like Billy, tearing around the room, bouncing off the walls. Because they made trouble for people, they were noticed and consequently got diagnosed and treated. Even though life for these individuals and their families continued to be challenging and stressful, at least everyone knew what the root of the problem was. Attention Deficit Hyperacitvity Disorder (ADHD) is the type of ADD Billy has and what we commonly think of as ADD.

But little girls like Jodi, sitting in the back of the class, not bothering anyone, were and are still easily overlooked. Jodi belongs to a group of individuals that we now understand do not or never had *hyperactivity*, and yet still have Attention Deficit Disorder. Dr. Kathleen Nadeau calls these kind of girls "people pleasers" who try hard to conform to teacher expectations. She says that often their ADD symptoms only show up at home after an exhausting effort to "hold it together all day."

ADD (without hyperactivity)

ADD children without hyperactivity have been described by Dr. Dale Jordan, a psychologist who has written a great deal about ADD without hyperactivity, as "lost youngsters who drift and float quietly on the edges of the environment." Dr. Tom Brown, another psychologist who has added a great deal to the body of knowledge about ADD without hyperactivity, emphasizes that ADD *without* is not just a mild form of ADHD, but itself is a severe condition. These children have all the extremes of difficulty in some of the same areas as ADHD children, but on the other side of the spectrum. Instead of being hyperactive, they are hypoactive—extremely underactive. Instead of not being able to stop moving, they have trouble beginning to move. Instead of acting impulsively without thinking, there is difficulty moving from an impulse to an action. And instead of seeking high stimulation, these children feel bombarded by stimulation. Rather than doing many things at the same time in order to concentrate, these children can only concentrate on one thing at time.

ADD can sometimes be confusing for the individual as well as the people around them because we usually associate intelligence with quick processing speed. ADD symptoms such as distractibility, both to internal and external stimuli, as well as difficulty with synthesizing and organizing ideas, coupled with general fogginess and confusion, make it difficult to process information in an average amount of time. Not only will this mask their level of intelligence, but people might even think they are slow. On the other hand, though, just because a girl is a good student and is thought of as smart, it doesn't mean she doesn't have ADD. It may just mean that a) processing speed may not be one of her problems, b) she may have a good support system; c) she may be working extraordinarily hard to do a good job; or d) her difficulties might impact other areas of her life more than academics. These will probably show up later in life.

> *A woman who is now the mother of four children says of her own childhood, "My kindergarten teacher told my mom that I wanted to know all about the moon and the stars, but that I couldn't remember to button my coat the right way or where I put it."*

One of the most telling signs of the ADD *without* child is disorganization. Just one look at her locker, her desk, or her room, or maybe even her handwriting might give you a clue that she may be struggling with this disorder. Dr. Nadeau points out that these girls who are "compliant at school but disorganized and hyperactive at home" are easily misdiagnosed. They also might be extremely sensitive to sights, and physical movements—highly distracted by both their internal and external worlds.

Socially, children with ADD w/o may have trouble as well. Because they have problems with small talk and with figuring out the rules of social interaction, they tend to become shy and withdrawn. Dr. Kathleen Nadeau says that little girls without hyperactivity "often appear awkward, painfully shy and unable to fit in." Additionally, these children often feel confused and in a fog. Sometimes it is hard for them to stay fully awake for the entire day.

ADHD Girls

Lucy— an ADHD girl: Sitting in the back of Mrs. Collins' room next to Jodi, is Lucy. Lucy is talking non-stop to some of her friends. She passes notes back and forth to her girlfriends about the cute boy two seats away. She is not paying attention to Mrs. Collins' long and boring lecture about the location of countries around the world. Instead she is giggling with delight at the thought of recess five minutes away, where she can try out the new hopscotch game she just thought of. At recess, however, another girl laughs at this new game, and won't play. Lucy is mortified. She breaks into tears, throws down the chalk, and stomps away. Mrs. Collins sees this, shakes her head, and thinks this is another typical "over-reaction" by Lucy. Mrs. Collins attributes this behavior to the recent divorce of Lucy's parents.

Why ADD Goes Undiagnosed Longer in Little Girls

Even though ADHD girls are more active and therefore more noticeable than ADD w/o girls, they too are identified and treated later than hyperactive boys, because they don't act out as much and cause as many problems. Another cultural stereotype that impacts ADHD girls occurs when they don't meet the "nice little girl" expectation. They are written off as "tomboys" instead of as having a learning problem. Or, because they are often very social, talkative, and emotionally reactive, they become labelled as "boy-crazy," "non-academic oriented," or "party girls." Dr. Kathleen Nadeau says that the hyperactivity of girls with ADHD is often manifested differently than in boys. Girls are often "hyper-talkative, hyper-social and hyper-emotionally reactive." She also says that the impulsive behavior of girls with ADHD is not tolerated in the same way as boys are. They are negatively viewed as "unladylike."

Rather than having an attentional disorder, many times their behaviors are attributed to emotional or family problems. For instance, in Lucy's case, if she is still undiagnosed by the time of her parent's divorce, it will be especially difficult for her to get an accurate diagnosis. In addition to her ADD, she will be reacting to this upheaval in her life.

Because ADD *without* girls aren't behavior problems, they often aren't identified at a young age, unless they also happen to have obvious learning disabilities. Another reason they don't get diagnosed, according to Dr. Daniel Amen, is that the cultural stereotypes that we have of little girls contribute to an under-identification. As in Jodi's case, the school system tolerates underachievement in girls that it wouldn't in boys. Also, I feel that ADD *without* girls usually fall into the "nice little girl" stereotype. Because they are quiet and nice, and often trying to please, they are actually meeting cultural expectations, and people either don't notice or are not as concerned with their subtle information processing problems.

Another way ADD is often detected is during an evaluation for learning disabilities. Because girls with ADD have fewer learning problems in the early grades in math and reading than boys do, according to Drs. Hallowell and Ratey, in *Answers to Distraction*, these girls are less apt to be diagnosed through this avenue.

The reason early identification of girls is so important is that years of being mis-labelled, mis-understood or just plain missed, leads to serious long-term consequences to their self-esteem, relationships, achievement and emotions. We will see these consequences as we trace the lives of Jodi and Lucy through childhood, their teenage years, and into adulthood.

Twelve Years Old and Still Undiagnosed ...

It's 3:30 pm. Jodi, twelve years old, is lying exhausted on her unmade bed, just trying to recover from a normal day at junior high school. Her clothes from the last few days are lying in heaps on the floor. Her books and papers are in total disarray all over her desk. She is unable to rest, however, because she is distracted by the bouncing basketball next door, and growing more and more upset by the minute. Her mother comes in, looks around, and gives her the familiar lecture of starting her homework on time and cleaning up her room. Jodi is thinking about the seventh grade history project and how stupid she must be because she can't figure out how to do it, even though her classmates are doing it pretty easily. Besides the project, she is facing another long night of homework. Jodi is hoping for the phone to ring, but she knows it won't. In junior high it seems harder and harder to figure out what to say to people or how to make friends. After she analyzes a conversation at school, studies the cracks in her ceiling, and makes a futile attempt at cleaning her room, she is dismayed to hear her mom call out, "Jodi, I hope you're doing your homework; it's 5:30 and almost time for your appointment with Dr. Evans." (Dr. Evans has diagnosed Jodi as depressed, and has suggested family therapy to find out the reason why.)

So how do we know that the psychologist wasn't right, and that Jodi isn't just depressed? It's not easy to tell ADD w/o from depression because many of the symptoms of depression look like ADD w/o, such as low energy levels, disorganization, and difficulty concentrating, as well as social withdrawal. However, in lieu of formal testing, which we'll talk about later, there are important clues which can be strong indicators of ADD w/o. Additionally, Jodi *may* be depressed, having had to cope with all these difficulties for years now, feeling more like a failure every year. The important thing to find out: is she depressed because she's disorganized, or is she disorganized because she's depressed?

Complicating the picture further, the psychologist is partly right, there very well could be family discord as well as an overfocus on Jodi's problems that no one has been able to solve. Again, this would be a *result* of Jodi's undetected ADD, not the cause of the problem.

So what are the important factors to consider when beginning to sort this all out? In Jodi's case, this is more than just a reaction to starting junior high, a big adjustment in her life. Signs of her difficulty were apparent from very early on. In Jodi's case, there is no chaotic family history, such as alcoholism or abuse, that would account for these ongoing difficulties.

Another important factor is the severity of Jodi's symptoms. If you compare Jodi to other children her age and ability level, you'll see that her difficulties are extreme, severely impacting her ability to work up to her potential. As we will see throughout the book, while all of us may have some of these symptoms some of the time, in ADD the symptoms are *severe and chronic*. And remember that even though ADD symptoms are severe and chronic, ADD symptoms in girls can also be *subtle, quiet, hidden and invisible*.

When girls have these strong emotions and reactions to the world, they are more apt to internalize these difficulties, and develop depressions and anxiety rather than acting out. Their stories are more likely to be of quiet failures of self-esteem and self-doubt. These are the seeds of the emotional legacy that will continue to grow as these children become teenagers and women.

Teenage Years

Lucy in the Sky without Diamonds (without protective factors)

Lucy is now a teenager and has been living with her mother since the time of her parent's divorce. Her mother was very disorganized, (probably undiagnosed ADD herself). They didn't have any extra money for tutors, or for after-school lessons that could have helped Lucy develop her special interest in art. After school each day, Lucy was pretty much on her own. She tried to study before her mother got home every night from work, but she usually got bored and ended up watching a lot of television, eating junk food, and subsequently gaining a substantial amount of weight. When she was about fifteen, a friend offered her some diet pills which she took. For the first time (the pills were stimulants) she felt awake, alert and focused.

Around the same time, she also began experimenting with marijuana and alcohol. She felt so relaxed at these moments and it felt so good to be with a group of people who seemed to like her and with whom she didn't feel any pressure. By this time she was fed up with school anyway, since no matter how hard she tried she somehow managed to mess up and get bad grades.

During the teenage years, organizational demands for adolescents increase. High school can be confusing; it can be overwhelming to have to move to many classrooms. The work itself demands more independent organizational skills. The social life of the teenager also requires more independent thought as the teenager is less dependent on the parent. As all variables in the lives of ADD girls increase, they find it increasingly difficult to handle the demands of their environment. Drs. Hallowell and Ratey, in *Answers to Distraction*, discuss the changes that occur in ADD girls around puberty. They say that this upheaval and hormonal change make these girls more vulnerable to the underlying ADD symptoms. They say often girls who have been quietly dealing with their symptoms up until this time often begin to display more drug and alcohol use, teenage pregnancy, shoplifting, eating disorders and high-stimulus-seeking activity.

ADHD girls might find themselves turning away from school, and may turn toward boys or socializing to compensate. ADD *without* girls might just move more into their own shell and become absorbed in their own ideas. Both groups of ADD girls might turn to drugs, alcohol or coffee, unknowingly self-medicating themselves in an attempt to concentrate, stay awake, relax, or ease social difficulties. *This is different than normal teenage experimentation, because it is often actually an attempt to gain control rather than lose control.* They also are prone to other addictive behaviors, such as sexually acting out, or may become vulnerable to eating disorders. They do this in an attempt to self-soothe, to be stimulated, or as a way to seek structure and focus.

As their coping mechanisms become strained, some of these girls will be identified as having some sort of problem, although they may not always be accurately diagnosed as ADD. For instance, they might get help with their anxiety or depression, or for communicating with their family. There will be other girls who, however, while continuing to struggle even more, will remain undiagnosed for a variety of reasons.

The reason they are not identified is because of the presence of protective factors in their lives that can delay the full force of their difficulties until adulthood. Dr. Tom Brown in his article, "Attention Deficit Disorder Without Hyperactivity," emphasizes the effects of having a high IQ. Special talents, as well as a high degree of family support and structure also mitigate and mask the effects of ADD. For example, a girl might have a family that provides her with tutors and guidelines for homework, and a structured activity schedule. Or maybe she has the kind of family that helps her find the right niche to allow her talents and abilities to flourish. Another girl may develop a coping strategy of working extremely hard, so that she is able to get by with average marks.

These protective factors, however, are a double edged sword for a girl with undiagnosed ADD. Even though they protect her from the full force of her difficulties as she's growing up, they also prevent other people from understanding her difficulties, and consequently getting the appropriate help.

"What is wrong with me, I must be an idiot," Jodi thinks to herself. "I'm sixteen years old and I guess I'm just not college material. I don't understand; I got high test scores, and my art and drama teachers think I'm so bright and creative, but I keep getting D's on my English papers. My teacher says that I'm just not trying hard enough. Whenever I open my mouth to express my ideas, nothing comes out right. On top of it all, I can't go to the party Saturday night because I haven't studied for the exam and I don't even know where my notes are, and my dress for the party is dirty, and I lost the directions and I can't call again 'cause she'll think I'm so stupid, and I'm just so tired all the time, and I act like a two year old, I said the stupidest thing in class yesterday ... Even though my mom helps me every night and gets me tutors, I still don't see how I'm going to make it through college. And if I don't go to college I don't know what I'm going to do. I'm so confused, I'm just going to take a nap ... "

Even though Jodi is struggling so much, an outsider might write her off as a typical teenage girl, as most are confused about their future, tired, or struggling with issues of self-esteem. Again, what is important here is *chronicity* and *severity*. Looking back we see this has been a continuous thread throughout Jodi's life. While the ADD symptoms themselves are not changing, what is new and developing is her negative self-evaluation as she is unable to understand her experience in any other way.

Every year that she remains undiagnosed, an ADD girl becomes more vulnerable to emotional, social and academic problems. As we have seen with Jodi and Lucy, a girl starts out with *primary* ADD symptoms. Each year that passes, the difficulties are compounded, resulting in *secondary* emotional effects, such as depression, low self-esteem, underachievement, and relationship difficulties. These effects will continue to grow and take on a life of their own when she becomes a woman, adding another complex layer to the original ADD symptoms she has already been coping with for years.

At some point the demands for these girls and the consequent pressures they feel and carry inside increase to where they are over their heads. No one knows what is going on: not their families, not their teachers, not their friends, not even themselves.

CHAPTER THREE

"Dance with the Lady with the Hole in Her Stocking" (Joni Mitchell)

A Portrait of the Inner World of Women with ADD
Before Diagnosis

The Secret World

Women with ADD often live in a secret world. Some people call it passing for normal. I call it being locked in a (messy) closet. Whatever the cute expressions, the painful reality is that many women with ADD have moved away from relationships or at least have kept a part of themselves locked away from other people, usually without even realizing it. Often their lives have taken on a secret tone, as if the way they live is in some way shameful. This feeling of secrecy and shame wipes out the possibility of enjoying or appreciating all their other abilities and qualities. Their inner world is a place that outsiders couldn't fathom, where the simplest activities— getting dressed, planning the day, or running a simple errand, are extremely difficult and frustrating. The cumulative effect of these daily experiences makes them feel like outsiders, separate from the world in some important ways— spending one's days not living life but instead coping with this silent thief of time and dreams.

In this chapter, we will be exploring the inner world of ADD women in order to better understand the complexity of their lives. We will then be better able to appreciate what happens when they meet the expectations of the outer world.

The Good News Is ...

Once these women are diagnosed and treated, many of the qualities they have developed along the way can help them get back on track. As a result of their struggles, they often develop a reservoir of strength, perseverance, and determination. The creative problem-solving ability they have developed as a result of not being able to do things "the regular way" can be of help when strategizing about effective solutions to their difficulties, especially once they understand what they have been coping with. As a result of their experiences, they often are compassionate and sensitive to others with difficulties.

More good news is that ADD is closely correlated with creativity, as one has the expanded ability to see connections between events or stimuli, that others don't always see. Without diagnosis and treatment, that creativity can sometimes go wild, creating the chaos that contributes to the feelings of being bombarded, overwhelmed and out of control. The good news is that with treatment this creativity can be directed and harnessed. This natural abundance of ideas and fresh outlooks combined with the positive qualities developed along the way, allows these individuals to access their strengths and talents, and move ahead in new, personally meaningful directions.

All Grown Up and Still Undiagnosed

Whenever I give a speech or seminar about ADD, I usually relate a story my friend Adriane told me about frogs, because I think it is very applicable to people who are coping with invisible disorders. This story goes that if you put frogs into cold water, and then very *slowly* turn up the heat, they won't notice that the water is boiling until it's too late to jump out and by then they've boiled to death. If they had known they were in trouble they could have easily jumped out and saved themselves.

Unfortunately, this story demonstrates what some adults with undiagnosed ADD cope with. They don't know how hard they are working, or how much of their energy is going into just *surviving.* They don't know that living is not supposed to be *that* hard. Too often, like the frog, by the time they discover this is not the way it's supposed to be they're already depleted, depressed, or overwhelmed.

For women who have grown up with undiagnosed ADD, it's as if their thermostat for enjoyment and sense of normalcy has been completely thrown out of kilter, much in the same way that too much yo-yo dieting throws off the body's metabolism. Eventually this makes it impossible to eat almost anything without gaining weight. These ADD women have spent a lifetime just trying to keep their heads above water. Their internal gauge, which registers how hard one needs to work to stay afloat, is seriously "out of whack." Unfortunately, there is no time for them to reflect on the reality of this. They are too busy either trying not to drown or trying to hide their problems from other people who might be able to throw them a life jacket. Surviving becomes the only goal. If they do survive, they feel they are doing well. Their goal becomes just to "not feel bad" instead of to "feel good."

This is understandable because they have never known any other way of living. Women say, "I can cope." "I can get by." "It's okay." And they do. They cope, they compensate, they have systems, they hide, they cover up, or they self-medicate with food or other substances. They overwork or severely limit their choices in life in order to control their lives. They organize their days around keeping their lives together, to the exclusion of friends, family, work, or recreation.

ADD is such a full-time job that some women have never had the opportunity to stop and figure out a way of doing things differently. They haven't discovered how to change the rules, what it means to feel comfortable, or how to live without feeling overwhelmed. They just don't have the concept.

Young Women

There are obviously a great variety of life paths that a young woman with undiagnosed ADD can take. As we said previously, the double-edged sword of protective factors often enables some women to pass for normal: go to college, develop a career, have a family. The protective factors, such as parental structure or high IQ, can prevent these individuals from getting identified or feeling the full force of their symptoms at an earlier stage in their life. This makes it much more difficult for them to understand the load they're carrying and to make sense of the tremendous difficulties they face. The more they've achieved, the more confusing it is for them and others close to them, to see the complex process they go through in order to maintain this success or achievement. We will examine this scenario in more detail as we resume Jodi's story later.

Other women, even if they've had little support in high school, still manage to go to college. Unfortunately, because they have no idea what is wrong, and what accommodations they could get to succeed, they are soon overwhelmed and either drop out or change schools several times.

Others continue to self-medicate with drugs or alcohol to counteract their low self-esteem, bringing them some form of needed relaxation, as well as a way to feel focused. Other young women might act out sexually with multiple partners or even tolerate destructive relationships in order to have the security of some kind of structure to come up against.

By senior year in high school Lucy had had it. She dropped out and moved in with her boyfriend who didn't seem to mind the way she was. He didn't get down on her like her mom did for making a mess. Secretly she believed her mom when she told Lucy she would never amount to anything and that she was a lazy, irresponsible slob. Lucy just tried to get through each day and worked hard to forget the "stupid" dream she once had of becoming a fashion designer.

For a while she liked living with her boyfriend, because even though he was becoming increasingly domineering, it felt good in a way to have someone tell her what to do. She took a job at a fast food restaurant and was soon overwhelmed. She got the orders mixed up, she was confused when handling money, and she got upset when customers got impatient. Everything seemed to be happening at once—people yelling, lots of noise, multiple demands for her attention. She often forgot important procedures which made the manager angry. Then she was late for work a couple of times. Eventually she was fired. Her family wondered how she would ever be able to do anything in life if she couldn't even hold on to this seemingly simple job. The experience confirmed for her what she had feared for a long time—that she was just plain stupid. She tried to figure out how to do what they all told her she must do:

"Change your ways"

"Change your attitude"

"Try harder"

"Concentrate on what you're doing"

"Be responsible"

Mostly she kept trying to figure out the answer to the question that kept ringing in her ears, "What's the matter with me?"

The Many Roads Taken ...

Until recently, before the growing public awareness of Adult ADD, Lucy probably would not have had the opportunity to recognize her symptoms for herself. Her life could have taken one of several different directions. She could continue to spiral downhill, drinking more and more, going from one bad relationship to another, never getting the help she needed. If she were lucky, she might at some time get help for depression and low self esteem. This might bring her some relief and some needed direction for a while. With this kind of intervention, maybe she could wind up working in a department store around the fashions she loved. If things continued to go well, she might eventually start a community college program. If she were really lucky, an observant college instructor might notice her difficulties, especially if a learning disability became obvious. In this way Lucy eventually could get some help for her ADD. On the other hand, she might go undiagnosed until she has her own child, who, when identified as ADD, causes her to recognize the symptoms in herself.

Women like Lucy without the benefit of education, often have to work at unskilled, low-paying jobs, which either on one hand are too fast-paced to manage, or on the other hand too boring for them endure. Either way, their talents, abilities, and strengths are pushed underground. Their self-esteem plummets and they often find themselves living with a chronic, low-level depression.

Other women in this situation, even in unskilled jobs, may find a good match between their personalities and a certain kind of working environment. Hitting the wall may be postponed for them. Dr. Pennington, in *Diagnosing Learning Disorders*, states: "Lower-status work can be highly structured and routine and not tax executive functions too much, but other aspects of adult development that require initiative, planning, flexibility, such as career development, intimacy, marriage and parenting may pose other problems."

Finally, if a young woman happens to be very talented in a particular area, and she's lucky enough to find a niche or an environment in which she can thrive, she might have a better outcome at this stage. She could continue along with a minimum of problems for a longer period of time.

"Hey Jod ... take a sad song and make it better ... "

Jodi's story is a representative history of an undiagnosed woman.

Jodi, despite her previous difficulties, had a different experience than Lucy. Even though on the inside she was struggling, she did get some help from a psychologist, who, even though didn't diagnose her as ADD, did suggest tutors and facilitated family support. This turned things around enough for Jodi to get through high school and develop her interest in drama enough to derive some sense of self-esteem.

College

After high school, Jodi went on to a small private college where she discovered that she liked the field of communications, especially radio and TV. Since she didn't have to work to support herself in college, she took her time graduating, taking the minimum required number of credits each semester. Some of the required courses in science for instance, were very difficult for her, and she received a few D's. In other courses, such as history, she devised elaborate systems for studying and processing the information. She knew that sometime around two in the morning her brain would turn on and she would study incredibly well. She got hooked on coffee and cigarettes and often stayed up all night, but she got through. Her teachers in the TV courses thought she was talented and she felt "really alive" in front of the camera. She didn't do much socializing, but instead put all her focus and energy into finding a way to show the world her real abilities.

After College

After college, a friend of her parents who had "connections" made arrangements for her to get an entry level job at a local TV station as a "go-fer" at first, but later as assistant to one of the writers. Her parents were proud of her and bragged to their friends about Jodi working in an exciting field like the television industry. Everyone agreed it was perfect for a creative girl like Jodi.

At first Jodi was excited too. After all, this had been her dream. What she soon found out, however, was that talent and interest in a field were apparently not enough. What seemed to be equally critical to success were the day to day, real-life working requirements that didn't always match her skills, strengths or interests. This entry level job required a great deal of paper work, keeping track of details, responding to multiple demands in a distracting environment, and a lot of boring tasks like filing. She was motivated, though, and determined to stick with it long enough to move up in the ranks to where she could really shine—in front of the camera.

Finally her big first break came and she was promoted to junior copy writer. Jodi had many great ideas for stories but she found she had a very difficult time communicating the depth of her ideas to anyone. In addition to this frustration, writing remained difficult for her. She found that in order to meet her deadlines, again, as in college, she had to stay up very late waiting for her brain to turn on so she could deliver the goods.

Her family thought she was doing very well. Every time they praised her, however, Jodi felt dishonest, as if she were fooling them. She knew how much harder she had to work than other people. Even though the final product was good, no one else saw the mess she created and coped with behind the scenes. Her anxiety mounted. She was growing exhausted. Each day she wondered, "Will today be the day I let down my guard and have my mask ripped away; will someone ask me to do something I haven't prepared for enough and expose me as the fraud I really am?"

Junior copywriters didn't have assistants; they did their own filing and typing and they didn't have their own offices. They worked in the middle of the room surrounded by ringing phones, typewriters, and lots of activity. Eventually Jodi couldn't find the important papers and information she needed for the stories she was working on. She spent hours searching for statistics or phone numbers she had misplaced and needed in order to verify sources.

The demands increased. People started teasing her and making comments about the state of disarray on and around her desk. She started hiding, taking as much work as she could home, in the hope that she would be able to concentrate better there.

One day, to the total bewilderment and disappointment of her parents who thought she was doing so well, Jodi just quit. Not knowing what the problem was, she had no way to solve it, and no way to understand what had just happened to her. She had no idea what went so wrong in a field she loved so much. Maybe it was her. Maybe she just wasn't cut out for a career in TV ...

Married Without Children ...

A year later, Jodi got married to a man who seemed very organized and had a secure job. Jodi secretly felt relieved to be out of a demanding work environment. Her husband was supportive of her creative instincts and Jodi happily began to explore all her many interests—writing, photography, acting and drawing. Before long she had ideas for many projects that would combine all these abilities in a new exciting entrepreneurial endeavor. Now that she had the time and space she just knew she would be able to put it all together.

Jodi took art classes ... and then wanted to put words to the creations so she took a class in haiku poetry ... there she met a very interesting person who told her about the local political situation, and she felt compelled to write an editorial on the subject ... she realized she needed more computer skills so took a class at a local adult education center and realized that she could teach a more interesting class than that ... and then she found out that she could become a producer at the local cable station on a volunteer basis ...

*and that was exciting because she could finally get her ideas across
in the way she wanted to on TV ...*

Five years later she looked around her bedroom floor and saw there
were about twenty uncompleted dreams sitting in piles strewn across
her floor—and another five or ten stuffed in boxes in the closet.

Married With Child

Jodi soon had a baby girl named Jessica, and began to hope that maybe
her true talents lay in childrearing and caretaking. She and her husband
both agreed that it was important for her to be at home during these
preschool years. She threw herself into the role and fell in love with the
baby and with being a mom. She read every book on childrearing and
enrolled in all the mother-daughter baby classes. Then came:

> *Co-ops and nursery school*
> *Volunteering and baking*
> *Driving and making clay*
> *Halloween and birthdays*
> *Christmas cards with baby photos*
> *Little girl's schedules and mom get-togethers*

All of a sudden there was a whole lot more than "you and me and
baby makes three."

And her little girl didn't seem like the others. She wasn't as easy
going as the other little girls. Her little girl cried all the time, overreacted,
withdrew, and got upset very easily. Gradually, Jodi felt more and more
overwhelmed, out of control, and depressed.

School Daze

Finally Jessica entered first grade. Jodi's husband was supportive at first
when she returned to work part-time, but when Jessica began to have
trouble in school, coupled with her husband's increasing complaints
about her lack of organization around the house, Jodi quit her job. But
things didn't get any easier. Secretly, she wished that she could get a
housekeeper, but how could she justify that since she only had one child
and wasn't working? Her days felt like a nightmare. She found simple
errands incredibly overwhelming and boring. No one understood why
an errand that should have taken only a few minutes, for her meant a
few hours of frustration and confusion. By the time she found her keys
and an unwrinkled shirt to throw on, and assembled all the "stuff" and
lists she needed, and by the time she stopped to get money because she
was out of cash and didn't have her checkbook, she was already frus-

trated and upset. Just going to the grocery store bombarded her with so many decisions to be made. The lines irritated her to such an extent that by the time she got home she felt she had just returned from battle.

When her daughter was in school, she would go out to have a cup of coffee, write in her diary and try to relax, but the conversations around her in the cafe overwhelmed Jodi and she couldn't block them out. She'd wind up moving several times, but again, she would be irritated by someone at the next table tapping his cup in an annoying way. She would go back home to try to get some peace, but the dog next door would bark and the war zone effect would start again. No wonder, then, when her husband got home and said, "Didn't you get to the cleaners?" she would blow up, slam the door and start to cry. He had no idea that she'd been to a war and back.

The Mother of an ADD Child

When Jessica was in the third grade she started to fall behind the other children scholastically. At the parent-teacher conference they asked Jodi to help keep her daughter organized and suggested an elaborate reward system to check off every day in order to structure Jessica's schedule. Jodi found herself unable to maintain this kind of structure and her daughter continued to fall more and more behind. She and her husband began to fight more and her entire extended family began to blame her for being a bad mother and being too lazy to take care of the house and her daughter. As she began to spend more and more time lying on the couch, she began to believe they were probably right. What seemed like millions of obligations swept through her mind as well as millions of ideas for new projects, but she felt paralyzed to move or take action. All the creative ideas that she had accumulated through the years lay strewn in piles all over her room. Her feelings of hopelessness increased and she dreaded the moment that her husband arrived home every day, knowing that a barrage of criticism would follow when he saw all the unfinished tasks.

Every couple of days, though, and for a few minutes each day, Jodi was surprised to find that she felt great. When it was just the right time of month, when there was just the right amount of stimulation without too much overload, it was as if a light switch had gone on inside her brain. She could easily get up, direct her energy and get her errands done effortlessly. During those times, she would sit down at the computer and start filling in a new calendar/planner. She felt in control and was determined to stay that way. The next day, as mysteriously as it arrived, the feeling would disappear. Her husband suggested that this obviously meant she wasn't really motivated or didn't really care.

She went into therapy to resolve the anger toward her husband that was obviously related to unresolved conflicts with her father. A couple of years of therapy later, she had resolved all the conflicts with her father and her husband, but, damn!—she still spent ninety percent of her time rummaging through her purse, looking for matching socks, or searching for those organizer/planners that were going to be so much help. Most perplexing of all was why, after all this therapy, did she still have this low-level feeling of anxiety, inner chaos, and depression?

Summary

One important point to remember when we are trying to understand Jodi and women like her with undiagnosed ADD, is that almost all women—non-ADD women—have difficulties meeting the complicated demands of today's world. Almost all women find that life today is complex, upsetting or frustrating, but they are still able to meet most of these demands reasonably well, and to some extent move ahead with their lives.

For the women with untreated ADD, however, the demands of daily life can be crippling. It cripples their self-esteem, their families, their lives, their work and their relationships. With undiagnosed and un-treated ADD, there will be some serious effect somewhere in their lives, even if it's often invisible and hidden. They don't always talk about it. Only those closest to them know the level of difficulty they confront each day of their lives.

In the next chapter we will examine, in depth, the effect of these experiences on a woman's developing self-concept.

CHAPTER FOUR

"Who am I? What's the Matter with Me?"

L et's think back and consider the development of that little girl growing up undiagnosed, with such a puzzling array of attributes and experiences. One of the most basic effects of these kinds of childhood experiences is to a woman's self-image. She often wonders, *"Who am I? Am I smart or am I dumb? Am I talented and creative or incompetent? Am I successful and interesting or immature and childish? Warm or intrusive?"*

These women often have difficulty developing a cohesive self-picture that makes sense, because as they grow, the pieces just don't fit together.

As you see in this picture of Mona Lisa, the pieces that make up her self-picture don't always fit together easily or naturally. Usually other people without these kinds of wide ranges in abilities go through life unconsciously putting together a picture of who they are, formed from their experiences. These experiences make sense to some extent; they're in a range that isn't out of the ordinary. Most people have some successes and some fail-

ures as they go through life. They develop some abilities and they notice some difficulties in other areas, but their experiences for the most part fall within a fairly narrow range. They might not be exceptionally gifted, but they aren't way off the scale in the other direction either. A person with ADD might have a wider range between their weaknesses and abilities.

As the non-ADD person continues on through life, the pieces continue to make sense. They don't get A's one day, and F's the next; they aren't called creative one day and lazy, unmotivated, and irresponsible the next. When people without these difficulties try to do something, their efforts usually pay off. In other words, there's a direct relationship between the effort and the results. This is because they have the necessary underlying, supportive organizational skills that help them pull it all together. This allows them to translate their ideas or abilities into the real world. They can then communicate those ideas cohesively to other people.

Because their discrepancies are much larger, people with hidden disorders are very confusing to themselves and perplexing to other people. Because their range can be very wide, individuals can't easily encompass and incorporate into their self-image both their strengths and their weaknesses. This is especially true before they know the nature of this challenge. On a day when things are going well, when they're "on," they may feel, and everyone else may think, that they are very competent or even talented. The next day, when a different kind of skill is called for and/or they're not "on," people might feel they have turned into selfish, preoccupied, unmotivated individuals. Have they suddenly become dumb, odd, hopelessly mean or controlling? If they only could just reach out and *embrace* both sides of themselves. Everybody could then perhaps see that they have not only abilities, but also difficulties. Acceptance would be easier for themselves and others.

When someone *is* diagnosed with ADD as a child, it still plays havoc in their lives because of the school and relationship difficulties it creates. There is still tremendous stress, and it still impacts self-esteem. But when it is explained and understood, it at least makes sense. It's comprehensible.

The problem for women is that most of them were *not* diagnosed as children. Even if they were hyperactive, they usually did not act out in the same way that boys did. They were apt to be labeled tomboys, written off in some other way without understanding the underlying attention deficit disorder. And for those dreamy girls without hyperactivity, it was even less likely that they would come to anyone's attention. Parents and even professionals would not have any way to understand their subtle information processing problems, their confusion or their disorganization. These women often grew up with absolutely no way to make sense of this baffling self-image. The wonderful pictures that they had inside didn't match the kind of reactions they got from the world. For them, these labels meant that no matter how much they tried, despite having equal abilities with other children, they weren't able to show what they really knew. Despite how hard they tried, they weren't able to measure up or please people.

A woman client tells of spending many Saturdays in her room as a child, because she wasn't allowed to go out to play until she cleaned up her room. She knew she couldn't figure out how to clean up her room, but she couldn't figure out why she didn't know how. She just knew that for some reason she wasn't doing it. So she spent all day locked in her room, unable to go out to play until she finished her work, but ... she couldn't finish her work.

The Inside and the Outside Don't Match

One beautiful woman I know said she feels like Pigpen, with a little cloud of dirt always around her. This poignantly demonstrated to me the difficulty women have of integrating opposite images into one self-concept.

In addition to the gap between what you feel like inside and what other people *see*, there is also a gap between the ideas someone has inside and what one is able to verbally express. It is painful to have wonderful thoughts with no way to organize or express them. It is as if the ideas of these women are padlocked shut, like having a beautiful car, but no keys, no gas—all dressed up and no place to go. Many of my clients express what one woman summed up like this:

"It's as though I have a symphony inside me, but all that comes out is a plunk on a broken-down old piano."

One more discrepancy in these women's lives is between their level of academic or professional achievement, and how they carry out the details of daily life.

I once went over to a woman friend's house, who was an "ADD with a Ph.D." She was standing frozen in the middle of her room, staring blankly at a tangled web of clothes and clutter. She had absolutely no idea of how to proceed, how to clean up the room.

Another women client of mine has just passed all the requirements for her Master's degree. However, she forgot to file the papers that would have allowed her to graduate.

For all these women these difficulties often unfortunately wipe out any sense of their real achievements. As we'll see later, the goal for women is to understand and hold onto opposite ideas about themselves at the same time.

These problems are often invisible, and even when there are visible signs, the level of internal difficulty is invisible. Since it is the daily tasks that are hard for the ADD woman, the routine ones that no one likes to do, it's even more difficult for anyone to understand that this is more than what all women struggle with. Until recently, no one ever heard about the neurological issues that cause ADD symptoms. No matter what conventional advice she hears, she's still not able to maintain any semblance of order in her life. As long as there are no other answers out there, she will continue to feel depressed, hopeless, and fall back into the three "I am's," described in the next section.

What's the Matter With Me?

By the time these women have grown up and lived without diagnosis for many years they start to ask themselves the question, *"What's the Matter With Me?"* I call these negative self-labels that women often use to describe themselves, the three "I am's."

"I am incompetent."

"I am immature."

"I am an impostor."

Let's examine these three basic areas.

"I am incompetent." Women with these kinds of difficulties incredulously ask, *"How do other women do it?"* (meaning Life).

They look at women who are able to lead regular, consistent lives as if they're from a different planet. They just can't fathom it. As Hallowell and Ratey say in *Answers to Distraction*, "They just don't have the equipment" to be able to provide this kind of structure for themselves. Hallowell and Ratey explain that "the ADD brain lacks the internal organization that naturally leads most people to structure their lives." As one client of mine said when it finally dawned on her that her friend had free time on the weekends, "You mean this woman doesn't have six months worth of unfolded clothes piling up around the house? She doesn't have stacks of unopened mail to wade through or unpaid bills to confront? You mean she's not constantly worried that the phone or electricity will be turned off or that the rent check will bounce?" For these women, it's unimaginable that these things don't happen to other people. Unless and until they've truly integrated the belief that this is part of the ADD, that it is the way they're built and this is part of a disorder, they will continue to feel very confused, and attribute their difficulties to some immaturity or lack of character.

Two reasons these women feel incompetent are:

1. The only basis of comparison they have is usually only non-ADD women.

2. Their basic feeling is that there is absolutely no way they can keep up with the demands of life. We'll be looking at this more when we talk about the actual Job Description for Women and we see what a poor match it is for a woman with ADD.

"I am immature." Many women ask, "When will I ever feel grown up? When will I get over this? When will I stop being so irresponsible?"

They berate themselves because the discrepancies between their levels of abilities and their difficulties are so much larger than average. Despite great maturity and competence in other areas, some parts of their lives often reflect a much less mature stage of development.

It is difficult to accept this in oneself or in one's partner as anything other than being stuck in childhood or still acting like a messy, irresponsible teenager. As we saw when we looked at the kind of discrepancies an ADD individual embodies, we now understand why it's so baffling and so easily attributed to a character flaw. And not just by others—but more significantly by ADD adults themselves. Even after diagnosis, without successful treatment these kinds of negative self-concepts are difficult to erase.

Dr. Ned Hallowell has said that he doesn't think that balancing your checkbook should be the measure of whether you're mentally healthy. In the same way, I feel that women have to understand that being able to keep your house a certain way, or staying organized a certain way isn't the sign of whether you're grown up or mature. Is it a sign of maturity to be able to see if you're blind, or walk if you have a broken leg?

One professional woman said in an interview, *"I feel like a stupid jerk. I feel like a two-year-old."* She berates herself with criticism for not being able to manage the details of her household or her business anywhere close to the way her other friends or associates do. She asks herself the questions *"Why can't I get it together? Why am I so undisciplined? Why do I say I'm going to do something and then can't do it?"*

"I am an impostor." *When will they find me out?*

Many women feel that no matter how competent others think they are, or no matter how much they achieve, they are really just fooling everyone. This stems partly from the large disparity between their inner and outer worlds. Other people often see the *real* competence of these ADD adults, but don't see the conflict inside these people. They don't see the "mess" in other areas of their lives, or how hard it is to achieve that outer picture. ADD women often believe they are fooling anyone who thinks well of them because without any warning the switch inside their heads could turn off, and their feelings of inadequacy would be exposed. They worry that they won't have enough time, that their systems won't work, that people will drop in unexpectedly. Any minute things could fall apart.

This accounts for the sense of impending doom that often is reported, that sense of inner chaos. Even if the achievement of these women is real, it feels tenuous and scary to them; they still feel like impostors. One person describes this inner/outer disparity as *"the counters are all clean, but the inside of the drawers are a mess."* This is a great metaphor for the exteriors that women often present while experiencing the interior feeling of messiness, disorder and confusion. Instead of taking credit for their "clean counters," they just feel that it's a cover. Even when they do take a risk, and let down their mask by letting people know what's going on inside, they are met with disbelief, invalidation, or ridicule. *The irony is that the more they achieve and the better they do, the less people are inclined to believe them, and the more they feel forced to then stay in the closet.*

Unsolved Mysteries

Throughout their lives, these women cope, compensate, and unconsciously devise ways to get by, to cover up and to keep their heads above water. They don't even know they are doing it. They cut back on sleep, they cut back on friends, fun, or achievement. If they do go ahead and socialize or work they then cover up what a toll it's taking. They often have an exquisite sense of not belonging: of hiding, pretending, and waiting to be discovered. *They are trying to solve a mystery without knowing what they're trying to solve.* Even the ones who do it best and longest—well compensated, often self-medicated adults—eventually hit a wall, physically or emotionally. They may eventually seek and accept psychological explanations for their difficulties. They get help at that point, sink more and more into depression or else become determined to use more will power.

Trying Harder

"I'm just going to try harder."

"I'm going to go home and DO it this time."
"I'm going to clean that desk."
"I'm going to get through those piles."
"I'm going to be on time this week."
"I'm going to balance my checkbook every month."
"I'm going to maintain those systems."

They are determined to work harder. They are trying to solve the problem in the same old way, but when this doesn't work, it can become demoralizing and debilitating. Remember, it's not that these women *can't* do the same things that other women do, or that they don't have the ability; it's just that they can't do it *and* also lead a regular, balanced life. It's not that they *can't* do it, but that they can't do it without a tremendous strain on their resources; without staying up to all hours of the night, without sacrificing all their free time.

Some of these women's lives are spent in "secretly organizing," just the way some people secretly eat or drink. They often feel that their dilemma is having to decide between two equally bad choices. The first is to tell or to hide and the second is to achieve or not to achieve.

To Tell or Not to Tell

1. To tell—If they stop hiding and let more of their disorganization show, they will get written off as spacy and irresponsible. They fear they won't be taken seriously and will be judged by their exterior difficulties rather than the strength of their ideas.

2. To hide—On the other hand, they can hide. This means many extra hours behind the scenes with a tremendous toll on their time and energy.

To Be or Not to Be

The other way women feel trapped between two bad choices has to do with their own achievement and ambitions.

1. To not achieve—They can *cut back* on their ambitions and achievements, or give up the idea altogether in order to try to control the demands coming at them fast and furiously. They give up the idea of focusing on themselves, because it seems like an impossibility; given the fact that they can't even keep up with the demands of daily life. So they spend their lives focusing on the routine tasks, which is the "hard stuff" for them. They wait to get that under control before they move ahead and attend to their own needs or their own lives. But that's not possible

without somehow changing strategies, because they're focusing on their areas of difficulty, rather than focusing on their strengths. Without some help, they will never get things under control, and focus on their strengths. This is the treadmill that they can't get off.

2. To achieve at a price—The other choice is to give up trying to control the uncontrollable, and instead try to maintain a higher level of achievement and self-focus. Unfortunately, this then often creates chaos for themselves and those around them. If they focus on their own strengths without the addition of structure and support in the form of some kind of coaching or organizational assistance, and without accepting and understanding their difficulties, chaos will reign and overwhelm them, ultimately destroying their feelings of success. Either way, it's a terrible trap.

Women with ADD don't have to make the impossible choice to either hide their problems and not have a life, or not hide and be written off. They don't have to make the choice of either cutting back on their ambitions, or going for it, with utter chaos as the result. Later in the book we will examine the process whereby a woman begins to expand her sense of choice and options and control.

We have discussed the feeling of internal disorganization, and next we will take a look at how disorganization manifests externally—in other words, the mess, the piles, and the clutter.

CHAPTER FIVE

Disorganization: The Disorder of Dis-order

"Disorganization causes the gifted and the well-motivated to fail ... It takes many forms and invades every aspect of daily life. It is pernicious. It is self-perpetuating. It builds on itself and it dooms fine minds to menial work."

This is how Sally Smith, in *Succeeding Against the Odds*, describes the effects of disorganization.

Disorganization in one form or another is the subject that women with ADD talk about the most in counseling: either the stress of living with it, strategies for dealing with it, or the emotions surrounding it.

It is important to take an in-depth look at disorganization as it will help us understand how the experiences of women with ADD collide with cultural expectations for women. We will see that the real-life effect of the primary symptoms of ADD is often disorganization. This disorganization leads to many of the internal conflicts and feelings of failure for women. With disorganization as their constant companion, further emotional complications result for women as they go through life.

Listen to how some people have described to me their everyday struggles with disorganization, and the level of difficulty with which they are coping..

> *"I disorganize so quickly. I turn around after a few minutes, look back at the kitchen I just walked out of and see all the drawers and cabinets open, the milk carton still left out on the counter. And I have no idea how it happened. People think I'm doing this on purpose or I just don't care."*

"I spend ninety percent of my time looking for things."

"They tell me to get a planner. I have twenty of them and can't find any of them."

"They say to make lists. I have hundreds of notes scribbled on pieces of paper. I find them in my pockets, everywhere."

Disorganization is a severely misunderstood and underestimated problem in the lives of millions of people. Every single thing in life takes organization—from doing the dishes and organizing your bills or your social life, to getting through the day on time and organizing your grocery list. Equally important, is the ability to organize your thoughts and ideas—writing a report, holding your own in an argument.

Disorganization affects cognitive abilities as well as the physical environment.

Without good organizational skills, it is easy to accumulate a huge amount of clutter which can overwhelm you by the end of the day. Poor organizational skills, combined with the extra ideas that the ADD mind generates, exacerbates the problem into one of constant expansion, rather than pulling things together and controlling them.

Remember again, these are not ordinary difficulties with disorganization. These are severe and chronic difficulties. And they are inconsistent. They enter a person's life in a pervasive, invasive, and insidious way. The automaticity with which other people organize just isn't part of an ADD adult's wiring. Dale Jordan, Ph.D., says in his book, *Attention Deficit Disorder,* that disorganization is the "earmark of ADD in adults."

Disorganization isn't a disorder or worth getting treatment for unless it's creating serious problems or consequences in one's life. That's how we distinguish it from creative or busy people who have these problems but aren't bothered by them to the same extent. For people with ADD, it's causing serious problems, impacting their ability to achieve their goals or to have any time for friends or family or serious relationships; it's seriously affecting their mood or self-esteem. It has impact, causing great pain by stopping people from not being able to reach their potential.

For a person with these difficulties, there is a constant drain on the resources of time and energy, often to the exclusion of the rest of life. A simple ten-minute task, with no emotional component (such as washing the dishes) turns into a long, drawn-out affair for the ADD individual.

Besides taking up valuable time, it can also contribute to a sense of emotional overload. Even women with ADD who say they *are* very organized are often obsessively so. These people are still centering their entire lives around the effort to "keep it all together," knowing if they let up on their vigilance in this area, they will be lost, like a blind person groping in the dark. For these women (and men) who must have everything in place to function, disorganization is still taking a toll on their lives, as the imbalance of focus on this area keeps them away from other creative, productive, or recreational pursuits.

"My Left Hand"

I recently hurt my left hand and had to wear a brace. People were solicitous and sympathetic, constantly asking if I needed any help. This was startling to me because it was nothing compared to my ADD and my organizational problems. The solution to this physical problem was simple– I just didn't use my left hand. But I can't just "not use" part of my brain. I can't just say, "Well, today, I'll just leave that part of my brain out of things. "Not using my left hand was inconvenient, but people obviously understood there was something physical that I couldn't do. There was no self-recrimination or hiding about it. No emotion was attached to it. Again, it was nothing compared to the invisible disorder I can never get away from. It doesn't matter how many creative ideas one has if they can't organize them or communicate them. Organization affects everything you do, say, and think. It permeates every moment of your life. There is no getting away from it.

Do You Suffer from TMS– Time, Money, and Stuff?

When I talk about disorganization I mean a variety of things for a variety of people. For women as well as men, time, money, stuff, and paper can dominate their lives, impacting their abilities to achieve their goals and feel like mature individuals.

"Time is just a white, wide open empty space with no markers; with no way to know how to piece it out."

Some people have more trouble with *time* than stuff, as the above quote expresses, feeling that there is no way to proceed successfully through one's day. This obviously affects arriving on time, as well as short- and long-term planning. It also affects prioritizing and sequencing one's day, week, and month. Not being able to plan one's day effectively can be very demoralizing. Poor time management adds a great deal of effort to any project and obviously reduces the odds of finishing a project at all. Even if the project is finally finished, and even if it's on time, the process one has had to go through to accomplish this may be filled with anxiety and tremendous stress. It can create an atmosphere of chaos, negatively affecting families or co-workers, as well as taking a toll in other areas.

Problems with time can seriously affect relationships and jobs. For instance, if an individual is chronically late for either personal appointments or work responsibilities, it sends the non-intentional message that one is not taking a person or a job seriously.

It is like traveling on a long journey with no road map. It can be done but it is so slow. It's like walking on a balance beam, one foot in front of the other, having to consciously and carefully plan the placement of each foot, monitoring the placement of each step, for fear of falling off.

Other people mention the difficulty of controlling and keeping track of *money*. For instance, the boring routine and attention to detail of balancing one's checkbook makes this a task that many with ADD just don't do. This, combined with the impulsivity of overspending or over-charging on credit cards, can leave someone with a chronic feeling of being immature and out of control.

"My bills are in unopened piles all over the place. I live with the constant feeling that the gas and electric will be turned off any moment."

As anxiety around this mounts, even less attention is given to this area, creating a dead end cycle of avoidance and disorganization. This eventually results in real-life problems, such as shutoffs, final notices and bad credit. It also creates problems with relationships, and trust.

Even today with most women working, many women even without ADD have issues around money, and taking care of their financial affairs. They aren't as knowledgeable about financial matters as they'd like to be, having control, power, and dependency issues. Coupled with ADD and feelings of being overwhelmed, this creates an even greater tendency to shut down and tune out in this area.

For some, disorganization is centered around *physical stuff*—papers, books, files, dishes, boxes, clothes—common physical objects that you come in contact with. This leads to a basic sense of confusion and of feeling trapped, almost as if one's hands were tied together. Your life is haunted by Disney-like, animated pieces of "stuff." People describe it as surreal or Kafkaesque. They feel that they are bombarded by "billions" of pieces of things that they can't control.

"I look down at my feet after a couple minutes of sitting in a

room and I see papers and all sorts of stuff accumulated in disarray, a mess all around me. How does this happen? Why doesn't it happen to other people? It's embarrassing."

"We have to just push all the stuff and papers to one side of the table to eat."

I've heard many people say that they "disorganize quickly." It is very frustrating, and equally frustrating for those around them. Other people in their environment might ask, "Why do you leave everything open? Why don't you put things back?" They don't understand that it was not a conscious decision. People with ADD say that they have no idea what has happened, or how it has happened, until they turn around and see that all the cupboards are open, that they've left out all the food and milk, and that there are things dropped on the floor.

Why do People with ADD have Organizational Difficulties?

The reason adults with ADD have difficulty with disorganization goes to the core of what ADD is. Earlier we discussed the primary symptoms, irregularities, and deficits involved with ADD, in relation to a person's *attention, activation, and impulsivity.* Because it is these areas that are involved with organization, difficulties here would then inevitably lead to *dis*-organization.

Following are some reasons for how specific ADD difficulties can lead to these problems.

ATTENTION

Difficulty Focusing on Routine Tasks

People with ADD need high levels of stimulation in order to focus. The brain's neurotransmitters, those information messengers, aren't functioning efficiently or consistently. It is during these routine tasks, without any high stimulation, that one becomes daydreamy, unfocused, and unproductive. A story told to me by a woman named Susan emphasizes this.

Years ago, before she was diagnosed, she lived in a house with an apple tree in the back yard. Every autumn the apples would fall off the tree, and Susan's family would have to pick them up, for otherwise they would rot on the ground. (She wasn't the type that looked forward to this— picking up the apples, making apple sauce, canning them for the winter— very un-ADD.) Her husband insisted, for at least the sake of the neighbors, that they pick them up. It was torture for her. She was slow and was upset from the second they started, obviously non-productive. This became an annual source of conflict between them.

Tasks like this with very little external stimulation or structure create a situation which can be of extremely low interest to the individual. This is where medication is extremely helpful. It turns on the brain and helps one focus when there isn't anything externally exciting going on.

Inability to Filter out Distractions

For people with ADD, this often means that there is not an effective filtering system with which to block out all the internal thoughts and external stimuli. The result is that a person feels bombarded by excess information; sounds, smells, noises, movement, and even internal ideas from one's own mind. Between work life and home life, things can mount so much that it feels like a tornado inside one's head. The distractions at work can increase so much that at home, one is trying to catch up on office work. But being at home is filled with such distractions, especially with children in the house, that not only does the extra work from the job not get done, but the household work isn't accomplished either. You can see how this could lead to another overwhelming sea of distress.

"When I'm inside my house it's like I'm right in the middle of a busy street. Each noise from down the block throws me off. If I have a thought and then the phone rings, I'm lost. Each tick of the clock drives me over the edge. People say, 'Just ignore it,' but I can't block it out."

"I was in Atlantic City for a conference. I had to keep taking time out to go back to my room so I could get away ... from the noise, the clicking, the coins; I was ready to lose it. It was a nightmare."

IMPULSIVITY

Excessive, Impulsive Shifting of Attention or
Excessive Shifting of Activities.

In a woman's home there are so many distractions, choices and variables, so many things to grab one's attention, that it can be difficult to pick out the most important thing to do first. It leads to tremendous inefficiency. In this unstructured environment, with so many pulls from so many different directions, it's hard to keep an organized household. Many women just can't figure out the proper sequence of events in order to accomplish a task.

"I start out to straighten the house but I notice we are out of towels so I go downstairs to get some more and I forget why I'm there when I reach the bottom of the stairs but I notice my shoes so I take them upstairs to the bedroom and then I see the travel article open on the bed because I wanted to plan a trip and since I remember now about the deadline I go to find the travel agent's number, but I am confronted by a mass of papers and scribbled illegible numbers so I start to dig around, and then I see the bills I haven't paid and think maybe I should go buy some stamps, but I remember I don't have any gas, and I can't find my keys ..."

"I just wander around all day, it seems. I don't get anything done. I just move things from one place to another."

ACTIVITY LEVELS

Activation.

Some individuals with ADD, especially without hyperactivity, have an activation problem as described by Dr. Tom Brown, in his article "ADD Without Hyperactivity". Rather than a deficit of attention, this means that one can't deploy attention, direct it, put it at the right place when one wants to at the right time. Often it means that they just can't think of what to do. Some people can't just think of an idea and act on it. They might not be able to act at all, or, as Kate Kelly and Peggy Ramundo say in *You Mean I'm Not Lazy, Stupid or Crazy?!* they might experience a "paralysis of will."

Dr. Thomas Brown explains that ADD people *without* hyperactivity have severe difficulty activating enough to start a task and sustaining the energy to complete it.

This is especially true for low-interest activities.

"The clothes from my trip a month ago are just still laying in a heap in the suitcase."

"I spend a lot of time in bed watching TV but my mind isn't watching TV. I'm thinking about what I should be doing but I don't have the energy to do it."

COGNITIVE DIFFICULTIES
Subtle Information Processing Problems

In addition to visible disorganization an ADD individual often has extreme difficulties with internal organization, especially of ideas. There are several ways in which information processing can be problematic. Dr. Tom Brown emphasized at the ADDA 1995 Conference (National Attention Deficit Disorder Association) that ADD causes significant but subtle diverse cognitive impairments. Dr. Martha Denckla speaks of "executive function problems" in *Attention Deficit Disorder* by Dr. Dale Jordan, and Drs. Hallowell and Ratey in *Answers to Distraction*, in their chapter on women, point to subtle information processing problems in women with ADD.

Following are four of the categories of information processing that I have seen frequently cause the difficulties that result in disorganization for ADD adults.

1. Loose, Shifting Mental Images

Dr. Dale Jordan in *Attention Deficit Disorder* describes in depth some of the reasons for disorganization in ADD adults. He uses phrases like "They can't maintain organized mental images... Their mental impressions change immediately... They have loose internal patterns... "The brain [of the ADD adult] does not maintain an organized impression of time, space or things within a given space." Even if these people have the activation needed to organize, they often can't remember where things go, or how they should look. Some people don't have a strong image in their mind which would allow them to put an object back in a particular place or in a particular way. Forgetting where things are can be extremely frustrating as one goes on a wild goose chase, wasting minutes and hours looking for earrings, stockings, belts, notebooks, or keys.

"I have a Ph.D. but I can't figure out how to clean my closet. I just stand there and stare at it. I don't remember where things go or what to do. I get so confused and overwhelmed."

Kate Kelly and Peggy Ramundo discuss the impact on organization from what they call "the erratic [memory] storage system" in ADD individuals. They emphasize that in order to organize, one must first be able to remember where one's belongings are and then be able to figure out what to do with them. They talk about the spatial problems often associated with ADD and point out that even when ADD adults have the motivation and slow down enough to confront their organizational tasks, they often "face the nightmarish task of figuring out what to do with his/her chaotic surroundings."

In addition, associated motor difficulties such as bumping into or dropping things often creates more mess in the process of trying to clean up than existed before. Kelly and Ramundo also speak about a "distorted sense of space" that adds to the organizational difficulties of ADD individuals.

2. Sequencing, Prioritizing and Planning, and Categorizing

Turning one's attention to very small categories is difficult and frustrating for many ADD adults. It is problematic to process all the information that comes into a household and put it into the right places. Most of these chores fall to women, and most people do it more or less automatically. ADD adults don't. Kelly and Ramundo also report difficulty in sorting and filing in ADD adults. They attribute this also in part to ADD adults' tendency to consider a multitude of options that make these small distinctions incredibly difficult.

"I am an executive at a large company where I must excel at long-term strategic planning. My husband doesn't believe me when. at home, I find it agonizing to have to sort the newspapers, bottles and cans for recycling."

Many people have difficulty figuring out what the next step in a task or project should be, or how to plan. They may look at the whole picture but don't know how to proceed with a job. They just can't figure out a good plan of attack, which is what Dr. Martha Denckla calls *"executive function problems."*

"I get up in the morning with no idea how to choose from what seems like millions of possibilities of things I need to do, how to organize my day ... so I just sit there."

"My non-ADD husband tells me how to clean the kitchen after a meal. First, put all the perishables in the refrigerator. Then you put away any other food in the pantry. Then you throw out everything that can go into the trash. Then you stack dishes and glasses together. Then you clean out the sink. At that point you start rinsing the dishes, stacking them again in categories before you put them into the dishwasher. This is how non-ADD people do tasks and organize their lives. This is exactly what an ADD person has such difficulty with. To them life contains millions of equal stimuli, with no order, no categories, no priority. Finding a particular bill or matching pair of earrings could be as baffling and frustrating as writing a report. It's all the same."

3. Synthesizing Ideas

For many people, trying to find the ideas inside their head that they need for a particular purpose can be as difficult as finding papers on a messy desk. What is difficult for many creative people with ADD is to pull all their ideas together, especially in written form, in an organized, logical, linear manner. Many have an extremely difficult time creating structure, a skeleton on which to build their ideas. This is what causes many individuals to overwork. They often have to spend many times more hours behind the scenes to pull together what is usually an excellent product. The level of difficulty involved is way out of proportion to the person's ideas or ability to address the subject. It's as if they have to go through many more cognitive processes to arrive at the end product. For example, a very bright young woman in college reports that she spent fifty hours to produce a five-page paper. This kind of difficulty is something I often hear reported by bright individuals with ADD.

There is often a limitless drive for information that leads to feeling overwhelmed because the person cannot organize the amount of material that they can generate mentally. This seems to come both from being unable to ignore any idea or connection that they make in their minds as well as a need (which I have observed) to understand the whole of a subject before they can understand any part of it.

4. Mismatched Input and Output

Some people *process incoming information slowly.* Because of this they just *can't match input and output.* When speaking to others, Einstein would say, "Talk slowly. I'm a slow thinker." This is a wonderful way to remember that slow processing has nothing to do with intelligence. However, it can feel as though you are "stupid" when you can't keep up with all the information coming at you. Sometimes the incoming information is out of sync with the internal processing speed. Sometimes, though, it's hard to know if someone is experiencing slow processing speed or is just creating more ideas than average. What happens sometimes is that the internal generation of ideas is more rapid than can be organized and expressed in a coherent fashion.

"I don't think I'm a slow processor. It's just that I create more ideas "per capita" than other people. It's impossible to keep up with them."

Kelly and Ramundo talk about people with ADD rapidly processing their own internal thoughts but having a slower rate of processing incoming information as well as organizing the information in order to express it.

Often ADD people just need a "bridge over troubled waters"— a coach, a partner, or a professional, to sit down and help them structure their day, help pick out a few things that they should focus on. Without that small bridge, they're trapped hopelessly on the other side, alone on an island, not even knowing that they can signal for help.

We will look at this in more detail later in the book. For women with ADD, every day feels like the height of the Christmas season: the kinds of stress and demands that all women report during this time of year are just regular days in the lives of ADD women.

Next we will examine the 'jobs' our culture requires of women in the course of a regular day, and the expectations that even the most "liberated" women have internalized and held sacred. We will look at the effect of disorganization on a woman, as she tries to live up to this cultural ideal.

PART II

HIDING

CHAPTER SIX

The Job from Hell: A Woman's Job Description

Can you imagine finding the following ad in your local newspaper?
Woman wanted to coordinate multiple schedules in very unstructured, distracting atmosphere. Must be able to process great numbers of details quickly and maintain very neat and well organized environment. Must keep track of all important occasions, including social obligations, birthday cards, and thank you notes to many people as well as be responsible for all subtleties and niceties of life. Must be able to choose quickly and easily from a great number of options. Applicant will be responsible for all record—keeping and for maintenance of all systems in the organization, as well as the upkeep on all equipment. For those interested, please call (911) n–o–t, A–D–D–D.

The Collision

We have looked at the various symptoms of ADD and traced the development of the inner world of the ADD girl growing up into a woman. Now we will place that woman in the middle of the cultural context in which she lives each day. We will see how ADD symptoms and disorganization collide with the role expectations for women in our culture.

Women with Attention Deficit Disorder often face a different set of challenges than do men. The role expectations for women collide directly with the specific difficulties that women with ADD face, causing a great deal of inner conflict and stress. *All women* are exposed to and often struggle with these expectations, but for ADD women, whose difficulties form the very basis of these expectations, the problems are compounded and intensified.

There still exists even today, an **unwritten job description** for women, both at home and at work, that requires great organizational skills. These job expectations create an internalized image of the "culturally ideal woman." Difficulty in matching this "ideal image" continually confronts the ADD woman leading to frustration and failure on a daily basis. This makes it difficult for her to be assertive, or to ask for what she considers "special" help.

Why ADD Impacts Women Differently than Men

Men with ADD face their own sorts of painful challenges and struggles in not meeting other cultural expectations, such as not always being able to be the stable, solid, breadwinner in the household. Below is a list of some of the ways ADD impacts women differently than men.

• Women have more sheer numbers of responsibilities that require organizational skills.

• Women have more tasks to do in general and more unrelated tasks from different areas of their lives to coordinate.

• Women's lives are often more diffuse, they have multiple role conflicts, and they often have more distractions to contend with.

• Women with children have more of the responsibilities for structuring the daily lives of their children (who often also have ADD).

• Men more often have wives or partners who organize their lives.

• Men more often have secretaries or other assistants organizing them.

• Men are often encouraged more than women from an early age to focus on a narrow area of strength and to pursue that.

• Men have not internalized these organizational cultural expectations to the same extent as women, so they don't feel the same sense of shame about their disorganization. As a result of this, they ask for help from other people more easily, which allows them to continue to focus on their talents and abilities.

• Men with the same difficulties are more often seen as endearing or absent-minded in general, while women with these difficulties are seen by themselves and the external world as defective or deficient in some basic way.

WHY ADD IMPACTS WOMEN DIFFERENTLY THAN MEN

Women have more tasks to do.

Women's lives are often more diffuse.

* Women with children have more responsibilities.

* Men more often have partners who organize their lives.

Men more often have secretaries or other assistants organizing them.

* Men are often encouraged to focus on a narrow area.

* Men don't feel the same sense of shame about their disorganization.

* Men with the same difficulties are more often seen as endearing or absent-minded.

The Ideal Candidate

Upon calling for more information about the job advertised (at the beginning of the chapter), one would receive a more detailed description of the ideal candidate, as follows.

Much of the work is boring and routine so applicant must be able to function well without needing high amount of interest or stimulation. Appearance is important; applicant must have a variety of well coordinated outfits. This job requires keeping up the appearance and maintenance of the building as well as attending to the subtle details in order to make the surroundings attractive for others. This position involves a great deal of entertaining and one must know the socially correct things to say at all times. Must excel at small talk, never interrupting or saying the wrong thing at the wrong time, never going blank, and always remembering people's faces and names. One must be able to converse on a variety of topics, remembering details from movies and plays, and of course be well-read, comfortable discussing both the recent bestsellers in fiction and nonfiction, as well as the current political situation. It is also important to not be reactive to people, but instead to maintain a calm demeanor throughout your interactions. The position may include the opportunity to care for children who have severe problems with attention and behavior. It could require the ability to be able to carefully structure their lives in order to give them the calm, supportive, organized atmosphere they need. The candidate will be held accountable for the children's success. Finally, the perfect candidate for the job will go above and beyond the actual performance of tasks themselves, to be an example to others on how to best perform these particular tasks. Slow, careful folding of napkins would be applauded. Enjoying grocery shopping, carefully picking the best vegetables, and finely chopping them would be most preferred. Of course, excellent calendar and scheduling skills would be most appropriate. We also prefer that you never say no to requests from volunteer organizations, charitable events, and of course friends or family. It will be important to attend as many of these organizational meetings as possible. Merit raises will be given to those who spend no time on themselves and instead focus all their time and energy on others. Going that extra mile means always saying yes and not asking for special favors. You must know how to cope and get by, and certainly keep any difficulties to yourself.

Would anyone with ADD (or even without, for that matter) deliberately apply for a job like this? Of course not. But yet, women with ADD cling steadfastly to this image and often remain determined to achieve this ideal standard.

Women's Basic Job Description

- Multiple task coordinator
- Central household information coordinator
- Household maintenance manager
- Creating a comfortable and attractive home atmosphere
- Billpayer
- Budgeter
- Housecleaner
- Food preparer
- Time Manager and Scheduler
- Event Planner, Management and Staff person
- Grocery shopper
- Clothes shopper
- Clothes coordinating
- Social Coordinator and Hostess
- Packer for trips
- Travel Coordinator
- Interior Designer
- Holiday Coordinator
- President of the Social Occasion Obligations Club
- Secretary of the "Hallmark" committee

- ("the right card to the right person at the right time")
- Chairman of the "Volunteer" committee
- The ADD organizer and Coach for children with ADD
- Charter Member of the "Welcome Wagon"
- ("We willingly open our doors to friends and neighbors")
- Household "mood" Engineer
- (setting the emotional temperature of the household)

. . . and this is often in addition to working outside the home all day!

The job description of running a home and family requires multiple task coordination that can be disastrous for a woman with ADD. You can see that these women's job descriptions and expectations bring them right up against their areas of deficit that we described previously. As Dr. Lynn Weiss says in her book *Attention Deficit Disorder in Adults*, "an ordinary day for a woman is a nightmare for a woman with ADD." Dr. Kathleen Nadeau, who writes a great deal about women and ADD says in an article on women and ADD in *ADDult News* that mothers with ADD "may be viewed by others as a 'bad mother' rather than as struggling valiantly with demands which are difficult if not impossible to meet."

The "F" word

These are the three main parts of the job description in which women experience feelings of failure: 1) failure to perform and conform to job expectations; 2) failure in their identity as women; and 3) failure in fulfilling their role as partner and mother.

Feelings of Failure to Perform and Conform to Job Expectations

Whether a woman is married and/or taking care of children at home and/or working at an outside job, or single and trying to keep up the demands of a social life, women with ADD often express feelings of failure to perform and conform to job expectations.

Brenda really loved staying home and taking care of her four children. But she was not able to take care of her domestic responsibilities anywhere near the level required. The distractions were overwhelming and she could not filter out the multiple demands on her attention to attend to cooking or cleaning while the children were present. She asks poignantly, "Why am I a failure at the one thing I want to do?"

Wendy, a single woman, speaks. "My friends don't understand why I'm so exhausted and overwhelmed after working all day that I can't go out with them at night. I don't really understand it, either. What's the matter with me?"

Feelings of Failure in their Feminine Identity

The feelings that women often express about the impact of these failings go to the very heart of their identity as women. Compounded over a lifetime, these experiences of failure in this role have a great effect on one's sense of "femininity." As one woman client said to me, *"I can't make small talk, or shop. These are two things that make me feel that I'm not like a woman."*

A beautiful young client, Lani, also expressed this feeling of not being feminine. Because acessorizing, coordinating, and the diffi-culty of dressing in the morning were such chores, she always chose very basic clothes. This interfered with the full and natural expres-sion of her personality, coloring her self perception for many years.

For Jamie, going to the grocery store can make her feel like ducking for cover from all the stimulation and choices. Going to a department store is even worse, where she is confronted by piano players, flashy displays and a dizzying array of colors, fragrances and choices.

Jamie has a very difficult time trying to hold in her mind what she needs to in order coordinate an entire outfit. She often just wanders around department stores for hours, leaving without ac-complishing anything. Not only does she feel that she wasted time and doesn't have anything to wear, but most importantly she feels like an abysmal failure—a woman who can't even buy an outfit, let alone enjoy it in the way that other women seem to do.

Feelings of Failure in Fulfilling their Role
as Partner or Mother

Rose was in tears as she asked me, "Aren't wives supposed to take care of the couple's social life, like setting up dates with other couples? I'm afraid my husband will leave me eventually because I don't perform these basic kind of functions. I just can't keep up with all of that."

Rose, an accomplished professional woman, admitted with a painful sense of "confession" her profound feelings of failure in her role as a wife and her fears that she is unacceptable to her husband, almost as if she had betrayed him. Even though her husband says he doesn't care about her role as social organizer she still has managed to have received this message from the world around her. She constantly observes how other women manage their lives and perform these roles well, or at least adequately.

Parenting raises a whole host of other problems for women trying to fulfill their basic role expectations, especially when this involves structuring the life of an ADD child. More specific suggestions for approaching this will be explored later, in the section on the Three R's. For now, we can begin to appreciate the tremendous collision that results when the woman with ADD is confronted with these parenting expectations.

Kay, a woman with ADD, had a son diagnosed with ADHD and attended a meeting to provide proper structure at school and home. One of the goals was to make sure that her son, Mark, completed his homework every night. On the nights that it wasn't done and Mark went to school the next day with it uncompleted, Kay was the one who felt responsible for this failure. Kay was the one whom the teacher confronted with the "bad news" at the end of the day when she came to pick Mark up. Kay's husband, Jerry, didn't feel the shame, embarrassment, frustration or daily stress of completing that homework, even though he didn't have ADD and might have helped Mark more easily. Mark certainly didn't feel the pressure of not getting the homework done, either. Kay, who had extreme difficulties with organizing her own life, became driven to the exclusion of all else to getting that homework done so that she could avoid a negative report from the teacher each day. She wound up being responsible for the homework and basically took over emotional ownership of this task. Obviously, the result was overload in an already overtaxed area of operation.

Women's (Unspoken) Job Description at Work

- Making small talk in the coffee–break room
- Serving on committees for fund raisers
- Baking or contributing food for special events
- Remembering co–workers' birthdays
- Sending get-well cards
- Spending extra time with someone in need
- Picking out going-away presents or arranging going-away lunches
- Socializing over lunch (engaging in non-work related conversation)
- Attending or arranging co-workers' baby and wedding showers

Women's Basic Job Description at Work

· Making small talk in the coffee-break room
· Serving on committees for fund raisers
· Baking or contributing food to special events
· Remembering co-workers' birthdays
· Sending get well cards
· Spending extra time with someone in need
· Picking out going away presents or arranging going-away lunches
· Socializing over lunch (engaging in non-work related conversation)
· Attending or arranging co-workers baby and wedding showers

Even at work, women face their own particular difficulties. While sometimes it is easier for women with ADD to be more successful at work than at home because there are fewer distractions and they are able to zero in on a specific talent or ability, work can often present its own particular set of challenges.

Even if a woman has found some measure of success in her job, it is often a painful reality for her to discover that it is often assumed (without question) that she naturally enjoys, is good at, has desire for, or has time for the kinds of activities listed above. A woman may feel subtly pressured to fulfill these kinds of non-work-related cultural expectations. The assumption is that, because she is a woman, she has these natural inclinations. This situation keeps these women swallowing feelings of failure, feelings of disappointing other people despite other successes. This keeps them from being able to feel the full flowering of their success in the workplace. They are still keeping parts of themselves hidden, "in the closet," saying yes to these "extracurricular" requests that eventually result in a feeling of being overloaded.

A woman on the job may feel a subtle pressure to be involved in volunteer work or being on special committees. It's especially difficult to say no to "charitable" causes that fund-raise or in some way aid others. "Sunshine committees" that take care of the niceties of life and help people who are ill or out of work can put a dark cloud over the woman who is already overloaded but continues to smile and hide.

A man these days is often asked to sign a card or even pick up a dish for a potluck, but he rarely is expected to take charge of or organize an event. If he takes on the responsibility and fails to do an adequate job, he is affectionately tolerated as meeting the cultural expectations for a man.

Women are less able than men to compartmentalize their relationships at home and work, so they might feel more pressure to invite business associates into their personal lives or to accept others' offers of such personal relationships.

One of the worst things for many ADD women is having to go to a business lunch and make "small talk." When men go to lunch, they are more likely to be focusing on "deals" and business. Women are often expected to discuss outside interests such as shopping or the theater or best-sellers which they may have no interest in or knowledge of. Women with ADD feel they have been unable to acquire or remember this kind of popular cultural information but that this reflects a personal failure. When this happens with business associates whose good opinion is of critical importance to them, they may spend most of these social occasions covering up what they feel are their inadequacies rather than feeling good about their areas of excellence. It feels particularly like a trap when a woman has worked hard to achieve excellence in her field, only to have to either "do lunch" badly or else refuse these social occasions and be thought of as a snob or as a little weird.

The areas that an ADD women struggles with are often those largely required to satisfactorily or easily perform the basic "job description" that today still exists for women. These difficulties are compounded by the cultural messages she receives as she grows up. As a result, she struggles daily with often intense inner pressures and conflicts.

Without even realizing it, the woman with ADD often deeply internalizes culturally transmitted images of behavior and performance that culminate in her pursuit to match the standard of the "culturally ideal woman." An ADD woman, no matter how successful she might be in other areas of life, when confronted continually with her areas of deficit, can experience a daily diet of stress, or frustration, or even failure.

We will trace this legacy and see how, over time, this small daily washing away of self-esteem adds to the feeling of not measuring up in some fundamental way. Over the years it silently erodes a basic sense of competence and self-worth, instilling a strong need for self protection.

CHAPTER SEVEN

The Emotional Legacy

Now you might be wondering at this point—"I just want to pay my bills, be on time and be able to see my desk again; why do I have to understand the emotional implications of all this?" Well, I could tell you just to go out and get a new, fancy datebook, but this time, just try harder! But I imagine that you've done this about a zillion times, and guess what? You're still disorganized, and you probably feel worse each time one of these systems doesn't work. Only by understanding the emotional components of disorganization will we then be able to have the tools to learn to live successfully with ADD.

We have seen the difficulties that many adult women have in fulfilling their job expectations and the sense of failure that often develops as they struggle to keep up with these overwhelming tasks. This is coupled with their attempt to match the dead-end pursuit of the idealized, culturally-approved image of what a woman should be.

In this chapter we will explore the two kinds of messages that women collect throughout their lives. The first are those general, culturally transmitted messages that a woman absorbs as she grows up. The second group of messages are more personal in nature, which she receives from the significant people in her life. We will see how these messages can eventually result in the emotional legacies of Shame and Guilt.

Cultural Messages

Cultural Messages are deeply ingrained rules of acceptable behavior that are often transmitted both through society at large as well as through the family of origin. They sound so simple that most women might think

Cultural Messages To Women

- BE "NICE"

- HELP OTHERS

- DON'T SAY NO

- DON'T ASK FOR TOO MUCH

- DON'T HURT ANYONE'S FEELINGS

- DON'T SET TIME LIMITS ON PROJECTS

- DON'T TRY TO GET OUT OF WORK BY ASKING FOR SPECIAL FAVORS

they are ridiculous, and that they can readily overcome them. But in fact, they are very powerful, and can easily slow or stop even the most determined person. They concern these four areas: helping other people, asking for help, fears about acting special, and conflicts about asserting one's own needs. These messages are articulated in some way from most women in therapy who are trying to make changes in their lives. For women with ADD these cultural messages can have even greater impact. It is absolutely essential for them to confront and work through them in order to create the necessary changes to make their life work for them. These changes have to be made at home, at school, in their jobs, and in their relationships.

General Messages To Women

- Be nice
- Be accommodating, rather than asking for accommodations
- Help others, rather than ask for help
- Don't say no to requests from people in need
- Always lend a helping hand

Here are some other cultural prohibitions or warnings women come to believe.
- If you ask for too much, someone will get angry or think you are trying to get away with something

- Don't try to get out of work by asking for special favors
- If you say no, you'll hurt someone's feelings
- You should never hurt someone's feelings
- If you set limits on your time and projects, people will think you just can't cut it
- Don't complain; keep your problems to yourself
- Don't act like you're better than anyone else

The following deeply held cultural values transmitted through the family of origin become ingrained in children's minds and continue to exert strong influence on women as they consider getting help or making changes in their life. In addition, every person's family has certain rules, rituals, and traditions that they hold sacred. These are extremely hard to confront and break.

"Willpower and hard work will get you through anything"

"Put up a brave front"

"Cleanliness is next to godliness"

"Don't start something you're not willing to finish"

"This is the way it's always been done"

"There's a right way and a wrong way to do things"

One of the first women with ADD I worked with in therapy was a young, bright college student named Carla. She was enrolled in a very technical course of study in which it was absolutely essential that she have extra time on exams. It took her months to be able to ask for the accommodations she needed. It was the first time I witnessed how, despite great motivation and with legal documentation of disability, something more powerful going on internally held this young woman back.

For Carla, like many women, this had a great deal to do with asking for special privileges or special favors. She had a deep belief that she didn't deserve what she viewed as an unfair advantage. Moreover, she felt even if she were granted this help, that would somehow diminish her in the eyes of her instructor. Carla didn't truly believe she was only asking for a level playing field. She believed rather that she was trying to "get away with something," to get out of work or fool someone. All these scripts from earlier days were swimming around in her head, causing tremendous conflict about asking for accommodations.

I've seen this over and over in my women clients. Women with ADD grow up hearing attributions and admonishments from parents and teachers. They are used both to explain mysterious gaps as well as motivate change in performance. These messages continue to exert strong influence over them as adults as they contemplate change—considering measures to help them restructure their lives. They need to get the help they need in their areas of difficulty so they can move ahead with their areas of strength. Unless the depth and source of these barriers are fully appreciated, an ADD woman (as well as anyone trying to intervene in helpful ways) will have a hard time understanding her apparent lack of follow-through.

After her initial resistance, Carla did make a cursory attempt to ask for help at school but she was rebuffed. At this point, instead of pushing through the process, she backed away. Carla, like many women who find themselves in this position of needing to confront a closed system with their needs, faced even greater *internal* resistance than external. A woman with ADD has struggled for years to get into a position of fulfilling her potential or beginning to feel the possibility of success. To have to admit vulnerability at the point of greatest hope would understandably be very threatening.

When women with ADD are afraid to ask for changes that would help make their life better, they feel this kind of stance will be seen as demanding or aggressive. They think this would lead other people to reject or resent them.

All the small talk and constant chatter made it impossible for Diane to do her work, and she knew there was an area away from her current work station that would be a less distracting place for her. But she hesitated to request this move. She felt the other women would think that she was standoffish, better than they were, or special in some sort of way.

It took a long time and a lot of support from the ADD group Diane was in before she could express these kinds of feelings and confront these internal barriers. After a few months of getting to know other women with ADD she became more de-sensitized to the reactions of the people in her office. Because of the support of the other group members, Diane was able to consider the option of moving to another location in the office.

Janis had her own office at work. Co-workers continually stopped by to ask questions or just to chat throughout the day. She had a hard time concentrating and getting her work done with all the distractions from the surrounding offices.

Theoretically, Janis could shut the door of her office if she wanted to. But she had a harder time even considering this option when figuring out how to improve her work life. She was concerned that it would seem rude to other people, even though it would have helped her tremendously to create a distraction-free environment. But she felt she couldn't say no or shut others out.

After a lifetime of hearing and seeing what a woman should be or do, cultural messages tend to become virtually unshakable thoughts that stay in a woman's mind. Though perhaps intellectually women don't believe these ideas, when they are pushed to take action that runs counter to these messages, they find themselves confronting powerful internal barriers. It is at this point that ADD treatment can become slowed or halted, even with diagnosis and medication.

Guilt

We've seen that exposure to cultural messages makes it difficult to ask for help. When a woman with ADD considers asking others to help her with things she believes she should be able to do on her own, the result is often feelings of guilt. Guilt is also often triggered when a woman considers asking for "special" accommodations. To take time away from helping others and focus on herself keeps her on a treadmill fueled by guilt. Women with ADD are often afraid that assertiveness (as they were indirectly taught on their way to womanhood) will be met with anger. On an unconscious level they would expect retaliation, confirming their worst fears. I hear this from women of all ages with ADD during counseling.

If they do manage to take the first halting steps, they are often rebuffed and then have difficulty in going on to the next level. This difficulty is partially from a lack of assertive skills, but also from a lack of belief that they deserve these accommodations. They haven't yet fully integrated the reality of ADD or discounted the messages they have internalized.

"Don't make trouble."

"Be grateful to be here at all."

"Don't bother anyone."

"Keep your problems to yourself."

"Just blend in."

"Don't make waves."

ADD women, like many women, may feel uncomfortable putting their needs before others, saying no, or not contributing to the group or the team. They put their own lives and needs on hold for as long as possible in order to avoid saying no to others or having to ask for special help. Even if they feel confident enough to defer a task or to make a space for themselves, they don't enjoy the resulting free time. They remain focused on what they have left undone and feel guilty about it. If the daily tasks are too difficult for them to complete, they're often unable to participate in other kinds of nourishing, fun, or replenishing activities either, because they've failed to do their work first. Certain kinds of work are never finished (because the tasks are so overwhelming and unending) and they never feel justified in blocking out any time for relaxation or fun.

An important part of the process of change, as we'll examine in more depth later, is to push that envelope and become gradually more comfortable enjoying life, even though some work is still undone.

Maligning Messages

Added to the culturally transmitted messages are the other deeply-embedded and more personal "maligning messages" which, because they are personal, are inherently more toxic. A woman with ADD has often been unconsciously collecting maligning messages since childhood. These stay with her and emerge at the most seemingly ordinary times.

Maligning messages come in the form of both "you" messages and "she" messages. "You" messages have been spoken directly to a woman since childhood, and are interpretations and evaluations of her perfor-

MALIGNING OF MESSY AND DISORGANIZED WOMEN

"She's a slob."

"She has no pride in her home or appearance."

"She doesn't take care of the children well."

"She's self-centered."

"She just doesn't care."

mance and behavior. "She" messages are descriptions she has heard about other girls or women who have the same difficulties she may have. She takes these as indirect criticisms and indications of her own failings, becoming painfully sensitive to these kind of statements.

"YOU" Messages

We've seen how an ADD girl can present a confusing picture to other people. As a result, she collects many negative labels and attributions along the way. ADD behaviors can look like something that she is "doing to" other people. Many negative labels absorbed at an early age remain tender, sensitive "hot spots," even when these children become adults. Children with ADD were blamed for things that they didn't know how to change; they were blamed for just being themselves. These kind of questions conveyed "you" messages to them.

"*Where were YOU raised? In a pigpen? This is a mess!*"
"*Why are YOU being so stubborn? Why don't YOU clean up your room? Why are YOU so slovenly? Why don't YOU care about the way YOU look? Why don't YOU try harder?*"

ADD women fear even when they become adults that if they push too hard to get what they need they will hear some "awful truth" about themselves thrown back at them.

"*You are stupid.*"
"*You don't belong here.*"
"*We made a mistake. You fooled us for a while.*"
"*You are too much trouble. You cause problems all the time.*"

Shame

A woman develops *shame* as the result of the cumulative effect of the kind of messages that have been used to describe her. No matter how bright or competent a woman is, the reminder of these negative messages continues to hold quite a sting. They create an internalized sense of self-blame, of not being good enough.

This following story of a former client of mine, Sharon, demonstrates poignantly how ADD symptoms can send waves of shame through a person, instantaneously triggering intense reactions. Despite maturity and success, an individual exhibiting her ADD symptoms in front of someone who thinks she is competent can send her into a state of anxiety and shame.

The Rhodes Scholar

Sharon was a fifty-two-year-old woman with two grown children, divorced after twenty years of marriage. All her life, she had heard maligning messages such as, "You're as slow as molasses. You'd forget your head if it wasn't attached." In spite of this, she went back to community college and started both to do very well and to have great difficulties. For the first time in her life, she became identified as having learning disabilities. When she finished community college, she went on to enroll in a well-respected, competitive university. She received accommodations for her learning disabilities and achieved high grades, despite having an extraordinarily difficult time in the process. She found that integrating and synthesizing a huge amount of material, continuously having to juggle, (i.e., figure out whether or not to drop a particular class, whether to get extensions, etc.) contributed to her feeling overwhelmed and anxious. In one way, she was thriving in this stimulating, exciting, challenging world; in another way, she was constantly feeling as if she were about to drown.

Through counseling she began to learn how to hold on to her successes, even when the process was difficult and she felt that disaster was around the corner. Sharon eventually also became aware that she had ADD, but at the time, she felt she was merely a bumbling sort of person. She used to call this her "muchness," because she was overflowing with ideas, enthusiasm, books, and papers. She did have difficulties but she also had corresponding qualities of being excited, interested, curious, and involved. She was beginning to be able to integrate and express the ideas she was being exposed to.

The pinnacle of her success came in her senior year when she received a letter that invited her to apply to become a Rhodes Scholar. She learned later that this honor had been offered in error because only students under a certain age were eligible. This technicality disqualified her, but that didn't matter to Sharon. This moment of triumph was naturally intense for her in the light of all her struggles. She experienced it almost like an internal earthquake, because it didn't match her inner experience of herself. For instance, just that day she had asked for an incomplete in a course because she was unable to complete the required work on time. She had papers all over her room, books spread over all the tables. She was interested in and following up on so many ideas that she wasn't always able to meet her deadlines. Of course, she was thrilled with the honor on one level, but still struggling to integrate this great accomplishment into her picture of herself.

Sharon grabbed the award letter along with the rest of her things and rushed over to the hallowed halls of the great university. She caught up with an old distinguished professor, an imposing figure whose opinion of her meant a great deal to her. Excited and a little out of breath, she said, "Professor Churchill, I want to tell you something very important. I was invited to apply to be a Rhodes Scholar! I want to show you the letter." She looked down at her feet, in horror, to see an array of papers, books, notes, her purse overflowing and—she couldn't find the letter.

She got down on her hands and knees and started going through everything, searching in vain as he towered over her. At that moment, sitting there, all the feelings of a shameful, incompetent, bumbling little girl flooded her. The feeling of shame, she said, started at the tips of her toes and traveled up her body to the top of her head. At that moment, it felt as if everything—all her successes—were just wiped out. The extremes of that pivotal moment demonstrated both sides of the ADD coin: on one hand, the success, the brilliance, the creativity, the competence and on the other hand, the bumbling, the fumbling, the disarray and the confusion.

Sharon looked up at Professor Churchill in tears and said, "Huh! What a joke! How could I be a Rhodes Scholar? Look what a mess I am! I even had to take an incomplete in your class today!" In her mind, she had undone for herself all the great success that she had achieved. Her professor, however, understood that they give Rhodes Scholarships to people who have overcome great adversity and have shown great perseverance in order to achieve. They are given to reward people who are committed to the pursuit of knowledge. Even though he knew she had taken an incomplete in his class, he realized it was her intense love of knowledge that led her off in so many directions. With all the wisdom of his years, Professor Churchill looked down at Sharon and said, "Listen to me, Ms. Oppenheim. It is because of *everything* that you are that has made them select you for this honor. Your thirst for knowledge and your perseverance cause you difficulty, but they're also what make you a Rhodes Scholar."

In that moment, this man had summed up the essence of this kind of discrepancy. The difficulty with staying on track because of intense interest in many things; the drive and excitement, even though they may cause severe difficulties, also made Sharon a special person in many ways. This story of the Rhodes Scholar demonstrates the battle with the deep reservoir of shame that can be triggered so easily, despite great success.

A few years after this incident, Sharon was able to say, "Now when something like that happens, I don't fall all the way to the bottom. I still feel embarrassed sometimes, but those feelings don't bleed into my self-concept the same way."

"She" Messages

"She" messages are those words one hears to describe other girls and women, who, like you, fail to meet culturally-sanctioned standards.

"She's a slob."

"She has no pride in her home or appearance."

"She doesn't take care of the children well."

"She shouldn't have had children."

"She's self-centered."

"She just doesn't care."

"She's a space cadet."

"She's let herself go."

"She's just not very interesting."

"She doesn't take the time to take care of herself."

Jodi is out to lunch with a group of women (all college graduates) who are discussing the latest bestseller. Jodi hasn't read a complete book in years. No one would guess this secret about Jodi. She's working hard during this lunch to keep up the illusion that, although she hasn't read this particular book, she still is well-read.

All of a sudden, the subject of Donna comes up. Jodi cringes inside because she knows that what will follow is the standard "she" message line about Donna: how irresponsible she is, how selfish, self-centered and lazy. She always seems to be too busy for anything. The kids never get a decent meal. Her husband has to do all the housework. She never sent a thank-you note for a present sent months ago. She hasn't reciprocated for any of their dinner invitations. "Can you believe that she's a lawyer? I can't imagine how any of her clients put up with her! She's so disorganized."

Jodi's anxiety level increases. She is sure that they must talk about her like this. "How should she react?" she wonders. Should she say, "I have those problems, too" or just keep quiet and stay undercover?

Hiding the "Shameful" Secret

Even if Jodi considers telling other people about her difficulties in order to get close to them or to get help, she might hear, "Oh, don't be silly!

You're so smart. I have that problem too. I lose my keys all the time." All
her feelings about being invisible, of not being able to make herself
understood, and of being discounted become activated and she often
retreats to the relative comfort of the closet. Inside her head, she hears
her inner voice repeating:

"You're just trying to get sympathy"

"You're over-sensitive"

"You're inventing problems"

"Who are you trying to fool?"

"What are you trying to pull?"

"Who are you trying to kid?"

Women grow up constantly exposed to messages about what's
right, what's acceptable behavior. When they fail to meet these standards, women often move into a "closet," hiding themselves from other
people. This results in great difficulty in ever getting help. If she feels it
is shameful to be disorganized, so shameful that she would not let
someone see the kind of disarray in which she lives, then naturally, she
would keep people away from her. This is a perfect setup for depression
and depletion and has a negative effect on relationships and achievement, leaving women feeling isolated, alone, and disconnected.

A client named Joan would not permit a friend, let alone a
coach or a family member, to come to her house in order to help her
get through the piles and backlog of materials, bills, and stuff. She
especially wouldn't let a baby-sitter in her house to care for her child
in order to start a lucrative career. When contemplating the idea of
getting some help, the imagined feelings of embarrassment and
hiding that would occur if someone helped her go through her things,
brought her up against a huge wall of shame.

This makes sense if one considers that every pile, every piece of
paper examined, and every unpaid bill discovered brings up a new
feeling of failure, a new recognition of opportunities abandoned, another reminder of a way she didn't measure up. These kinds of feelings
prevent her from having the kind of help necessary to move ahead.
Unless these kinds of emotions are understood by the individual and by
everyone trying to help her, she will eventually run into a brick wall.
Before a coach, a friend, counselor or family member can intervene
effectively, they must understand the level of difficulty that a woman
may have employing strategies that sound completely reasonable to the
person suggesting them.

Emotional Flow Chart

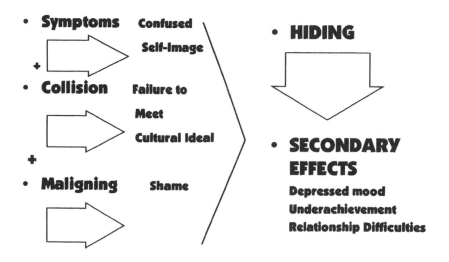

Summary

A woman often develops a desire to avoid triggering those old maligning messages at any cost. In order to maintain any appearance of competency that she has managed to achieve, she slowly but steadily, even without her full awareness, begins to hide parts of herself. Shame is one of the major stumbling blocks that prevents a woman from moving forward and getting the help she needs.

Until she examines these behaviors, she may well be unaware that she is acting in order to avoid triggering negative responses. Consequently, she won't understand why she avoids taking steps to restructure or redesign her life. The negative messages she receives often take the form of an inner, judgmental voice that can stop a woman in her tracks, no matter how smart, how strong or how resilient she might be. This inner voice severely restricts a woman's ability to get assistance, to receive special accommodations or to rearrange her environment. It feels too risky—she is just too vulnerable and raw in these areas. Exploring these particular fields of sensitivity may trigger her feelings of inadequacy by bringing back earlier childhood pain and humiliation of being "weird," "stupid," a "spaz," not fitting in, of being globally wrong in some way. The laughter and ridicule of others are there lurking inside her. Fear of the retribution exacted by these inner voices causes her to avoid triggering them no matter what the cost to herself in terms of hiding more of herself. This makes it more difficult to get the extra help or emotional support she needs, freeing up time and energy to focus on her many strengths.

As you see in the Emotional Flow Chart, ADD symptoms of inconsistent attention, impulsivity, and activation can lead to a confused self-image, laden with disorganization. The collision of the women's job description and the cultural expectations create for a woman failure in meeting the cultural ideal. Along with this, she hears maligning and cultural messages, which create the emotional legacies of shame and guilt.

The effect of all this cumulative experience is often a decision by a woman, at some level, to hide a large chunk of herself from other people and move to protect her self. This keeps her locked tight inside that closet, for fear she will be scrutinized, found out, publicly exposed and humiliated. She then becomes trapped on a continuous treadmill, unable to get the help she needs to restructure her life, unable to break through the guilt and the cultural messages against asking for special treatment.

The lack of time and energy, feelings of depletion, and hiding all combine to create "secondary effects" on women's lives, namely underachievement, a depressed mood, and difficulties with relationships.

SECONDARY EFFECTS

Depressed mood
Moving away from relationships
Underachievement

CHAPTER EIGHT

Secondary Effects: Underachievement and a Depressed Mood

The shame, guilt, and need for self-protection that we've just examined contribute a great deal to what I call the secondary effects of ADD symptoms. The effects of the primary symptoms of ADD (inattention, impulsivity, over or under activity level) consist of difficulty in doing routine tasks such as housework, schoolwork, jobs, and, of course, disorganization. The secondary effects of ADD impact women primarily in three areas: a woman's **achievement, mood, and relationships.** In this chapter we will discuss these first two issues, Achievement and Mood.

Underachievement

Shelly was a good student in high school. She did well in college also, although overworking almost to the point of exhaustion. After she graduated, she took a job with a local social agency. She did all right there; however, the paper work became overwhelming and eventually she left in frustration. She changed careers a few times, looking for just the right fit, but never really found it. She always would bog down at a certain point and never stayed long enough in one place to really move forward. She took a few other jobs through the years usually with the same results. She got married, had a baby, and a few years later went back to work again. However, she never could excel at anything. Shelly started seeing high school and college classmates' names in the paper.

President of this company, Director of this agency. "I was as smart as those people," she thought. I wonder why they made it and I didn't."

The ADD woman may shy away from making a phone call to get the information she needs to move along in her career. She fears that she will be called stupid, or scolded if she has already received this information and misplaced it. She may fear being laughed at or thought weird if she has an interesting new approach to a problem and requests assistance in carrying it out.

With each fleeting year, the woman with ADD becomes more aware of other people passing her by, people of equal or lesser abilities. These others have been able to proceed in a single direction, stay on course, mobilize their energies in order to build a career. The woman with ADD has no way to figure out, especially before diagnosis, why that happens or how to get herself on track. We can see how the web she feels tangled in traps her in the same place instead of allowing her to move back on track. Each person she meets or hears about who relays a history of achievement often causes a stab, a pain of diminished self-esteem, or grief over lost opportunities, and eventually even a feeling of hopelessness. Without diagnosis and treatment, she continues to feel trapped. A woman's inability to extricate herself from her entanglements and expectations makes her despair of ever finding a way to achieve and pursue meaningful goals. Hallowell and Ratey, in *Driven to Distraction,* put the pain of underachievement number one on their list of common themes heard from people with ADD.

I have identified three areas of achievement in which secondary effects of ADD particularly affect women. The first I call **Getting Stuck,** second is **The Assertion Blues,** and third is **The Mask of Competency.**

Getting Stuck

Even though women obviously are in more positions of power now than in previous years, still they find themselves confronted with having to do more paperwork and more detail work than do men of the same ability level, as they work their way up. Once ADD women can rise above entry and mid-level positions, they often are able to do very well; they can see the "Big Picture," conceptualize wonderfully well, and they (finally) have secretaries. There is often a double organizational wall that confronts women; they may face both the traditional "glass ceiling" in organizations as well as difficulties with organizing which keeps them trapped in the position of having to organize for those in higher positions.

Sometimes women feel that when their organizational skills do not match the requirements of their jobs the mismatch is a personal failure, rather than just a poor match between person and job. In these cases, women usually assume that they are "not good enough" and should therefore move downward to an "easier job." In reality, it may be that they need to move upward to a job that does not require them to scale down their thinking to match the limits of the job. They may need to develop a support net beneath them to handle the detail work that would allow them to express or present their ideas in an organized way.

Maggie had an entry-level position in a service business. She constantly berated herself for not being able to do small tasks even though all her ideas, projects and concepts were so big. She used to say to herself, "I'm a failure, I'm not even able to do these basic tasks. How am I going to be able to move ahead?" instead of thinking, "I need to do a different kind of job where I can shine and grow and use assistance to do this other kind of work." Maggie eventually took the examination necessary to enter a very demanding professional field and obtained an almost perfect score.

Women often confuse their strengths with their deficits. They see them as one big glob of ability that defines them. It is critical that women continuously sort out, separate and isolate their strengths from their weaknesses. Many women seem to operate on the premise that "something's wrong with me." They say, "I can't think that small. I can't do that kind of slow, boring work. I can only write huge reports. I can only think of big ideas. Something's wrong with me. I need to get smaller and smaller. I need to give away the exciting, big parts of this so I can do the small, required, detailed tasks."

Without any kind of organizational assistance, they either quit the jobs that require larger conceptual thinking (which is their strength), and find jobs where they can manage the organizational demands (not using their conceptual abilities), or they keep thinking they're bad because they're not able to meet the demands for smaller thinking. These women need not get smaller, they need to find ways to continually get bigger and discover how to provide a cushion of support underneath them as they use their real abilities and conceptual strengths. They must constantly find ways to keep pace with their achievements so they can continue to grow. Of course, this applies to men as well as women but usually men are in a position of having more support, both at home and at work.

Think of this as "The Organizational Package." This is a separate set of duties that need to be handled but perhaps they are only ten percent of the essential function of a job. They shouldn't dominate your choice of careers if ninety percent of your skills are a great match that would let you fulfill your dreams. When you understand this you can then present yourself with confidence. Every day I work with ADD women I see creative, competent, talented women who have had to turn down their dreams, thinking they just weren't smart enough to pull it off. Actually they just didn't have the "organizational package," the skills that a good secretary could have covered for them.

The Assertion Blues

When we examined cultural messages, we saw the reasons that women have trouble with assertion. Now we see the effect of that as it impacts achievement for the woman with ADD. For instance, when they hear "no" to a request for accommodations, they sometimes tend to accept this without pushing the issue further. Sometimes women don't have the assertive language skills to turn a request into an assertive statement without becoming aggressive or retreating into passivity. They're not always comfortable or accustomed to stating their needs in a calm, non-defensive, non-apologetic way. In addition to these troubles with assertion itself, often these women haven't progressed far enough through the grief cycle or integrated the idea of ADD to where they own the idea of ADD in a deeply personal way. They haven't reached the point yet where they don't have to apologize or overexplain.

When that identity is still new and belief in ADD is still shaky, it's hard to push through to be assertive, especially in questioning authority at school or at work. I repeatedly saw how long it took women with ADD to be able to ask for even simple, reasonable accommodations, such as for extra time, for note-takers or for a non-distracting environment. Because of my work with these women, I was able to understand the strength of these difficulties: the embarrassment they had to overcome, their perception that they'd be seen as trying to get away with something.

The Mask of Competency

A woman's need to keep up a mask of competency makes it difficult for her to expose vulnerabilities in order to get the help she might need to do her best work. If she's doing well, she often feels she is managing to fool people. When her difficulties aren't obvious to others, the last thing in the world she wants to do is announce that she has problems and needs some special help. She tries to hide her difficulties, often feeding into that tendency to overwork and creating a gulf between herself and other people. It feels so good to finally be seen as competent she doesn't feel she can risk setting limits when people ask even more of her. The problem with this is that people aren't going to say, "Oh, you're doing a great job! I'm not going to ask you to do more." What happens is that the more they do well, the more is asked of them. It's a double bind or Catch-22; the better they do, the more difficult the organizational demands become, and also the more difficult it is to keep up that front. If they set a limit on the amount of work they take on or talk about their difficulties, that might wipe out the good work they have done. They often feel they would disappoint people who have good opinions of them and create a situation in which, from then on, others would only see their limitations.

It reminds them on some level of what they experienced as children, when it often seemed that the trouble they caused or the problems they had wiped out other people's good feelings about them. They were such confusing children, with inconsistencies or sensitivities they often frustrated those around them, especially those in authority. This explains why women are often willing to go to extremes in order to keep people from seeing those parts of them. Again, that often creates the very thing they were afraid of, not being able to keep up with the demands. Because they're not getting assistance or accommodations to help them maintain their success, they are eventually drained so much that either things are left undone or are done poorly—or they just simply leave.

Depressed Mood

By the time many women with ADD are adults, they often are already depressed. Sometimes this depression is a coexisting, full-blown mood disorder of its own, which is not related to the ADD. Women also have, on top of this, a variety of hormonal changes related to PMS, pre-menopause, or menopause, that intensify the feelings of depression and anxiety, even when they're on medication.

Women can experience a chronic, low-level depression as the result of the ADD: coping without knowing what they're coping with, having low self-esteem and feelings of being trapped, helpless, or bombarded.

Four areas that I will discuss affect the mood of ADD women.

We start with the concepts of being *overwhelmed, overloaded, overworked.*

Then we will explore how being *non-assertive*, and having *negative self-talk* add further to the problem.

Finally, we will also see how some ADD women can be *highly reactive with quickly changing moods.*

Overwhelmed

The word that I hear more often than any other word from women with ADD and disorganization is "overwhelmed." We've seen how the tasks themselves that often fall to women are so difficult for a person with ADD. The tasks in and of themselves cause feelings of failure and the feeling of being overwhelmed and never able to finish one's work. The tasks themselves bring about a certain level of chaos and confusion. This feeling of not having control is often a contributor to a feeling of depression. A woman with ADD just doesn't have the kind of skills and structure and equipment that would allow her to feel that sense of control. So it's not the same thing as when things get messy and out of hand for other people, as they might after a busy weekend. Other women feel at some level that they can just come in, roll up their sleeves and get everything cleaned up and back in order.

For the woman with ADD, though, there is more going on than that. First there is her perception as she looks around the room that there are millions of separate items, taunting her. In addition to that, there is often a huge backlog of disorder contributing to the feelings of being over-whelmed. Most importantly, she feels that she doesn't have the skill to easily, automatically move in and get things back where they belong. This feeling of not having control, even when one has a strong motivation or desire, is a strong contributor to depressed feelings.

Overload from Not Saying "No"

Barbara, who had successes in many areas throughout her life, "con-fessed" (as if to a crime) that she was unable to meet the demands of charitable and civic organizations who had solicited her volunteer assis-tance. She had actually said "no" to them. Other women in the group then admitted to her with relief that they, too, have "shamefully" consid-ered lying about not being able to give time or else they have taken on these obligations for "good causes" which resulted in failure. These kinds of obligations seem to take on an aspect of religious devotion; failure to give selflessly to others carries an almost sin-like feeling.

Another setup for depletion and overload for women is the difficult time they have in saying no to requests from other people. Women often feel that they have to take care of other people's requirements. If other people's needs compete for attention with her own, a woman lets her own go. A woman with ADD pressed for time often relinquishes her personal nourishment, fun, career or friends, because it's the only area she feels she has enough control over to eliminate. Because her life is so overwhelming, with so many competing demands from work, children, partner, and her environment, she's got to eliminate something. What happens is that she usually cuts out any path that leads to her own satisfaction and sense of completion, or gives her a sense of her own strength. As she cuts herself out in order to eliminate the sheer number of demands and tasks, she continues on a downhill spiral, leaving her more depleted, less nourished, and more overloaded.

The stress of staying up all night in order to complete tasks or the constant overworking with no weekends off, is a setup for complete emotional and physical exhaustion. Some women try to cut down on sleep; sometimes they don't eat lunch because they're trying to find time any way they can in order to finish their work and meet the demands of other people.

Women balance the budget of time on their own backs. Their resources are already overtaxed, as we've seen, because they can't say no to other people very easily. They often think that they'll just wait until the demands stop; then they'll focus on themselves.

"I'll wait until people at work stop giving me so much to do."

"I'll wait until people at home stop asking for things."

This, of course, never happens. Instead, ironically, the more efficiently they meet other people's needs, the more the demands increase. Because of that need for approval and the need to cover up areas of difficulty, women often escalate their need to perform, to keep up, to not disappoint anybody by letting them down. Instead of saying, "No, I can't handle this, this is my limit," they just hope that one day the demands will stop. However, the more that people at work, for instance, view them as successful and competent, and the more is requested from them, the better it feels on some level. Because of this kind of reinforcement, these women try even harder to meet those demands, often feeling increasing pressure to perform, yet becoming more and more depleted. This struggle would make one feel that one is disappointing people by turning down requests. "They'll know I've just been fooling them and they'll lose all their faith in me." So women keep on saying yes.

Overworking

Constant overwork and overload in order to prevent reminders of those painful messages from childhood failures is another setup for depression. These women will go to great lengths to prevent the maligning messages we talked about earlier, or even hints that they're not competent.

"You know you don't measure up."

"Who are you kidding?"

They fear that someone will find them out, that the impostor will be discovered underneath their fragile sense of competency. To prevent hearing "You're not good enough," they'll keep saying "yes" for even a morsel of good feedback. It's hard for them to believe that they still can be viewed as competent, successful, and well-respected *and* at the same time still set limits on the amount of work they do. Ironically, by overworking like this, eventually they are *not* able to keep up because they become depleted or overloaded. This creates a self-perpetuating cycle and a self-fulfilling prophecy of failure.

It's easy to see that living with ADD as a woman, especially before diagnosis, is a setup for being overwhelmed, depleted, overloaded, and feeling low self-esteem, helplessness, and hopelessness. This all adds up to depression.

Assertion Difficulties and "Toxic Help"

Another setup for depression comes from the difficulty with assertion that can develop as women mature. It's often difficult for women to set limits. This is especially so if people are nice to them or helping them get organized, or if they feel that others already doing so much for them. They feel guilty about being helped and soon start to feel they're a burden and that others will become fed up and leave them. Feeding into this also is their early experience with messages from others that they are too much bother, or simply causing trouble. It makes it particularly difficult for a woman to say no or to set limits about how she will permit herself to be treated or spoken to while she is receiving help. It's hard for a woman to say to someone who is trying to help her, "I really appreciate your help today in this area, but at the same time, I also feel angry about what you said yesterday." It's hard for her to understand she can be appreciative and accept help but also have a right to her own feelings. She must not permit what I call "toxic help" along with the assistance. Toxic help happens when the helper says things like, "How can you live like this?" At the end of a "helping" session piles of stuff may be off the floor but the ADD woman's self -esteem might be on the floor instead. A woman has to learn to be able to separate out what was helpful from what was not.

SELF-TALK

ADD Happens

BLUNDER
DISORGANIZE
SHUT DOWN
Negative Self-Talk

"I'm so stupid!"
"Forget all this garbage"
"It's just an excuse"
"What's the matter with me?"
"What a jerk!"
"I'm a mess"
"It's hopeless"

DEPRESSION

For instance, *"I appreciate your help today but I find that when you lecture me or say things like "how can you live like this?" it is very counterproductive and not helpful. So maybe we can find a more effective way."*

Negative Self-talk

Negative self-talk also contributes a great deal to the development of depression. Negative "I" messages are the result of years of difficulty in various areas of life, which are confirmed by the maligning messages of others.

"I'm no good."

"What's the matter with me?"

"I act like a two-year-old."

"Why can't I act like a grown-up?"

"Why can't I do these things that other people can do?"

As you can see in the Self-Talk illustration, after a steady diet of experiences like this, you can eventually feel depressed *in addition* to coping with ADD. Then it's even more difficult to move and to get things done, which further makes women characterize themselves negatively. All of the old negative messages from the family, even if they're no longer receiving them now, are locked inside. ADD adults tend to characterize themselves as the source of the problem and when ADD symptoms cause problems, they say things like:

"I'm a jerk."

"I'm so stupid."

"I'm a slob."

"I'm so irresponsible."

"It's hopeless."

"I don't deserve to be a mother."

"My children would be better off with somebody else."

"How stupid could I be?"

Add to this negative talk the overwhelming tasks, the brain chemistry, overwork, exhaustion and this self-barrage and you have the perfect prescription for depression. Later when we discuss counseling we'll see what happens when the this self-talk becomes more positive.

Reactivity: the Pressure Points

Don asked his wife Susan if she would run to the store after work and pick up some shaving cream for him. Susan looked at him blankly. "I can't, honey. I just don't have enough time. I have so much to do!" "But it only takes five minutes," he replied. "What's the big deal?" "It's not a big deal to you maybe, but to me ... " and then she burst into tears.

It's easy to understand, considering the kind of experiences that we've examined, why a woman would be reactive. I conceive of it as if these women start out each day with ninety percent of their coping vessel already filled. Combine this with chaos, disorganization and the energy it takes to cope each day, and it's easy to see that it wouldn't take much to put someone over the top. It might be confusing to a person who requests what seems like a small task, but to the ADD individual it may seem equal to climbing Mt. Everest.

In the above story, Susan might be at the point at which she has no more room to incorporate one more task. And on top of that, it's not five minutes. As a woman said to her partner, "It seems like five minutes to you, but it might turn into more like two hours." This kind of task might entail forty-five minutes of trying to get out of the house because she doesn't know where the keys are, or the money is. On the way out she may drop something and become further involved in the tangled web of ADD. People often describe this as "walking through molasses" or having their hands tied together. So Susan, with all the best intentions, might react in anger, frustration or tears to her partner's request. This kind of behavior makes her feel worse about herself. By screaming out in anger at someone she cares about who doesn't deserve it, she feels more immature, or like a failure or a bad partner. This adds to her low self-esteem and increases her vulnerability to depression.

Quickly-Changing Moods

People with ADD experience quick drops in mood that seem to be easily triggered. I think part of this has to do with the discrepancies we've mentioned previously. Until her core feeling about herself is more stable and she's able to embrace both her strengths and difficulties, a woman's mood may drop or rise depending on which one of those extremes are being pulled on that day. Great success—she feels high in mood. Visible failure a few hours later even the same day—she drops to a low level. In addition, a woman like this might be exquisitely sensitive; something irritating in the environment throws her out of kilter and her whole body goes into a state of mini-panic. If she is concentrating intently and the phone rings, it feels as if everything is wiped out of her brain, as if the computer screen has crashed. Obviously, her mood goes down.

When a woman starts to embrace all of herself and her self-picture becomes more steady, she doesn't flip-flop back and forth so much between, *Now I'm smart, now I'm dumb, now I'm good, now I'm bad.* Eventually these kinds of emotional reversals diminish and the sense of self remains more constant. Then you are able to look at the difficulties on one side and the strengths on the other and understand that they are all part of you.

"So Tired, Tired of Waiting ..."

Women often feel that they have to wait until their lives are in control before they start to focus on themselves. They want to wait until their lives are in balance before they allow themselves to move in a nourishing, replenishing, satisfying direction. As we saw earlier, they're so used to coping that they consider themselves a success when they are merely able to survive. They consider themselves doing well when they're not severely depressed. They're like those frogs that we talked about. They have no idea of how much emotional support they deserve, or how much physical support they can dare ask for. They question, *"How much is too needy? When is someone going to figure out it's not worth the effort and leave me?"* They "keep on keeping on," spending more time and energy, draining their resources, and overworking, in order to do things that leave them depleted. In this way, they sometimes create the very situation they've been trying to prevent.

As a result of being drained and depressed, women can push people away more than if they just admitted the truth and worked with their partner to get help for their original deficits. Instead, by not eating or sleeping, by overworking, becoming depressed, reactive, and overloaded, they wind up with the relationship difficulties they were trying to avoid. It's akin to money going out with nothing coming in, never balancing the accounts, running a big deficit. Eventually it catches up; you're overdrawn and emotionally in debt.

Summary

Being overwhelmed, overloaded, and overworked, being non-assertive, having negative self-talk, and being highly reactive with quickly changing moods all can leave one locked in a state of depression. Guilt prevents you from enjoying life until your work is done. Since your work is never done, this also often prevents you from enjoying your life. When you must fight to hold it all together and hide your struggle from other people, you may find yourself with an inner sense of chaos that makes you feel very vulnerable. Even when you feel "all right" for the moment, you never experience a sense of peace and relaxation because you have such a tenuous hold on organizational balance. This reminds me of people who say that they are "one paycheck away from being homeless." They know that if something goes wrong with their car, or if a child gets sick, they'll lose their fragile grip on life. It's with the same sense of insecurity and with the same anticipation of disaster that people with ADD often approach everyday life. Even when things are okay for the moment, they know it would take very little to upset their delicate balance.

Underachievement and depression are two painful results of ADD. Especially if undiagnosed, a women with ADD will have a very good chance of not reaching her potential. She can likely get stuck in low and mid-level jobs that require her to use her lesser developed skills rather than her broader ones. This, along with inability to say no, due to the cultural messages she has received, stops her from getting the help she needs to focus on her strengths.

CHAPTER NINE

Secondary Effects: Relationships

Vanessa, a young, beautiful young woman in her twenties, had known from her childhood that she had ADHD but never took it seriously or got treatment, until the time she became my client. Over the years she watched as her friends graduated from universities and started building their lives and careers. She knew that she was just as smart as they were, but had been unable to achieve in school or to get her emotional reactivity under control in order to consider the possibility that college was an option. Up until the point at which she became my client, whenever she had encountered someone from high school who had graduated college, this young woman would answer their inquiries about the college that she had attended with a lie. She would name a prestigious school that she had graduated from. The original ADD difficulties that had led her away from the college path were compounding rapidly. Each time she lied, she increased her feelings of shame and lowered her self-esteem. Her difficulties now were not just about ADD, but also about lying and the anxiety of hiding and avoiding people because she feared of being found out. This compounded her feelings of isolation. In addition to her original problems of attention and activity regulation, she now thought of herself as a liar. The simple original difficulties of attention led to such pain of underachievement that all these other secondary effects compounded the difficulties, weaving the web until it became even more tangled.

The Tangled Web We Weave

A woman who grows up with ADD often makes a series of small, subtle decisions that leave her in some way apart from others, on the outside.

This moving away, conscious or not, has the cumulative effect of compounding the original ADD difficulties. The ADD difficulties take on a life of their own, complete with emotional meanings that trigger an entire fabric of new difficulties.

The fact is that many people with ADD (especially without diagnosis and treatment) move away from relationships for one reason or another. By mid-life they turn around to find they don't have anyone they are close to; they feel isolated. Many people feel like outsiders all through their childhood and teenage years, on into their twenties and then mid-life. We're going to look at some of the reasons why a person might continue in this interpersonally unsatisfying way, often unconsciously, for self-protective reasons. The secondary effects discussed so far, such as depressed mood and underachievement, continue to feed into each other in a negative way as well. These effects often combine with the difficulties that relationships bring to increase feelings of isolation and depression.

A woman is often locked in interpersonal patterns that are dissatisfying and frustrating. Depression, in turn, adds to the feeling of moving away from relationships, which affects achievement and self-esteem. None of these effects are separate, but all interwoven. These feelings may have become so intertwined with the sense of self that it becomes very difficult (although essential) to sort them out and untangle them.

For the purposes of our discussion here, let's divide relationships into two categories. First, we will look at relationships with acquaintances, friends, extended family and colleagues. Because of shame and need for **self-protection**, a woman might begin to **misperceive** other people's reactions to her ADD symptoms and also **disconnect** from them. Second, we'll discuss the choice of intimate partners, and the resulting emotional legacy.

Self Protecting

One of the main reasons women with ADD can have difficulties with relationships is that the emotional legacy of shame and guilt cause the ADD woman to push away from people. She feels a need to protect herself, both from bombarding stimulation as well as the vulnerable self-image that she has developed. She does this through hiding and separating from relationships.

We all need to protect ourselves, but we have to find healthy ways to do it, not in ways that create more vicious cycles, isolation, depletion and cutoffs. Without some of these issues worked through, the only means left to us are automatic self-protective devices that distance us from others. Often women haltingly take one step out of that defensive posture, put their hand out, get too close to the fire and shrink back instinctively. It takes a while to desensitize and to keep moving forward instead of moving back into the closet.

When an ADD symptom threatens to appear or does occur, it can send a woman into a mini state of panic. She'll be discovered, her cover will be blown! It's like being a spy in a foreign country. She's constantly wondering with each particular symptom such as blurting out or forgetting, if this is the clue that's going to give her away. Will it erase her reputation for competency and with it any goodwill and approval that she's worked so hard to achieve? Will this be the moment when she's finally going to disappoint someone and they will uncover her mask? If such a woman loses a phone number, for example, instead of asking for the number again, she will often spend hours searching frantically for it (to the detriment of everything else in her life). Instead of saying laughingly, like someone without this sensitivity, "I forgot that number again!" she'd rather spend hours covering up what she feels to be a terrible failure.

Because disorganization is such a core issue for her, a woman with ADD might spend hours organizing and cleaning up, before even considering inviting friends to visit. On the other hand, she might avoid inviting people over at all to escape the shame. One client told me that, even though she had wanted to invite coworkers to her house throughout the ten years she had known them, she had never dared to do so. She had a deep sense of regret about what she had missed.

This fear of being unmasked is so strong at work that ADD women might be reluctant to ask for accommodations such as a quiet, private workspace or secretarial assistance. This affects her ability to do her work as well as increases her feelings that she is hiding from other people. The woman who is hiding her difficulties at work often feels on the edge of being found out. The wrong statement at the wrong time, interruption, blurting out, not remembering what she wants to say, dropping something, breaking something, forgetting something, all trigger shame and fear, again moving her away from relationships.

Feeling Misunderstood

When these women feel they are misunderstood or are seen as odd, those old feelings of shame and need for self-protection are activated. This further moves them away from people.

A client of mine, Joan, started to form a friendship at work with another woman. She was feeling good about this because one of her goals with ADD was to try not to isolate herself, but to make more friends and have a good time. After a weekend which was filled just trying to keep her life together, she was exhausted. Even though she hadn't done anything out of the ordinary, she felt as overwhelmed as another woman might have felt after a full weekend of special events and activities. She told her friend at work on Monday, "I'm really tired." When the friend inquired, "Oh, what did you do? Must have been a great big weekend!" all she could think of was that she had gone out to dinner and the movies with her husband on Saturday night. The friend laughed and said, "How could you be so tired? You didn't do much!"

Someone else being ridiculed for being unable to keep up an expected pace would have shrugged it off, but for this woman it triggered old wounds. Gradually she began to move away from this relationship. She did not know how to explain why she was so different in her energy levels and capacities especially since they both had high-level jobs in which they functioned equally.

ADD women often move away from relationships in the initial stages of forming friendships because of their difficulty in making small talk. Many people with ADD experience difficulty with finding the words that they want to say when they want to say them. Sometimes it is as difficult to find the words in your messy mind as it is to find a paper on your messy desk. Kate Kelly and Peggy Ramundo call this a "reaction time irregularity." They point out that a person with this difficulty might look rude or disinterested when they actually may be having "trouble retrieving things from memory in a demand situation."

In addition, ADD individuals have difficulty regulating their rate of speech. They are also prone to interrupt, blurt out or shut down. Often they are not as well-read as other people, and often feel unable to participate in discussions about cultural events or politics. There is a cultural expectation for a woman to make small talk; it's the way that women start to make friendships and test the waters, a vehicle to reveal oneself. The woman with ADD does not want to be found lacking, though, so her natural instincts lead her to protect herself in defensive ways. Sometimes she avoids these situations, cutting off opportunities to get to know people. The feeling of not being able to reveal themselves makes it even more difficult to move into a deeper relationship. The amount of energy they need to invest in organizing and getting themselves together makes it difficult to keep up with the ordinary social and recreational events that other people do. ADD women feel such an energy drain just trying to keep their lives together. Because they feel so different from others, even if they do begin to form a relationship, they soon begin to feel misunderstood.

Two Choices

A woman often feels that she has an impossible choice to make in relationships. She could "come out" and be open about her difficulties, but this would shatter her fragile sense of competency. The second choice seems to be to continue to hide, spending inordinate amounts of time and energy compensating, covering up, feeling like an impostor. If a woman does take that little step and tries to explain herself, her attempts at honesty are first met with disbelief. Because people often take her explanations to mean that she thinks she's crazy or stupid, common reactions she might hear are: "You're just overreacting, don't be ridiculous, I've got those problems too." In an attempt to bolster her they say, "Don't be silly, you're so smart. I lose my glasses too." Then a woman finds herself in the unenviable position of trying to convince someone who thinks she's okay that she's actually defective. She often feels that it isn't worth the effort to pursue this line of communication. These confusing situations move them back more and more into the closet. When the ADD woman gets treatment and her inner feelings change about ADD it becomes easier to talk about difficulties. She will begin to accept that she won't always be understood but she can continue in relationships anyway. At some point she needs to separate out those who are not supportive and not pursue those relationships, as well as understand that other people can provide nourishment and relationship benefits even if they don't understand her perfectly. ADD women can still get what they need from relationships without expecting perfect acceptance and understanding from others.

MISINTERPRETING

Misinterpreting is the next big area that causes problems in relationships. Without checking out people's reactions, we often misinterpret the way that people react to ADD symptoms; this causes us to behave in ways that actually do push people away. These are self-perpetuating cycles, actually creating the problem we're trying to avoid.

Creating the Problem

The Secondary Effects Chart shows that when the original ADD symptoms occur, a woman might be so self-conscious that, in response, she behaves in a way that might create negative feelings in other people. She mistakenly assumes that it was because those original ADD symptoms

SECONDARY EFFECTS

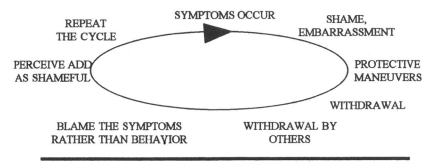

REPEAT THE CYCLE

SYMPTOMS OCCUR

SHAME, EMBARRASSMENT

PERCEIVE ADD AS SHAMEFUL

PROTECTIVE MANEUVERS

WITHDRAWAL

BLAME THE SYMPTOMS RATHER THAN BEHAVIOR

WITHDRAWAL BY OTHERS

were so bad. This creates the very situation that she wanted to avoid, because it wasn't her original ADD symptoms that were so unacceptable, but instead her defensive behavior that actually created the negative feelings in others. People react to her behavior, but she thinks it is the ADD symptoms causing all the problems. This misinterpretation initiates an emotional downhill cycle. Because, for a woman, these ADD symptoms seem so out of place and out of character, she becomes focused on them and often withdraws from other people out of shame or embarrassment. Her behavior becomes very baffling to others and her ability to do her work is impaired.

Misinterpreting with Friends and Family: The Need for Isolation

Another thing that women do in relationships is to isolate themselves in order to reduce the amount of stimulation. People without hyperactivity are often not high stimulus seeking. Instead they're bombarded with stimuli, often needing to get away from people. This is again an area where women have to learn to understand the difference between a healthy means of self-protection and defensive behavior that pushes people away. Women do have a legitimate need to protect themselves from bombardment and they should plan what they are going to do when they have an "ADD attack," when they get overloaded. They do need to regularly recharge and isolate themselves from people. Unfortunately, they do this often without explanation. It's so embarrassing to them to explain or arrange for their special needs, but it's healthy to have a reduction in stimulation and to plan to achieve this in ways that don't move you inexplicably away from people.

Women often walk away, tune out, withdraw or abruptly say no, because they don't know how to talk about what is going on and they feel embarrassed about being different. This behavior pushes people away; other people react to your behavior, not your need for "time out." The person with ADD leaves with a sense of not being connected and a sense of being misunderstood. They are misunderstood because they're not explaining themselves.

Patty "overloaded" each Sunday when she and her husband traditionally went to have brunch and spend the entire afternoon with her husband's large extended family. This included several sets of brothers and sisters, and many children of various ages and several family pets. The teenagers played music, the children played video games, the men and women discussed politics and women prepared and served food and cleaned up. There was a football game perpetually on television. Even though Patty liked most of her relatives, she found these Sundays a strain. Keeping up small talk as well as hiding her ignorance about the current political situation combined with the incredibly distracting and overwhelming noise level left her on the brink of tears after about an hour.

In addition, her sisters-in-law always discussed the latest fashions and engaged her in talk about these things, which left her feeling badly about her lack of "feminine know-how." An hour after breakfast, she would slink away, either into a back room where she hoped she wouldn't be missed for a while, or if it was nice weather, go for a long walk and try to regain some sense of balance. She became increasingly self-conscious, though, about appearing standoffish and became more and more convinced that they considered her weird or an outsider.

So her original need for reduced stimulation took on a life of its own, creating more negative feelings about herself and perhaps negative feelings about her behavior from her family. Patty needs to be able to describe what she needs in these situations and find a way to take care of herself while still staying connected to people who are significant in her life.

Healthy self-protection is vital, and it needs to be built into your life. The balance to work toward is not to clam up, tune out, or leave the room, but protect yourself without apologizing, putting yourself down or moving away from other people. We will look at ways to do that later on.

Misinterpreting at Work

Even if a woman has managed to be successful in the business world, she often has to confront the kinds of cultural expectations for women that she thought she left behind at home. However, they follow her even into this area, where she was trying to channel her strength. Because she feels insecure around these other demands for small talk, volunteer work, etc., she might start avoiding people in the office and just focus in isolation on her work. But when she starts avoiding people, she knows it's not what's expected of her and she might actually look like she is "snubbing" others. She might get up as soon as people walk in the room. She might not socialize with them outside of work or be able to convey a sense of interest and caring about other people.

She might be so bombarded by all the stimuli that she might not be able to function in a nine to five traditional setting. Because she starts to feel self-conscious about these behaviors, it's easy for her to imagine that her co-workers are beginning to think badly of her, that she's a snob or unfriendly. She might wonder if this influences their opinions about her competence. Whether they are or not, it's hard for her to know. Her perceptions of their feelings about her are colored by her feelings of failure in this role.

Avoiding People

Julia, a bright young woman in a small management agency, felt she had difficulty getting her ideas out clearly in small groups. She would either talk too fast or not be able to contribute appropriately to the discussion. She became focused on the idea that one supervisor in particular thought that she didn't measure up. Julia started to avoid people who were at these meetings (and specifically this supervisor). Julia started feeling more and more convinced that they didn't like her at this company because of her difficulty in expressing ideas in meetings.

When in counseling, Julia started to examine this situation and began to understand what she might be doing to create it. She saw that this other woman was probably reacting to Julia's avoidance of her. When she lost some of her defensiveness about this, Julia was able to see that her *behavior* was pushing people away, rather than her ADD symptoms, which in this case really hadn't affected their opinion of her capabilities. They thought she was bright. Because of her past experiences, she had overfocused on this as a reason why others wouldn't like her. It was actually her behavior unrelated to ADD that was causing her relationship problems.

My Story

My personal story is the perfect example of what I've been talking about.

I worked at a large counseling agency with a lot of demands for completing forms and filling out paperwork. I was so sensitive about my handwriting because of all the years in school of getting papers back with big red marks on them, that I lived in fear of checking my "In Basket" every day to get back my forms after they were processed by the clerical staff. In the past, I had been what I called "clerically abused". At another agency, one member of the clerical staff had put me down and complained about me, and was very upset with my performance. She called me sloppy and careless. At that agency, my forms would come back to me with words like, "I can't read this! Careless errors!" with those big red marks again.

Many years later at another agency which had a really nice clerical staff, I still expected the same thing to happen. I approached each day with a great deal of anxiety, as if I were still in the seventh grade and going to get my work returned to me with red ink scrawled across the forms, saying, "This is a mess! This could have been done by a second-grader! Be more careful!!" Even though I am not naturally prone to paranoia, no matter how good my work actually was, I became convinced the clerical staff talked about me and didn't like me because I had messy handwriting (which is ridiculous if you look at it objectively). But all those years of experience were working on me unconsciously. Instead of going to them and talking about it, (they really were lovely people) I started to avoid them. Eventually, they probably did think I was not a friendly person. So perhaps at some point, I was reacting correctly to the fact that they weren't friendly to me. Whatever the reality of the situation was, I had created a very different scenario due to my past experiences.

Eventually, when I understood my behavior and understood my difficulties, I was able to talk about it. Not only did this harmful cycle of emotions get broken, but I actually received more help with my work because I was able to talk about the difficulty that I was having. The secrecy and shame attached to the original problems take on a life of their own. It's very important for women with ADD to understand how, when shame and guilt and a desire for self-protection kick in, they color your perceptions. They create interpersonal difficulties as well as prevent you from getting needed assistance.

DISCONNECTING

Another reason that women move gradually away from relationships is that they simply, as one woman put it, "disconnect."

Starting Relationships—Not!

Relationships simply bring too many more things to do and to consider, just adding to stress and feelings of being overwhelmed. Women feel, at some level, that developing more relationships or even a few relationships to a deeper point, will put them over the top. Even if they find a relationship that's potentially fulfilling, it just seems to them that it's not worth it. As we said before, they'll balance the time and energy demands on their own backs. It seems so difficult to say no to other people's demands, even if it's at the expense of any kind of nourishing relationship. In addition, the guilt they feel about "not playing until they finish their work," feeds into the feeling that they don't really have time for this kind of pleasure when they have left so much undone.

The sheer time involved combined with the shame about not fulfilling these expectations just increases the lack of connection. Cutoffs from family can even occur. I've heard many middle-aged women with ADD talk about trying to explain in vain to other family members about their difficulties, which fall on deaf ears or receive blank stares. Taking care of older parents is difficult, but when you have ADD and can't find a way to explain your apparent lack of caring in the same way that other siblings might be able to, it causes great guilt and anguish.

Joe and Cindy were a middle-aged couple who both had ADD. Because they couldn't find a way to explain their difficulties, they just cut off from the family who couldn't understand why they weren't able every weekend to come to take care of their parents, fix the house, keep up the car, and mow the lawn, as their other adult siblings did. They couldn't begin to take care of their own lives, let alone find a way to take care of their parents. Without knowing what else to do, they just cut off from the family.

This cutoff response increases the difficulty in other relationships, inside oneself and eventually even between the couple themselves. Without understanding it or even noticing it, this is the option that individuals sometimes choose. People like this spend their lives treading water. It's working on some level if they're not drowning, but on another level they can get pretty tired out if that's their only strategy. Get lifejackets, get life rafts, reach for someone's arm! We'll see later how this couple could reconnect.

Maintaining Relationships—As Time Goes By

What happens more than cutoffs, though, in terms of disconnecting, is that more small occasions and important events are missed with other people: missed thank-you notes, missed birthdays, invitations not reciprocated. The connections just aren't kept up and eventually they're gone. ADD individuals might feel so embarrassed or guilty about not keeping up those connections, they might imagine feelings of disgust or maligning statements being made about them. The anxiety just causes them to avoid these people more and more.

At some point, both anxiety and avoidance kick in, as well as the reality of not maintaining connections for many years. This leads to that place in life where you turn around and realize that many of your meaningful relationships have slipped away. You haven't really noticed because treading water, trying not to drown, takes all your focus and energy.

Embarrassment

We've talked about one reason that women disconnect, the shame of having people over to their house. That's a big theme. They feel their house is so over the average level of messiness that they would absolutely be thrown into a panic if they had to entertain. This greatly impacts women with children because there are many occasions in which they have to have the kids' friends over—or they often have to join organizations like Girl Scouts where they feel they must fulfill their obligations. Any kind of outside involvement brings more opportunity to have people to their house, again another reason to move them away from getting involved in the first place. Instead of finding alternative ways of reciprocating or finding ways to discuss this, they just make excuses and pretend, until people finally stop calling on them.

The Messy House

Kris was in a panic because her daughter wanted to have a sleep-over. Her husband wanted to have a couple of people over this weekend. Her new neighbor, it seemed, liked to drop over every now and then to say hello. Even when close friends or family offered to help her organize her house so that she would feel comfortable in these situations, terrible feelings of shame and embarrassment overtook her and she refused. When a part-time job opportunity arose after school hours that would have necessitated a baby-sitter coming into the house, and even though it was something that she very much wanted, she had to turn the job down. Kris' feelings of failure at this basic job of keeping her house in a certain way had great ramifications in her life.

Without knowing what they're coping with as they grow up, these women swallow cultural messages whole and internalize cultural images that they just can't match. That's why it goes to such a deep level, beyond their intellectual understanding, and why women confront such barriers of shame and guilt when they try to solve these difficulties.

Intimate Relationship Choices

Women who have grown up with ADD, especially undiagnosed, are often influenced by their experiences to choose particular kinds of partners. It's especially important to understand this because when they finally do get treated and begin medication, the partnership that has been serving them well in certain ways often radically changes. What follows below are patterns that I've noticed in the choice of intimate partners for ADD women.

Chaotic Partners

An ADD individual's outer life can often look chaotic and her inner life can feel chaotic. As we know, however, when viewed through the "lens of attention," (a phrase coined by John Ratey, M.D. and Andrea Miller in their article on the subject) this appearance can be a result of their attention deficit problems and not a deeper psychological disturbance. Before she understands the reason for her often chaotic lifestyle, a young woman may find herself attracted to partners whose lifestyles are also chaotic. First of all, these partners might be more likely to accept the chaotic environment that the ADD woman often creates. These individuals might also be as confused and lost in a fog as the ADD women feel that they are. Unfortunately, these partners are often leading chaotic lives for other, more serious reasons. For instance, they might have a serious mental disorder that might cause disorganization, or a personality disorder that makes them unpredictable or erratic. In many cases, ADD women might be attracted to someone with a serious substance abuse problem. The probability of becoming involved with someone like this is increased because many individuals with ADD self-medicate with substances before they are diagnosed and medicated. This increases the likelihood that they would socialize with others with the same problems.

It's easy to see how disorganized people can appear similar on the outside to some extent, even if the disorganization stems from a different source. The emotionality and reactivity can also look very similar in these potential partners, but they are due to very different experiences—they are not the same kind of people. Once women with ADD become diagnosed and begin to get treated, they understand these differences and realize their partner isn't one they belong with. In time, they will often move away from these kinds of partners, but it's often a difficult process. It takes these women a long time to understand just where they do belong and what kind of people they really want to be with. It can be very confusing for a long time.

Unavailable Partners

Some women with ADD choose partners who are unavailable, either physically or emotionally, because that way they have fewer demands placed on them.

I worked with a woman whose husband had a demanding professional life and who was home very little. Her friends used to say to her, "You're so understanding and patient!" but this woman experienced his absence as a relief. "If he were here all the time, I wouldn't be able to handle it. I wouldn't be able to meet all those demands." Women with ADD feel they have to find extra time anywhere they can so they're either going to take it out of their own hides, as we've seen earlier, or pick a partner who is not going to come with a full plate of expectations.

A variation of this is a woman who might have become involved with someone who is available emotionally and then, for the same reasons, find herself keeping her partner at a distance. On a deep level, this woman might feel that if a partner got too close to her, she would be found unacceptable in some way. The partner might now see her outside mask, but if he got too close and saw the way she really lived, if he saw the real mess, he'd see how difficult any life together would be. She may feel that if this side of herself were revealed, she would be so unacceptable that he would ultimately reject her. It's easy to see how a woman who feels like this might keep a potential partner at arms' length. This harkens back to the deeply-ingrained feelings of shame from childhood which leave women believing that their "failure" to meet traditional role expectations, their discrepancies, so disproportionate to their abilities, are sufficient to wipe out all the good things they can bring to a partnership. They might believe that it would be so impossible for them to create a way of working it out or living together that they take themselves out of the running. It requires a long time to work toward this in a relationship when a woman has such depths of feelings about the personal way she lives. But once women integrate and accept these kinds of difficulties in themselves, they are able to work toward letting their partners know them fully and allowing other people to help them.

Caretaking Partners

Both women and men with ADD will sometimes find that they have unconsciously chosen partners who function as caretakers. These partners structure and organize their lives for them so much that these ADD adults might not even hit an "organizational wall" until something happens to disturb this relationship. If a mental health professional or the woman herself doesn't understand the actual, real-life functions that the partner had been providing it would be very difficult to understand the possible overreaction to the loss of the relationship. The loss of a caretaking relationship for an ADD adult, then, involves more than the "normal" sense of loss at the end of a relationship. In her case the vital structures of daily life are disrupted when this kind of relationship ends.

Of course, this kind of caretaking can cross the line into dependency and co-dependency. It's critical, when getting the help she needs from her partner, that a woman doesn't accept what I call "toxic help" along with the assistance; and that she doesn't give away too much of her sense of power and control. When this partnership works well, it can help a person achieve and get the kind of coaching functions they need from their spouse. It can also, though, overprotect them for so many years that they develop a sense of incompetence and set themselves up for a huge fall if something disrupts the relationship.

Controlling partners

Another form of intimate relationships that I've seen women form is with controlling partners. It is easy to understand how this might happen to a woman who feels that she is floundering around with no sense of internal structure. It would be attractive to come up against someone who can provide a strong structure. This can work up to a point, if a partner is able to provide firm limits and structure or is very systematic and organized. The danger is that he might cross the line to become controlling and dominating. A woman might get involved with someone who's organized to the point of being obsessive-compulsive and who, because he couldn't tolerate her disorganization would be abusive or subtly put her down. As we saw with the caretaking partner, both can work up to a limit, as long as the interactions remain positive, complementary, and consciously worked out.

Living with ADD has a great effect not just on a woman's cognitive or attentional processes, but impacts every area of her life, especially her intimate partners, friendships and relationships with family members.

PART III

EMERGING

CHAPTER TEN

Diagnostic Dilemmas For Women

W omen with ADD feel as if they spend much of their lives treading water. Despite years of trying to keep their heads above water, they sink deeper and deeper, feeling trapped and helpless. Many women with undiagnosed ADD are unable to explain for themselves or have anyone else help them understand their experience. It may be incomprehensible for others to believe that a seemingly successful woman, or a woman who has never been hyperactive, may have ADD. Instead, they may be written off as having typical "women's emotional problems" or serious psychological disturbances. If there are some outward signs of success, it just makes it more baffling to those around them. And if they have been visibly struggling, it just reconfirms other people's opinions that they are indeed weak, incompetent, or helpless.

When ADD women aren't treading water, they are running. Eventually, they may either hit a wall at ninety miles an hour, or they'll just keep cruising along and gradually run out of gas, coming to a dead stop.

Common Difficulties Diagnosing Women with ADD

There are three reasons that make it difficult for a women with ADD to receive a correct diagnosis.

1. **The personal histories of girls and women don't always conform with what is normally considered a typical ADD life course.**

2. **ADD is sometimes the cause of another disorder** (or causes symptoms of that disorder). The ADD is the cause, and the other

disorder is the effect. The other disorder is diagnosed, and the ADD gets missed.

3. ADD looks like many other disorders and often co-exists with another disorder. Because the language and presentation of ADD looks like other things, professionals often diagnose another disorder other than ADD. Sometimes, however, a person can have both ADD and the other disorder as well.

For these reasons, it is easy for ADD to be underdiagnosed, over-diagnosed, or actually completely misdiagnosed. My main concern, and hope for the reader, is that women will get correctly diagnosed.

The ADD individual's inner sense of chaos is hard for others to see. Other people sometimes don't believe them even when these women try to reach out to others and explain it. They're often told they are overreacting or over-sensitive. When they do decide to go for "professional help," they might choose a mental health professional who doesn't understand this disorder. To a therapist not used to seeing ADD in adults it might be seen as something in the "family dynamic" causing her to act out at home, or she may be termed as "passive-aggressive" toward her husband. Perhaps a therapist will see it as a more severe psychological disorder. They might diagnose depression, and not realize that battling the ADD caused the depression. The cause and effect can be confused.

Unfortunately, not getting help for the underlying disorder and being misunderstood in this way can create a downhill feeling of desperation as a woman searches in vain for an answer to her difficulties. I have seen many women who have been in therapy for years working on some valid family and secondary psychological problems, but never working on their basic underlying problem— the ADD.

When a person with ADD goes to a doctor or therapist seeking help, they describe the difficulties in maintaining order in their daily lives over and over again. They talk about their decisions, their disorganization, their routines, the feeling of being overwhelmed, and their feeling of lack of control. They might talk about the same general things that other clients do, about relationships or feeling depressed, but underlying everything is the severe feeling of not being able to solve their real-life, daily problems. And this is despite achievements in other areas. As I've emphasized repeatedly, it's the discrepancy between these kinds of difficulties and the achievement in other areas that makes it hard for someone who is not experienced to understand how her troubles could be related to something cognitive or attentional rather than something psychological or emotionally-driven.

Professionals inexperienced in seeing ADD in women unfortunately have a tendency to discount the woman's self-identification of ADD. A woman with ADD sometimes presents an overwhelming amount of material, and a confusing picture can emerge for a mental health professional. These women might not always be taken seriously. Her initial inquiry into ADD might be too quickly dismissed because of her lack of stereotypic history. She might be seen as denying her depression or her real feelings. This, coupled with her tendency to not be assertive with authority figures, might make her accept a therapist's opinions, feeding into her already insecure feelings at that point.

With the recent media attention on Adult ADD, luckily now both professionals and individuals alike are more aware of ADD. It is becoming easier to get a diagnosis; it's much more accepted now that adults can have and be treated for ADD. However, women, and especially non-hyperactive women, still have difficulty getting diagnosed. Professionals are just starting now to understand this disorder in women.

Following is the first of the three reasons that make it difficult for a woman to get diagnosed—when a woman's past history and a present story doesn't "add" up to ADD.

1. A HISTORY LESSON

The histories of girls and women don't always conform with what is normally considered a typical ADD history.

When a woman goes to a counselor, psychologist, or psychiatrist to get help, one of the first things this mental health professional will probably do is ask for a complete childhood history of problems as well as their present life difficulties. From the complete story that she relates, the therapist eventually makes a diagnosis. The first problem a woman with ADD might have in getting diagnosed is that her story sounds nothing like what many professionals view as ADD.

Childhood Histories—Non-Hyperactivity

If you went to a therapist complaining of depression or being overwhelmed or overloaded, and there's absolutely no childhood history of hyperactivity, it could make it difficult to get diagnosed with ADD. You may, in fact, have the other opposite experience of not wanting to move much at all, or have difficulty in moving directly from an impulse to an action. There might be great discrepancies in your energy levels. You might not be hyperactive on the outside, but may feel an internal restlessness that you don't display.

You might present a history of being dreamy, disorganized, distracted, or just plain shy. Or you might not have acted out because you were socialized against doing that. Since you didn't cause any trouble for anyone, no one was disturbed enough to consider that there might have been a problem. This history does not sound like the hyperactive symptoms most therapists think of as ADD. It sounds closer to other things. POSSIBLE MIS-DIAGNOSIS: depression.

Childhood Protective Factors

Many women have had in their life what I call "protective factors," which can lead therapists into thinking there wasn't or isn't a problem. The problem was there, however, it just hadn't surfaced yet because these factors were "protecting" the individual. Again, in this case, the ADD symptoms wouldn't be obvious in the history of the individual.

We talked earlier in the book about how protective factors can cloud the diagnostic picture, which requires severity and chronicity. There are many circumstances in a person's life that can delay the full impact (severity) of ADD symptoms until later, when organizational demands get greater and the complexities increase. Many women grow up in structured environments and don't "hit a wall" until college or marriage, or when they go to work or have children. They may not find out until later in life that they are unable to achieve or function in the same way as others of the same educational or ability level.

Therapists look for "chronicity," in other words, how chronic or long-term a "problem" has been. If they don't see chronicity, if the problem looks like it has happened recently, then they might not feel that ADD is the problem, because chronicity is one key element of ADD diagnosis.

For instance, let's say you are a newly married, young woman in your twenties. You go to a therapist, worried and anxious, because you find yourself being completely disorganized, unable to keep up the demands of your new life. As child you led a very protected and structured life. Your mother kept a very organized house. You also went to Catholic schools where they kept you very organized and structured. Your new level of disorganization might appear to be the result of your new marriage. In actuality, the protective factors of your life prevented the ADD from becoming an obvious part of your history. POSSIBLE MIS-DIAGNOSIS: Adjustment Reaction with Anxiety (as a result of the new marriage).

Other protective factors, such as being very intelligent or being talented in one area, can also be misleading to a therapist. If you were very bright, your intelligence may have covered your organizational or attentional weaknesses, and you could have come out looking like an average student, instead of a very bright one with ADD. Or, if you were very talented in one area, that may have focused you to the point where you difficulties weren't noticed as much.

Blurring the picture of recognizing ADD in an adult are various ways of living that individuals create—in order to achieve a certain level of success.

Unconscious Strategies that Mask ADD

Coping	Compensating	Self-medicating
	Over-controlling	
	Over-organizing	
	Assisted Living	
	Underachieving	

Coping

Sometimes adult women may not present themselves as having any or many obvious ADD symptoms such as disorganization, but they still may have ADD. It is especially hard to diagnose ADD when other circumstances mask the difficulties. Some women, without even knowing it, have developed exceptional "coping abilities." They may have achieved much in their professional life, and/or have successfully managed a family. Their level of coping and/or compensating has been developed to such a high degree that they've managed to do well in spite of their ADD. But they've paid a price. They many eventually end up seeing a mental health professional for depression or anxiety. Eventually the demands or stress of the process by which they cope has become too hard and the woman might finally hit a wall. They may be getting through their daily lives, but the pressure of doing the little routine things is intense. So while these women might not present as underachievers, they can still have ADD. It's hard for a professional to diagnose ADD in these women who do present well to the world, or to believe the severe, daily difficulties these women describe.

These people are achieving despite inner difficulty. It is very hard, even if they get diagnosed, for professionals to think that they even need to be treated, because it is felt that they're doing all right. "Doing all right" is not a very effective basis on which to evaluate whether someone needs treatment. A person who is coping may then be doing very well at their job, achieving excellent results. But it is the inner process, not the final product, that needs to be examined. The level of difficulty needed to sustain this achievement and the impact on them emotionally and physically needs to be considered.

A nurse was tested and found to have ADD, but the psychologist felt that this woman didn't need medication because she had a job in which she was getting good evaluations. Her career provided a very stimulating environment where she could move around a great deal. "Perfect," the therapist thought, for a person with ADD. What this diagnostician didn't see was the overwhelming bombardment and demands this nurse felt in what she perceived to be a chaotic environment. Even though she was doing well, the process was unsatisfying to her, very anxiety-provoking, and both emotionally and physically draining. When she was treated with medication and made some adjustments in her work day, she felt great relief.

Self-Medicating

You might be a person who seems to manage well but, when the therapist inquires further, it might be discovered that without knowing it, you might have been trying to "fix" your own brain chemistry, by self-medicating. You might be drinking excessive amounts of caffeine each day, through coffee or colas in an attempt to stay alert, awake, and focused. You might find out that you've been using other substances that act as stimulants as well—nicotine, diet pills, antihistamines, or even cocaine.

Instead, or in addition to taking stimulants, you might find that you've been self-medicating in order to keep you relaxed, in order to focus with pain medications, alcohol, marijuana or food. These substances are often taken at night to sleep, in order to counteract the stimulants taken earlier in the day to stay awake. This is obviously not a healthy cycle, and despite the positive short-term benefits, has too many negative long-term effects.

This kind of self-medication, of course, could then appear to the therapist as a substance abuse problem, which it may be by then. The important point to remember is that the self-medication allows ADD individuals to achieve at a "normal" level, thereby masking the true level of difficulty caused by the ADD.

Compensations

Some ADD adults might be compensating very well without even knowing it; their life works as long as they maintain their compensations. This is often a fragile balance, however. If their compensations aren't carried out or if their systems are disturbed in some way, more of their true difficulties would emerge. They have found ways to get around their difficulties in order to achieve a level of success, but beneath this mask of the well-compensated adult, you may see someone who holds things together in an unhealthy way or with a great deal of anxiety. They are afraid that they will "lose it" if something is disturbed.

It's important to distinguish between the person who is compensating in ways that are negatively affecting her life (even though the same compensations are helping to diminish the effects of the ADD) from the person who compensates in effective ways. Occasionally ADD serves a person well without further treatment because of a combination of factors, such as the ideal career, a high degree of talent in a specific area and family support. In this ideal scenario a woman would be able to channel her ADD strengths and minimize negative effects in healthy ways. This would, of course, require that a woman be comfortable with asserting her needs and overcoming the shame and guilt associated with "breaking the mold."

Over-controlling/ Underproducing

One way some people mask their ADD symptoms is to anchor their lives with extensive systems and controls. They may seriously limit the amount of activities in their life in order to keep things under control.

Half the Job— Half the Money

A woman named Jean came to see me. From the outside, she seemed quite successful. It had been hard for her to be diagnosed because, unless someone looked deeply, they wouldn't know that her life had been completely dictated by her undiagnosed ADD. At some point she had to leave the large corporation at which she had started her career. She eventually went to a mid-size company and then to a small one. Finally, she was unable to take the kind of constraints or demands in working for someone else, so she started her own business, which she ran out of a home office. She was doing well. She wasn't disorganized, and didn't leave things unfinished. What she didn't do was make as much money as other people of her own ability level. She controlled her environment in a way to handle things, but realized that she was only able to do half the work that other people were able to do—if she wanted to maintain the quality of her work, and meet the organizational demands of running a business. Because she would become disturbed and actually non-functional if anyone touched or moved anything in her well-designed environment, she found herself unable to take advantage of office help, which could have helped her to increase her work load.

As we mentioned before, some individuals with ADD function like a blind person, who would be totally thrown off if you interfered with her systems by moving something in her environment.

Overorganizing

As an ADD individual trying to get diagnosed a professional might well ask you about the level of disorganization in your life. You might honestly respond, "I'm very organized. I'm never late, in fact I'm always early. I never forget appointments and my house is very tidy. I have a place for everything." It would be difficult then to see you as having ADD. or difficulties with shifting attention or impulsivity. But, and **this is the key**, if you look more closely at your daily life, you may begin to understand that your whole life may been **centered** around organizing—you feel that if you don't, everything will fall apart. It's very hard for you or a professional to sort out at this point in your life the difference between your *personality* and your compensations.

Just saying that you are organized doesn't mean you don't have ADD. You might be focusing on organization to the exclusion of everything else. This could become obsessive, agonizing about the placement of every one of your possessions. Or you might stay up to all hours of the night preparing carefully for the next day's ordinary routine, in order to successfully be on time and fully prepared. Unfortunately, this is a difficult way to live, often at the expense of your family or other areas in your life. Again, the important diagnostic distinction is to determine, not whether you are able to stay organized, but rather, to determine the amount of time and energy this takes, compared to people who don't have these difficulties with disorganization.

Assisted Living

Another reason it can be difficult to get a diagnosis of ADD, especially for a woman, is when a woman has a relationship with a "caretaker." A caretaker is someone who naturally and willingly fills in the gaps for an ADD person, and takes care of the details of daily life, preventing the full impact of her condition to become visible. (Many women, coincidentally, are "caretakers" for men.) This can be an effective compensation. However, problems will appear if, a) her own sense of competency is compromised by the situation; b) if power and control issues begin to surface; c) if the caretaker begins to have resentment. (One of the couples I see call this the "R" factor. When the "R" begins to build, it's time for the caretaker to cool it for a while, and focus on themselves.) Obviously, if the relationship ends, a women's systems can begin to fall apart. When her newly emerging disorganization appears at the same time as her depression and anxiety over the lost relationship, the ADD might continue to still be missed.

Underachievement as a Compensation

Finally, some of the sexual bias that still exists in regard to women might make a professional predisposed to judge a fairly successful woman as having achieved a great deal when she may in fact be severely underachieving. Her level of ability may be far greater than she has been able to display, because of her life long difficulties. As she was growing up, the cultural or family stereotype of gender expectations may have minimized concerns regarding her life choices and levels of achievement. If she now voices disappointment about her accomplishments, especially if she has achieved what most people think is a fair amount of success for a woman, she may be seen as overly ambitious, aggressive, or perfectionistic

A highly intelligent woman can continually have her ADD mis- or undiagnosed; and she can continue to harbor the painful sense that she is severely underachieving, without understanding the reason why.

2. CAUSE OR EFFECT

In many cases, the ADD is the **primary underlying disorder** that produces symptoms of a different disorder which clears up when the ADD is diagnosed and properly treated. In other words, living with undiagnosed ADD can produce symptoms that are seen as evidence of a separate and diagnosed disorder. In fact, what one is seeing is often just an **effect of the ADD.**

Depression

Depression is probably the most common disorder that can mask ADD. This depression could be a co-existing problem that would need treatment along with the ADD, or it could be a result of the ADD—whose symptoms would disappear once the ADD was dealt with.

A woman may have distinct periods of a "major depression" in which she may feel hopeless, and lose interest and pleasure in her activities. I have usually found this to be a co-existing condition, needing its own treatment. Frequently, however, women experience less intense, low-level feelings of depression for several years. These low-grade feelings of depression can co-exist with the ADD, but they are often the result of struggling for a lifetime with undiagnosed and untreated ADD. It is understandable to see how a woman could develop a feeling of burnout if they have been carrying this unknown "problem" with them their whole lives.

A third difficulty in diagnosing depression from ADD, is that ADD symptoms may look like symptoms of depression. When a person complains of difficulty concentrating, of being disorganized and lethargic, or even restless and agitated, these are all symptoms of both depression and ADD. If the depression is a result of the ADD, it will often be helped when the ADD is treated. If it is truly a separate disorder, the depression will need to be treated, in addition to the ADD.

Does a woman who describes symptoms of disorganization become depressed first, or is she depressed because all her life she's had difficulty organizing, and concentrating? Making matters more difficult is the issue of non-hyperactivity. When a woman describes feeling cognitively depressed, sluggish, and unable to put things into action, these again are symptoms that look like either disorder.

One can see that depression is a condition easily confused with ADD; it can coexist with it, or it can be the result of a primary attention deficit disorder.

Anxiety and Avoidant Disorders; Social Phobias

Like depression, anxiety disorders are also difficult to separate out from being a symptom of ADD. You can develop anxiety disorders just from living with ADD, and people often have both. Living a lifetime feeling insecure, that things are going to fall apart, that it takes an incredible amount of energy just to keep your life together, can eventually create an anxiety disorder.

Again, a way to differentiate between anxiety being its own entity or being the result of ADD is to note the language people employ in describing their feelings. Do they talk of "impending doom, the sense that things are going to fall apart?" Is this free-floating anxiety, or is this a description of a cognitive state where someone can't stop? As one ADD woman said, "thousands of thoughts are speeding past." She can't grasp them. The internal world is so fast and unorganized that it feels like a chaotic state. Is that what one is reporting or is one reporting a real fear? Is someone having a mini-panic attack that comes from being startled, when one is hyperfocusing, or is this more of a general fear unrelated to a cognitive state?

Women with ADD, especially those without hyperactivity, often avoid people or situations in order to control their environment. We have seen that they may feel the need to protect themselves from the bombardment of extra obligations, and the stimulation that comes as a result of relationships. They sometimes avoid relationships because of the sense of shame they have in the way they live. Or because their hair, clothes, jewelry, or other "womanly" things aren't "up to snuff," they may avoid many social situations. These individuals could be seen as having a full-blown avoidant disorder, when, in fact, they could just be trying to cope with their ADD.

Family problems

Family problems might be the effect of the stress of living in a household with undiagnosed ADD. Blame and resentments can accumulate for years in this situation. The disorganization and the problems might be looked at as the result of someone's primary emotional difficulty, instead of as diagnostic of ADD. This happens frequently when a child with ADD has his behavior problems attributed to a conflict in his family. Often there is conflict in the home by the time he is diagnosed but the original source of stress was the undiagnosed ADD. If the mother has ADD as well, the same difficulty can arise. Since we know ADD is hereditary, there would be a good chance that either the mother or father of the child had ADD.

A woman seeking diagnosis and treatment and the mental health professional with whom she works must try to differentiate between cause and effect. If the ADD is the cause of the family difficulty, the treatment would obviously be different.

Obsessive-Compulsive Disorder (OCD)

Obsessive-compulsive disorder can coexist with ADD. OCD is an attempt to order the inner sense of chaos. Again, we ask the same question. "Is the behavior anxiety-driven, which would be the case in the OCD, or is the behavior an attempt to maintain an organized environment to function in?" The latter, of course, would indicate more of an Attention Deficit Disorder.

Substance Abuse

ADD could be the reason why people abuse substances, as they self-medicate in order to focus. If you treat the ADD, the need to self-medicate will often disappear, and with it the substance abuse.

Many times in this situation, however, the primary underlying ADD will be missed in diagnosis and only the substance abuse will be addressed. In these cases, treatment for the substance abuse will often fail. However, if a person does go into recovery, eventually they may realize there still is something that hasn't been addressed, the primary ADD.

People who have abused substances in order to "fix" their unknown ADD, are in great need of proper medication. Unfortunately, these are the very people many doctors hesitate prescribing for, fearing they will become addicted to or abuse the medication. While this is a legitimate concern, and needs to be approached cautiously, all of the experts that I have read or heard maintain that when the right medication is prescribed and monitored correctly, these people are greatly helped and, in fact, do not abuse it.

Dr. Daniel Amen says that adult children of alcoholics display symptoms that can mimic ADD. Many alcoholic parents may have had ADD and were using alcohol to self-medicate.

The ADD-like symptoms in an adult child of an alcoholic can result either from growing up in an alcoholic or ADD household or from actually inheriting ADD or a tendency toward alcoholism.

3. WHEN ADD LOOKS LIKE OTHER DISORDERS

The third reason for the **misdiagnosis** for women with ADD, (the first two are history and cause or effect) may be the most common. ADD simply looks like other things. This is even more of a problem for women, especially women without hyperactivity. As was the case with depression, the language used by a woman with ADD to describe her feelings as well as the style in which she conveys these experiences can sound like more serious psychological disorders to therapists not familiar with ADD in adults. A woman with ADD may tell her story in an emotional, excited, expansive way and relate great difficulties in living. She may be **overpathologized**, in other words, thought of as having a more serious disorder than she actually does.

Another cultural reason why women are misdiagnosed is because it is not uncommon to discount reports of women who have many physical conditions and stage-of-life issues to deal with. Therapists can write off symptoms of mood, and concentration variablity to PMS, menopause, or just that "plain old, female sensitivity."

On the other hand, the reverse may be true, and some people may mistakenly attribute these natural conditions to ADD. Of course, a person can have more than one condition, or a combination of conditions.

I will now explain some other psychological conditions that ADD might be confused with, due to the similarity of the symptoms. It is always important to remember that these conditions can also co-exist with ADD, and/or may actually be the condition a person is suffering from—instead of ADD.

A brief, narrative description of some of the conditions will be followed by a more detailed explanation for why a certain disorder may be too easily attributed to a woman with ADD.

The behavior of a person with ADD could be interpreted as **narcissistic**. What looks like self-centeredness, self-focus, or preoccupation could just be difficulty blocking out one's thoughts and needs, or difficulty in meeting the demands of life. *As I've said, it's important to be self-centered when you're drowning.*

If a therapist is inclined to see women as **hyperemotional**, again, that could predispose them to miss a diagnosis of attention deficit disorder. They would be seen as **histrionic**, hysterical or perhaps exaggerating their difficulties. If a woman is reporting high achievement, but severe difficulties in areas that sound trivial, such as daily routine activities, that might indicate somebody who is exaggerating, and not seeing things clearly.

The language that people use to describe their inner state can be easily misconstrued, for example, a woman reports **instability** in her mood, relationships, job, or basic identity. People sometimes describe a feeling of **fragmenting**, a sense of self which is falling apart, a sense of impending doom, where they can't hold things together. Without understanding that this can be describing a *cognitive experience*, not an emotional one, a person could seem to have a more severe personality disorder instead of attention deficit disorder. The critical distinction between ADD and serious disturbances of personality lie in the meaning that these descriptions hold for the individual. Drs. Hallowell and Ratey go into depth about these differences in *Driven to Distraction*.

The confusion between a person who is severely disorganized because of ADD as distinguished from someone who is disorganized due to a serious mental disorder is demonstrated in the following story.

One woman who came to see me had seen a therapist many years before who wanted to hospitalize her, perhaps feeling that she was a schizophrenic. On a home visit the therapist had seen an extremely disorganized home and thought it must be a manifestation of a severe mental illness. Indeed, this client was severely disorganized at home, but she was certainly mentally healthy. She held down a high-level job, and took good care of her child. But she was functioning with much distress because of her disorganization. She certainly did not have a severe mental illness, although her house could have been seen as symptomatic of that diagnosis.

Following are some other common psychological disorders that can look like ADD. Remember, a person may have these disorders along with ADD, or just have these disorders outright, without the ADD.

Dependent Personality Disorder

As we have seen earlier, women might form relationships with caretakers and when that relationship ends would naturally have an extreme reaction when they lose this kind of support. They may actually stop functioning. They could become disoriented, go into a state of panic that would seem to indicate a severe dependency problem. Indeed, they were dependent on this person, but it was for daily real-life functions, not for some deep psychological need. Without the every day support, their life has ceased to function.

It's very important for a professional to determine whether a client is describing their inner feelings about themselves, or describing real-life, daily problems. A woman can seem to have a dependent personality, when instead they're an ADD person compensating with a caretaker or organizer. When the relationship breaks up, it looms much larger than even the normal emotional difficulty of breaking up. This kind of total reliance on another person is not a good idea and can lead to negative consequences but this has to be distinguished from a personality disorder. Of course, ADD doesn't preclude having a more serious disorder of this type, but it usually clouds the issue.

Passive-Aggressive Women and the Men Who Love Them

A woman could be seen as passive-aggressive if she were constantly late or always forgetting vital tasks for her family. A therapist could look for the reason that a woman is "acting that way" toward the family, especially if she is not acting that way at work (which might be easier for her to function in). A therapist must find out the meaning of the forgetting and the inattention with the spouse or in other relationships. At that point, especially when the suggestions in treatment are not followed, it might be psychologically interpreted by the therapist as a resistance to the therapeutic process.

Passive-aggressive means unconsciously not doing something. A woman may be acting out some kind of anger by not doing something— by forgetting, by not making dinner, by not responding to invitations, by not picking up her husband's cleaning, by not taking care of what someone's asked her to do. It feels to another as though someone's doing something to them.

A woman's role as mother is usually to organize the life of a child; it is she who will be looked at with concern when the structures agreed upon are not followed. Since a woman is predisposed to accept the responsibility for her child's failures, she will often join in blaming herself. After many years, the woman's "scattered" image in the family might become solidified to the point where she has become the identified person with the problems.

A woman may present symptoms that look like other things to the therapist: she may look like she is sabotaging herself or has a fear of success; it might look as if she has anger toward her husband or unresolved conflicts with her father. Women often present such a complicated, confusing picture. A mental health professional would try to understand what purpose her behavior serves in a relationship, or what is going on in a relationship might become the focus of the inquiry.

A boy in junior high starts to have a lot of trouble, but might not be hyperactive, or might be getting average grades even though he's smart, so no one would understand this might be an ADD. Someone looking at this might view it as a relationship problem between the parents getting projected onto the kids. Any structure set up might not be followed through by the mother to help the child and the focus can then shift from the child to the mother as the problem. The parents can begin fighting over the handling of the child and the mother's lack of follow-through. Things can deteriorate into a cycle of blaming and fighting, and it can certainly look like (and now would be to some extent) the child is having difficulties as a result of the parents' conflict. The original source of the problem- the child's ADD- could continue to be missed. The mother would continue to feel more guilty and depressed. This is very common when one parent and the child have undiagnosed ADD, and is most likely to happen in women without hyperactivity.

*ADD often **coexists with another separate disorder** and is frequently missed in light of the more obvious disorder.*

Bipolar Disorder

One mood disorder condition very hard to distinguish from ADD is called bipolar disorder or manic-depression. A person could have distinct periods of mania that look like ADHD, or the ADHD could look like mania. In bipolar disorder, you have periods of grandiosity, of extremely driven activity, fast talking, over abundance of ideas and schemes. This can easily appear to be a person with ADD, unless you have much experience seeing both types of conditions. They are very different, however. ADD people can seem to go from high to low several times during a single day. They can be distracted easily out of one mood state into another where they're feeling upset or angry or worried. The phone can ring or someone can catch their attention, and all of a sudden they'll be distracted out of one mood into a different kind of feeling state. ADD is environmentally triggered, whereas bipolar mood cycles have more of an inner-driven quality to them. Bipolar cycles are much more distinct cycles of extreme highs and extreme lows, each of which can last for days at a time.

I worked with a client who had been diagnosed as bipolar and put on lithium but continued to be very agitated, depressed, and reactive. What she described painfully and repeatedly was a deep sense of underachievement. She was very bright, but with both dyslexia and ADD, the ADD never having been properly treated. She was coping with an overwhelming number of daily tasks and organizational tasks of life.

The original cause of many of her problems was the ADD. Many of her other symptoms had arisen out of the ADD. The psychiatrist that she went to refused to see her symptoms in this light. Every week she would describe her lost hours, her disorganization. It was clear that she couldn't go any further without a correct diagnosis and treatment. Besides needing the correct medical treatment, i.e., medication, she needed to change her pattern of self-recrimination. She attributed her difficulties and mistakes to having a "bad character" and of not being motivated. Eventually, she saw a doctor who treated her properly for ADD. The new medication, along with education and counseling, helped her a great deal more than her previous diagnosis of and treatment for bipolar disorder.

I want to reiterate that it is even more dangerous to misdiagnose a serious disorder such as bi-polar, calling it ADD. It just so happens that the disorders can look alike, and can be confused.

Histories of Abuse

I think one of the most difficult circumstances to separate out from ADD for a woman is **when she has grown up with a history of abuse.** Any of the following traumas could initiate behaviors and symptoms in an adult, which could imitate ADD: child abuse, sexual abuse, physical abuse, emotional abuse, verbal abuse. It is especially difficult to diagnose these women accurately because both groups have difficulty clearly remembering many of the events of childhood. Furthermore, women with both ADD and abusive childhoods report chronic and severe problems their lives, especially in areas of concentration and distractibility, and we know that chronicity and severity are two main diagnostic criteria for ADD.

Other Physical Conditions

Of course, there's a wide range of physical conditions needing to be sorted out and eliminated before someone jumps to the conclusion that they have ADD. There could have been an early head injury, or more recent injury or illness that might especially account for something that hasn't been a chronic condition. It could be aging, with a person having a normal loss of memory. Someone may be going through menopause or another kind of hormonal change that could account for symptoms. It could be Alzheimer's disease coming on, if symptoms occur later in life. That's why the chronicity has to be so thoroughly investigated. There are other circumstances such as thyroid condition, and other kinds of hypoglycemic conditions that need to be addressed.

Narcolepsy, a sleep disorder, can look very much like unaroused ADD according to Dr. Edna Copeland. Dr. Thomas Brown also points out that many individuals with ADD without hyperactivity are borderline narcoleptics. They may not meet the full criteria but often struggle to stay awake during boring tasks or tasks like reading that require concentration. These must be looked at carefully to distinguish and treat. This is why an entire health profile of the person has to be studied before any diagnosis is reached.

Learning Disabilities (LD)

Learning disabilities can mimic or accompany ADD. Learning disabilities are distinguished from ADD in that Learning Disabilities are actual permanent impairments in specific processes whereas ADD is a neurochemical disorder. Because of its "chemical" nature, ADD can be treated with medication. Learning Disabilities cannot. They can only be accommodated and compensated for. In many situations, individuals have both ADD and learning disabilities. There are many important questions one has to ask in trying to differentiate between a learning disability and Attention Deficit disorder. Why can't someone pay attention? Is it because of ADD or do they have a auditory processing problem? Why don't they read? Is it because they can't concentrate or get bored, or do they have trouble distinguishing words? Why is someone's handwriting illegible? Is it they can't form the letters properly or are they unable to keep up with their rapid thoughts?

If a person is being treated for ADD and it's not helping significantly you may have to look further for possible LD. Ritalin or other medication will not cure a learning disability.

Overdiagnosis of ADD

While we have focused on people underdiagnosed with ADD, they can also be overdiagnosed. Sometimes a person who is highly creative can display ADD symptoms when they don't have ADD at all. Or an energetic person with an extremely busy life can look appear to have ADD, but does not. And there can be an overdiagnosis of ADD instead of a really serious psychological disorder, as we have previously discussed.

It's important that people who may have some organizational difficulties, or other ADD symptoms, don't get diagnosed with having a disorder when there's not really a problem. A woman could be very creative, with what may be just exaggerated creativity, and the way of life could look similar to ADD. A woman could be very messy, with her things all over the place, but this could be a part of just a visual life style, a "right-brain" way of seeing things. Only if it is a problem for an individual, or a significant problem for those close to her, should she be diagnosed. If the person can function fine, if she can find her possessions, if she is enjoying this exciting, creative kind of life, then there is no problem. If she is thriving, feeling good, having meaningful relationships, and is financially in control, then there is no problem. On the other hand, symptoms shouldn't be taken lightly, as they could indicate some other kind of neurological, psychological, or physical problem. However, if a person displays symptoms, that doesn't mean one needs to rush into expensive testing. Seeing a professional, experienced in adult ADD, should be your next step. Nowadays, there has been enough exposure about adult ADD to find a knowledgeable professional in almost every area of the country. They can assess all the symptoms and begin to differentiate between what looks like ADD and what could be another condition.

Summary

Many women, and men, have been coping and compensating so well for so long that it may be hard to see their struggle under the surface. To complicate this further, when they seek help, women are often over-pathologized. Like many individuals with ADD, they may complain that the world feels like it's about to fall apart, which to clinicians can sound like a severe psychological disorder. In fact, ADD can mimic many other disorders such as depression, anxiety disorders, family or marital problems, thought disorders or drug abuse. In some cases, these disorders are the result of coping all one's life with an undiagnosed attention deficit disorder. That is why it is so important to be properly tested and diagnosed by professionals to sort out causes from effects in order to provide corrective treatment.

The longer the ADD goes on, the more difficult it is to separate ADD out from other things, with the potential for a mis-diagnosis. Further complicating the issue, women might be very competent at work but report more problems at home—where it may be more chaotic. This could be a false "lead" for a professional, guiding them toward a "family" or "relationship" problem. Or, a professional could misinterpret the confusing picture that an ADD woman may present. She may complain for years of low-level depression, low self-esteem, feeling out of control and overwhelmed. The language she uses to describe her internal states, such as, "everything's going to fall apart," may be misunderstood. She may be overpathologized by a mental health professional who may be predisposed to see her as chronically depressed, dependent, hysterical, narcissistic or passive-aggressive, depending on how she presents herself.

Other mediating circumstances, such as family support, structure, or high IQ, coupled with a lack of hyperactivity, can easily cloud the picture of chronicity and severity that's required for diagnosis; and in this all-too-common scenario, the woman's inquiry into ADD might be quickly dismissed. The underlying attention deficit disorder that might be contributing to her difficulties or at least coexisting with them may be undetected. A woman's lack of assertiveness might also play into the difficulty of getting diagnosed, as she might accept the authority's dismissal of ADD too easily.

It is also wrong to insist that you don't have other difficulties and assume that every problem you may have is an Attention Deficit Disorder. As we'll talk about in the next section, you want to find a diagnostician that you can trust, and put that information together with what you have read. And if you're uncomfortable with that professional, if what they say creates feelings of being unheard or what they say goes against what you have read about recent ADD discoveries and what you feel deeply inside, go talk to somebody else.

In the absence of severe mental illness or other neurological problems, in the absence of other great stressors, family problems or other things that would account for severe difficulties with disorganization, you must keep going in pursuit of your diagnosis for ADD. If you feel, in spite of other great achievements or abilities, even after therapy, that you're coming up against these problems over and over again, continue to pursue the correct diagnosis. If you're spending your life looking for things, if you're overwhelmed, out of control, buried with paperwork or details, unable to take care of routine household tasks, look for the ADD. If you're spending all your free time just trying to get some sense of control, if maintaining control is the focus of your life, if the impulsivity and attention/activity levels are chronically and severely causing you depression, anxiety or low self-esteem, keep going until you find some help. Find someone who can help you sort out and help with your difficulties—whether it's depression, anxiety, your family, learning disabilities, or if it's ADD.

Diagnosing ADD is not a science. In fact, it's a combination of art and science. Remember, ADD has many faces and it looks very different in women and men. Even in women with ADD, symptoms manifest very differently. Most people don't identify ADD with the non-hyperactive attributes of sitting on the couch not moving, slow processing, confusion, or fogginess. Most people still think of ADD as hyperactive little boys who've been acting up, or, aggressive, hyperactive, high-stimulation-seeking men. It's going to be hard for you, a woman with symptoms of ADD, to find someone who can help and understand you. But you must keep trying.

CHAPTER ELEVEN

Self-Assessment for Women and Paths to Diagnosis

U P TO THIS POINT, we have covered what happens when a woman is having difficulties, and doesn't know if it is ADD or something else going on. We have also shown how easy it could be to get misdiagnosed, as ADD is similar to so many other disorders. Let's presume that you, as a woman, think that you fit some of the characteristics we've described. You might be asking yourself, "what are the steps I have to go through to get to diagnosis?"

While women share many primary and secondary symptoms of ADD with men, they do have some significant issues in regard to ADD that differ. One of the difficulties, up until now, has been the lack of a self-assessment tool designed specifically for women. Despite the presence of other excellent self-assessment tools for Adults with ADD in general, I felt there was and is a need for a new way women could begin to identify themselves. Many women screen themselves out early on, even when they start to get an inkling that some of these characteristics describe them. When they look at various diagnostic descriptions they often feel that even though they saw a few words, a few lines, or even a chapter that might apply to them, the majority, of material was "not them." They then fall back to their previous position that they were just being lazy, disorganized, or depressed.

This is especially true for women without hyperactivity. Picasso's image of a Sleeping Woman represents the way a woman without

hyperactivity may look and feel as contrasted to a more hyperactive, and consequently more easily identifiable ADD individual.

Self-Screening

As we have mentioned, the concept of ADD in adults is still a relatively new phenomenon. Only recently has it started to come into the mainstream of possible diagnosis for mental health professionals. With the publication of many new books on adults with ADD, as well as the conferences, newsletters, and support groups popping up throughout the United States, word is beginning to spread. This neurological condition really exists and it is the cause of many people's difficulties.

It is so important for women who think they may have this disorder to be as educated as possible. Just as it is important to be an educated consumer when purchasing a major item like a house, car, boat, or computer, today it is equally imperative to be an educated consumer when it comes to health care, especially when you are dealing with something that is new.

The first thing to do is go through a preliminary self-assessment. This means reading about ADD (which you are doing now), perhaps going to some lectures, and completing some initial self-assessment checklists. If you still think you are on the right track, the next step would be to obtain a professional diagnosis. If you are having difficulties that don't seem to fit ADD, but are still disturbing to you, I urge you to seek professional help anyway, as you can be treated for depression or other interpersonal difficulties aside from the ADD.

Before seeing a professional for a diagnosis, I recommend a preliminary self-screening, or self-assessment. Drs. Hallowell and Ratey, in their book *Driven to Distraction*, have their Twenty Criteria. This is an excellent way to get a sense of the severity of your symptoms. Edna Copeland has a well-known checklist called the *Copeland Symptom Checklist for Adult Attention Deficit Disorders*. And Dr. Thomas Brown has a new checklist called the *Brown Attention Deficit Disorder Scales (BADD)*. Dr. Kathleen Nadeau also has a checklist, called the *Adult ADD Questionnaire*. I also like the self-assessment that appears in Dr. Dale Jordan's book, *Attention Deficit Disorder (ADHD and ADD Syndrome)* because it targets and assesses disorganization as a primary effect of ADD.

If you have most of the symptoms described in the following list or any other of the checklists, or if you have some of these symptoms to a severe degree, then it is worth pursuing a professional evaluation.

Solden Self-Assessment for Women with Attention Deficit Disorder

Copyright © 1995 Sari Solden

Every woman has the kinds of feelings or problems listed in this checklist at some time or another in her life, and to some extent. The important question is: do you have them more severely than the average person? Have they been present for most of your life? Do you feel these particular symptoms are the major reason you may be having difficulty in your achievement level, your self-esteem, your relationships, and your mood? If your overwhelming reaction to this list is a big Yes!, you might want to consider professional consultation about ADD.

Stimulation, Filtering System

↗ Do you feel bombarded in department stores, or grocery stores?
• Do you feel overloaded and exhausted after a day at the office?
↗ Do you feel overloaded from the noise and activity at parties?
↗ Do you often shut down in the middle of the day, feeling assaulted?
↗ Is it impossible for you to shut out nearby sounds and distractions that don't bother others?

Time, Money, Stuff (TMS)

• Is time, money, paper or "stuff" dominating your life and impacting your ability to achieve your goals?
↗ Are bills and important papers and forms piling up unattended?
↗ Are you spending a majority of your time coping, looking for things, catching up or covering up?
↗ Have you never learned to balance your checkbook?
↗ Is your car constantly filled with all sorts of stuff?
↗ Do you feel that you can't clean up without a tremendous amount of effort?
• Do you often feel life racing out of control, that it's impossible to meet your daily demands?
↗ Do you have trouble meeting deadlines, planning and prioritizing tasks?
↗ Do people frequently get annoyed with you for being late or forgetting appointments?
↗ Is packing for trips a nightmare?

✓ Despite your best efforts, is it impossible for you to maintain systems?

✓ Do you spend much of your energy on organization, to the exclusion of many other things you'd like to do?

✓ Are you too embarrassed to have someone come to your house to clean because they would see your mess?

• Are you too embarrassed to hire someone to help keep you organized because you think you're beyond help?

✓ Do you start each day determined to get organized?

Relationships

✓ Do you avoid people because of all the clutter in your life, or your disorganization?

• Have you stopped having people over to your house because of your shame at the mess?

✓ Have you been thought of as selfish because you don't write thank-you notes or send birthday cards?

✓ Are you called a slob or spacy?

✓ Do you feel like you are "passing for normal"?

✓ Do you feel like an impostor?

✓ Do you often go blank in conversations?

✓ Is small talk difficult for you?

✓ Are there times when you can't stop talking?

✓ Are there times when you can't help yourself from interrupting others even though you know you shouldn't?

✓ Do you have difficulty discussing world events?

✓ Have you had difficulties with sexual relationships because you can't concentrate enough?

• Have you often formed relationships with people who function as caretakers?

• Do you have special fears of abandonment or winding up alone because you don't think you could meet the demands of daily life by yourself?

✓ Do you hesitate to get close to intimate partners for fear that you couldn't manage the demands of marriage and children?

Emotions

✓ Can a request for "one more thing" from you put you emotionally "over the top"?

✓ Do you feel overloaded, or depleted?

✓ Do you feel depressed because you can't get everything done in your life?

✓ Have you felt this way for a long time? Since childhood?

• Do you find that you can't maintain a balanced life and meet the demands on you?

✓ Do you engage in negative self-talk about your disorganization or forgetfulness?

✓ Do you feel you are irresponsible?

• Do you worry excessively, have an inner sense that things are going to fall apart?

✓ If someone disturbs one of your systems, do you have a strong angry reaction?

• If the phone rings while you are concentrating, are you thrown into a state of "mini-panic"?

✓ Can you be distracted from one mood to another easily?

✓ Do you feel you are on a treadmill that you'll never get off?

Staying Alert: Energy Levels, Activity Level

• Do you drink an excessive amount of coffee or cola every day?

• Have you abused stimulants such as cocaine to stay focused, or alcohol or marijuana to self-medicate?

✓ Do you feel like a couch potato or a tornado, at either end of a disregulated activity spectrum?

✓ Do you feel as if you are in a fog?

✓ Is your motor always running?

• Do you feel that your mind is hyperactive, always thinking of new ideas?

✓ Is it very difficult for you to sit still or feel relaxed for long periods of time at meetings or lectures?

Ideas, Synthesizing

• Do you feel that you have many more ideas than other people?

✓ Do you feel that you can't synthesize, organize or act on your ideas in an orderly way?

✓ Do you have difficulty prioritizing?

✓ Do you have difficulty reading and remembering basic facts?

✓ At the end of the day, have you collected a multitude of notes scribbled on random pieces of paper?

Achievement

✓Have you watched others of equal IQ and education pass you by?

✓ Are you starting to feel despair of ever fulfilling your potential and meeting your goals?

✓ Are you clueless as to how others lead a consistent, regular life?

• Are you unable to figure out how to focus on your abilities because you're already drowning in demands?

• Do you find it very difficult to meet the demands of a 9 to 5 job?

History

• Were you called a daydreamer as a child?

✓Were you called messy, spacy, lazy, selfish, oversensitive?

• Were you ever diagnosed as having learning disabilities?

✓ Were you clumsy, bumped into things a lot?

✓ Were you either extremely shy or extremely social and talkative as a child?

• Were some of your grades in school way out of sync with the other grades?

✓Even as a child, did you have problems organizing your locker, your drawers, closet, or room?

• Were you promiscuous as a teenager?

• Did you change schools or colleges more than average?

✓ Did you change majors several times?

• Do you change jobs frequently?

• Have you changed life paths frequently, had more and different jobs than other people?

Women's Issues

✓Do you have difficulty keeping track of your jewelry, makeup and clothing accessories?

✓Is it very difficult for you to shop in department stores?

✓Do you have difficulties with impulsive or compulsive shopping?

• Do you find it overwhelming to help your children organize their school and social life?

• Are you unable to provide the structure required, especially if your children have ADD?

✓Do you find yourself using food or sex compulsively as a way to focus or soothe yourself?

✓Do you find yourself shifting from one activity to another when you are trying to do household tasks, without accomplishing much?

If you answered yes strongly to many of these questions, I would encourage you to pursue the question of whether you have ADD.

After Self-Assessment

Let's say you've done the above self-assessment, and you feel you're on the right track. The next thing that would be helpful to you (especially if this book is your introduction to the subject of ADD) is to read some of the other books listed in the appendix and do the self-assessment checklists in those books. They will inform you even more, to give you a better idea if it sound like you may have some symptoms of ADD. I find it's very useful for a person considering further assessment to *write things down* that seem to relate to them as they read. Try to think back to your childhood all the way through to the present and jot down difficulties you may have experienced. Think about any unusual inconsistencies in school, job changes, social relationships, or experimenting with substances. Especially think about the organization of your daily life.

Think about the severity of your symptoms. Look at the periods of time when things were going well, and try to figure out what kind of support you had at those times which helped your life to work. Try to remember when things might have stopped working well, when you might have hit a level of demands in your life which caused you not to be able to function as well. Talk to your family. If you have a partner or children, talk to them. If your parents and brothers or sisters are available, talk to them about what they remember.

O.K. You've done the checklists, the reading and you feel more convinced than ever that ADD may be the source of your difficulties. Now might be the time to get professional diagnosis and treatment. At this point there are several different ways you can proceed.

Talking to a Professional

You now have several options, any one of which can be positive or negative, depending on your particular situation and history. The most important criterion, however, is that *whoever you see should have as much experience as possible in treating Adults with ADD*. Ideally, for a woman, a professional should have seen many adult women with ADD.

There are three areas in which you will need professional help in order to receive a complete diagnosis and treatment. Sometimes you might find a professional experienced in all three, but often you will find it necessary to see more than one person as you continue to be treated. First, you will need professional assessment and diagnosis. This will include not just diagnosis for ADD, but for other difficulties that might be impacting you as well. Second, if you are diagnosed with ADD, you will need a medical doctor to prescribe and monitor the appropriate medication for you. And third, you will then need ongoing education, support and often counseling, especially in the beginning stages.

Paths to Diagnosis

There is no absolute test for ADD, but there are different schools of thought about what an adult has to do in order to be diagnosed. I think it's better to take a slow approach. Learn as much as you can, get some education, go to some CHADD meetings, and do your self-screenings. After a while, you'll get a "feel" for what ADD is all about. Then go for a professional opinion.

If you're already involved with a therapist, talk to her about your reactions to your self-assessments. If she has the expertise, she may be able to assess you herself or recommend another mental health professional who specializes in ADD. It's important for the professional to spend a lot of time with you to separate out the psychological from the neurological symptoms. Dr. Thomas Brown emphasizes that assessing ADD *without* hyperactivity requires extremely careful listening and questioning during the interview. He states that identifying the cognitive symptoms of ADD without hyperactivity requires much more subtle measures than "the simple observations or reports of overt behavior, which can identify hyperactive-impulsive types of ADD."

If you don't find someone who understands, go somewhere else. It's important to be open-minded and listen to what they have to say about the other possible causes of your difficulties. But also trust yourself. Many professionals don't have the experience yet to see ADD. Trust yourself and find a professional that you can trust and work with in a partnership, as you both try to understand your difficulties.

If you have been thoroughly assessed by a therapist who specializes in ADD, through interviews, histories and self-assessment tools, she may at this point recommend a full battery of neuropsychological tests. These can better explain the ways and areas in which your brain functions well, and in which areas it has more difficulty.

She can either refer you to a psychologist who does this kind of testing, or if she is a psychologist herself she may do this testing. Another route she may take after her assessment may be to refer you to a medical doctor for a confirmatory diagnosis and medication evaluation. This can either be to a general practitioner who is experienced in ADD, or if you are experiencing major depression or other kinds of serious psychological difficulties, you are going to want to be treated by a psychiatrist. She or he should be an expert in this kind of medication and treatment.

In other cases, you may start out discussing your feelings about ADD with your general practitioner, or a psychiatrist who makes the diagnosis and prescribes medication for you. This doctor may or may not also require that you get full neuropsychological testing first. If this doctor is not going to provide follow-up education support or counseling along with the medication, you should be referred to someone else for that. The combination of a mental health professional and a physician often works well.

The third way you could approach diagnosis is to begin with full neuropsychological testing followed by a referral for medication. Again, ideally, this should be followed by provisions for follow-up counseling, coaching, support or education.

There is disagreement in the field about the paths to diagnosis. Let's try and sort out the factors that might make a professional recommend one approach for you instead of another.

Clear-Cut Histories

Many adults have a strong history of ADD without many other complicating factors. In these cases, after a full assessment and history, the diagnosis can be relatively clear to a professional experienced with adult ADD, especially if she is also clearly able to rule out other co-existing disorders. Often there are reasons, however, why it's important to follow a different route, even though more expensive and time-consuming. This is most appropriate when a professional is unsure that ADD is the cause of someone's difficulties after this initial assessment period. This could be because of childhood histories or current coexisting difficulties that cloud the diagnostic picture. Neuropsychological testing is expensive, and there is no absolute yes or no answer as to whether someone has ADD. Often test conditions themselves, as Drs.Hallowell and Ratey point out in *Driven to Distraction,* provide the exact conditions of motivation and stimulation that a person with ADD needs in order to pay attention. Sometimes then he or she will do much better on these tests than real-life difficulties would suggest. However, as long as that is understood, the tests can provide a great deal of valuable information and, more importantly, can be of great value to the individual beginning to absorb and understand the reality and meaning of her ADD.

What is Right with Full Testing

There are a group of people who, because of some of the childhood histories we've discussed, have a more difficult situation to assess. Learning disabilities have to be sorted out, You might have physical disorders, other kinds of mood disorders, or personality difficulties clouding the issue that you want to be sure you can rule out. In these cases, there are a lot of good reasons to go for a more in-depth, full battery of neuropsychological testing.

Another very important reason for testing is for legal accommodations. In order to get certification for legal accommodations at school or at work, you will need a full battery of tests. You can also get extended time on some professional exams. These are excellent reasons to get the full neuropsychological testing.

There are less compelling, and, I feel, more optional reasons to get full testing but they can be of great value if a person has the resources and is so inclined. Some people, even if they know they have ADD, want to understand what their neuropsychological profile is. They want to know in what exact areas their strengths and weaknesses are. It is always helpful to know more about yourself. After you've had some introduction to ADD, and some time to absorb it, and have developed a relationship with a professional with whom you are discussing the ongoing management of ADD then, especially for the above diagnostic reasons, it's a very helpful step to go for the full battery of tests.

These tests and this process is useful to break through denial, especially in young adults The right kinds of tests help them understand that they have ADD, and they really start to integrate it in their lives. The tests can also help family members to understand it.

Unhelpful Ways to Get Testing

I have found that people often get diagnosed with ADD in an unhelpful way. A person could just read something about ADD, go to a psychiatrist right away, get a prescription, go home, and that's it. Or, someone goes right in for a full battery of tests with a psychologist who says, "Yes, you have ADD," and then goes to a psychiatrist, gets medication and goes home. No counseling. No guidance. Either one of these scenarios are helpful up to a point, because at least you'll know you have ADD. If you're so inclined you'll read a lot more about it, get involved with some people, and develop a network. For some people, that can work for a while. It can even work very well, depending on your initiative.

For most adults, though, it won't be enough. If they get the diagnosis and medication too quickly, and just go off on their own, they won't become involved with other people and continue to become educated about their ADD. They won't have the necessary time to absorb and integrate this new kind of identity. They won't have someone to work with on restructuring their lives, and confronting the difficult situations that come up when they try to make the necessary changes. Eventually, they're bound to feel disappointed.

Medication is an important phase of treatment, but since diagnosis is really the beginning of treatment, the way it's handled can set a significant tone. The pacing of treatment is very important. For many people it is not helpful to immediately get on medication, with little discussion of themselves, or their life or relationships. It takes time to get the right "ADD education," start to sort things out for yourself, get a diagnosis, possible testing, and then get a prescription. A person should then slowly and carefully explore the feelings and changes associated with the medication, as a new phase of life will have begun.

Diagnosis is the start of treatment because, as Dr. Ned Hallowell says, the "treatment begins with hope." With diagnosis, an ADD person will feel relieved and is on her way to understanding. A whole variety of feelings will accompany diagnosis. In my opinion, the best chance of success in treatment will occur if these feelings are explored with a caring mental health professional. They will be able to discuss your problems, explain your feelings, and answer the myriad of questions that will accompany your treatment. This is a critical juncture in your life, and all too often it's done in a quick, clinical manner. Although the testing may be thorough, I've too often seen test results that aren't thoroughly gone over in enough depth. Tests are only helpful if the results are carefully explained. They should illuminate your strong areas as well as your difficulties, what can be done to help, what's effective, what kind of strategies you can use, and where to go from here. Unless you get this supportive information, merely going through a complete battery of tests, while spending several hundred dollars is not really going to do you a lot of good.

But testing is not necessarily for everyone, especially as a way to begin. Timing is critical, as well as testing, in the context of the entire ADD treatment plan. I personally feel that the approach and route appropriate for each person needs to be determined on an individual basis. Have they been involved in educating themselves about ADD for a while? Are they ready to try medication? Is there family involved? Do they need a counseling or supportive relationship as a follow-up and to accompany medication trials? In addition, many people cannot afford neuropsychological testing but need help very badly. If these people can be accurately diagnosed without testing, they should be treated and carefully followed.

At the end of the book is a complete list of sources which should help you find references in your area. For starters, there are local CHADD groups (Children and Adults with Attention Deficit Disorder) in almost every area of the country. They could help you find a referral. If you use a computer with a modem, there is a forum for users with ADD on CompuServe with over forty thousand participants. They can help you as well. Mental health professionals in your area, your family doctor, or doctors who work with children can probably give you direction as well.

"Tips When Seeing a Professional"

Here are some tips when you go to talk to someone about all of this. First of all, take your notes in with you, and don't be afraid to use them. Also take a **tape recorder.** Ask them if you can tape the session in order to remember what is said, or ask them if you can take notes. Make this experience work, because you may get a lot of confusing information and you'll want to be able to go home and process it afterwards.

If you have tests taken, **make sure you get a thorough explanation of them, why they are giving the tests to you, and a good explanation of the results.** Beforehand, have someone sit down and tell you what the test consists of and how this will be helpful to you. What are they trying to show with each of the tests? When they explain the results, get a good understanding of your strengths as well as your weaknesses. Get some suggestions as to where to go or what to do now that the test is finished. What you don't want is to feel as though you are a part of a mill, where you are whisked in and out: "Here's some medication, thank you, good-bye, and have a nice life." This is for life, the beginning of a long, slow process which should be approached in a very human way. You have the right to ask for that and to find someone with whom you feel comfortable. If they do recommend medication, it should be handled slowly and thoughtfully; it is a big adjustment to begin medication. The person you work with doesn't have to know everything about ADD to start you on your path, but it is important to have someone you feel comfortable talking to, as you begin this process.

Summary

Sometimes it might take a few steps before you understand the whole picture. If you feel like you're **being dismissed,** or being told that you don't really know what you're feeling, or that this couldn't really apply to you, and you still think you have ADD, ask the professional to explain her position. If you think that ADD could still be the source of your difficulties, continue to look for someone else who might give **you a second opinion.** On the other hand, **don't ignore the fact that you may have a different disorder (that needs treatment) that may look like ADD.**

This is new; we never viewed people and their problems like this before. We never understood; we thought disturbances were always from emotional and family causes. We never understood that people have very different brains, different blueprints, different brainprints, just like fingerprints. People are just beginning to recognize how much we're influenced by our brain chemistry, and our brain wiring. Everyone is different, everyone has variations. All the different chemical transactions that go on in our minds—our behavior and emotions—are reactions to our brain chemistry. We're seeing now that cognitive differences and subtle variations are causing an effect in our lives that could account for our difficulties. We used to only focus on early childhood experiences, and never considered how much our psychology and our lives are responses to our own particular neurology.

We're just beginning to explore these differences and their impact on us. Right now there's a big shift in the understanding of this, and it's going to continue. Even though it is starting to become accepted, there's still a tremendous dis-belief and lack of knowledge about ADD in adults, ADD in women, and especially, ADD in women *without* hyperactivity.

CHAPTER TWELVE

An Overview of Treatment: Getting Started

The Grief Cycle, Medication, Women's Issues

L ET'S BEGIN WITH a diagram, All Roads Lead to Success, an overview
 of treatment that we're going to follow through the rest of the book.
When I say "treatment," I mean getting better, whatever that means to
you. Treatment does not have to mean individual psychotherapy each

ALL ROADS LEAD TO SUCCESS

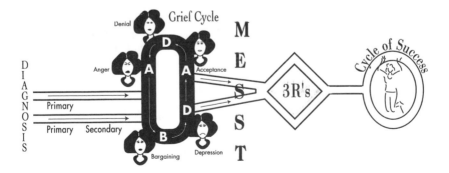

Some take the high road and some take the low road, but you
have to stay on some road to lead to success.

week, but might indicate a combination of medication, coaching, support, or counseling, with couples, individual or group work, depending on each person's particular history and present situation.

Each individual on the road to successfully living with ADD might take a different route; depending on their history might meet with fewer or more roadblocks or detours on the way. The important thing is to always get back on the road and continue onward. At the end of the journey, though, expect to find yourself there, not a different person, but just more of who you really are. For the trip to be successful, you will need fuel (medication) and good company (you can't do it alone; you can't do it with "toxic help"). You will also need a map to know where you're going, what signposts to look out for along the way and how to tell if you've arrived. Most importantly, you must be sure you are headed where you really want to go.

After the Diagnosis: An Overview of the Process

Sometimes the primary ADD symptoms are what bring an individual through diagnosis and into treatment. A woman feels she can't get her life on track, or that her home life and work at home are too difficult and time-consuming. In other cases, the secondary symptoms lead the individual to seek help. These are difficulties with mood, self-esteem, relationships, or achievement that are related to ADD. In either case, the moment of diagnosis often brings a feeling of great relief and hope, especially when the diagnosis is given in the context of education. Medication should be accompanied by emphasis on the whole picture of ADD and some options for continuing counseling or support.

As soon as diagnosis is made, the ADD individual begins to work her way through what is called a Grief Cycle. This concept was originally conceived to describe how people confront and come to terms with terminal illnesses. It has since been applied to any major life change. Dr. Lynn Weiss, in *The Attention Deficit Disorder in Adults Workbook*, as well as Kate Kelly and Peggy Ramundo, have applied the grief cycle to the process of accepting ADD. I have my own description of what I've seen happen as people go through this cycle in one form or another. There might be an obvious working-through of the cycle, or the process might be more subtle, but eventually all people diagnosed with ADD must work their way through all the stages.

Also in this early period after diagnosis, people begin to learn how to manage their primary ADD symptoms. Some of the tools and interventions I describe in my MESST Model (later in the chapter) will help them with this life-long process.

- Medication
- Education
- Support
- Strategies
- Therapy

A woman diagnosed with ADD can follow this model on her own, but eventually she will need to enlarge her support system to include other people in a variety of ways. She may attend support groups, join ADD organizations or employ the support of coaches, family members or a counselor to facilitate this process. The important areas of focus as a woman progresses and continues to integrate what she discovers about herself (her strengths as well as her difficulties) are seen below. I call them.

The 3 R's of Living Successfully with ADD

- **Restructuring one's life**
- **Renegotiating relationships**
- **Redefining self-image**

If all goes well, at some point I see people moving through a grief cycle to start a whole new cycle of success. We will carefully examine the road to success as we move along.

By following the bottom line on the Road to Success diagram, as you can see, a person may have to take a less direct route to achieve the same goal, or to arrive at the same destination. In addition to the primary symptoms, for example, a woman may also carry with her the emotional legacy of shame and guilt that we've talked about. She may still be affected by many of the secondary effects, such as difficulty with mood or relationships. These may interfere with her ability to move through the grief cycle or with employing techniques or tools necessary for change or managing her ADD symptoms. A woman who brings this more complicated life experience with her might need professional counseling, either in an individual, group, or couples setting.

A woman might find herself stuck without knowing why, confronting internal barriers that make it difficult to continue making the changes that she desires. In addition, any change in a person's life or in a family brings about its own stresses. Even if changes are positive, people close to her may resist or react in unexpected ways. Professional facilitation can help support and maintain positive changes. Later, when she starts to have new success and begins to be more assertive in her relationships, she might need new skills and support. For all these reasons some form of counseling periodically is helpful as an individual continues her life learning to live successfully as a woman with ADD.

THE GRIEF CYCLE

Illustrated in the diagram of the Grief Cycle are the stages of grief and the feelings that go along with them.

The Grief Cycle....

| DENIAL | ANGER | BARGAINING | DEPRESSION | ACCEPTANCE |

...becomes a new cycle of
SUCCESS!

Denial

After the period of relief that can accompany diagnosis, one might enter a state of denial. People at first might either deny the reality of ADD, or accept it superficially, but continue to question if it really applies to them. Even if they say that they have ADD, they have not yet integrated it in any kind of deep or meaningful way that will help them adjust. Even after diagnosis, when their ADD symptoms emerge, people often fall back into an "I'm stupid or irresponsible" stance. Even if they give lip service to the idea of ADD it takes a while for people to integrate it into their self-view.

As with any new life-altering event, label, or change of self-view, the person diagnosed with ADD often goes through an initial period of shock. This shock can persist for a long time, unless they've had a lot of time to investigate ADD before diagnosis. If the individual has been reading, integrating and thinking about ADD, applying the information to herself, and has become convinced that ADD is her problem before diagnosis, then, of course, she may have already worked through some of these feelings. If, however, the first mention of ADD is followed too quickly by diagnosis and medication, the person might believe that they are moving effectively through the grief cycle, but they might have to go back through the cycle again in more depth.

Another way that people deny their ADD, in this first stage of the grief cycle is to deny the impact (as opposed to the reality) of it. They deny the effect that it has had in their lives, that it's going to continue to have in their lives, and especially the changes that they will have to make. This happens most frequently as a result of a quick diagnosis followed by medication prescribed without any in-depth education or follow-up counseling. A person in this situation won't have an understanding that this condition or treatment involves more than just taking medication. Also, if they do not fully appreciate the reality of ADD, they will not be able to understand the potential strengths that can accompany ADD and learn to capitalize on them. Skimming the surface of the grief cycle prevents a woman from immersing herself in a process which can be an exciting and fulfilling challenge.

Anger

After a woman understands that she does have something called ADD, and has had it for a long time, she begins to look back and see how deeply it has affected every area of her life. At this point she will often move into the next stage, which is anger. She often feels anger at lost opportunities, looking back at the paths that she didn't take. She focuses on the point at which things started to go off course and begins to feel anger at a system that let her down as a child. She may feel angry at her family who didn't help her or teachers who misunderstood her or people who blamed her. Or she may just feel angry in general that this is happening to her and that life has been so hard even though she has been unable to understand why, or how to fix it.

It is helpful for an individual to see that anger is a natural part of the grief cycle and that it is important and necessary to go through it in order to move beyond it and continue in a positive direction.

Bargaining

When a person understands that she has ADD, she is naturally encouraged and excited to learn that she can take medication that will help. She says, "Okay, I have ADD, but I'll just take my medication and I'll be all right." She figures that taking medication will take care of the ADD. Unfortunately, medication for ADD is often promoted (especially by the media) as a magic pill. Medication is a cornerstone of treatment, as we will see, and is often essential, but it is not magic or perfect and not sufficient as treatment. Because the benefits of medication don't always match a person's expectations, disappointment and discouragement often set in.

Depression

When the medication doesn't cure everything; when, even if ADD individuals feel better and many areas of their life are greatly improved, they still have many of the same difficulties. They then begin the next stage in the cycle. A state of depression can result at this point because they've found that things are still hard. The difficulties can be seen as even harder at this point because the whole experience can be so disorganizing in itself. They're caught in between two worlds for a while and they can't go back. They want to forget about ADD, go back to the way it was. Even if the system wasn't working very well, at least it was familiar. They've seen other people with ADD and by now they know that there's a long road ahead of them, but the process seems like too much to deal with. Often they are not yet getting enough of the support that would make it easier to make necessary changes. As a result of not getting enough support at this point, they may feel isolated and lonely, which also contribute to feelings of depression.

These are all signals that point to the way out of depression and indicate the kind of support necessary to engage in order to continue to move through the cycle. In addition, as a result of the new focus they achieve through their medication, people are able to see much more clearly. This often means they can see problems in a relationship they might not have had the energy to face before or to deal with. They may now face the fact that they have to deal with more conflict and work through issues that may have been buried for years. There may be events in their own past, many feelings that they now begin to face. It is natural at this point that they start to feel all the loss—of dreams, hopes, and opportunities. Like all the emotions a woman feels as she works her way through this cycle, these are all natural and necessary. It means that she is integrating the idea of ADD, getting to know herself and understanding her past in a way that will lead to a more satisfying way of life.

Acceptance

With the right kind of support, counseling, education or merely with the passage of time, people move to a new level that we call the acceptance phase. Sometimes they go through the other phases over and over again without reaching acceptance; sometimes they move to acceptance and then go through another entire cycle again. But at some point, they will have integrated in a deep way the idea of themselves as a person with ADD. At that point, they stop thinking of ADD as a matter of willpower or moral failure. One of my clients, even a year after diagnosis, refused to see ADD as anything but bad character on her part and would continue to berate herself with each emergence of ADD symptoms.

At the stage of acceptance, eventually people start sorting out their primary ADD symptoms in a less reactive way. They learn that although they can manage their ADD symptoms, they will still occur. They learn to recognize their responses to the ADD which they can begin to change so that they don't make things worse for themselves.

Eventually they learn to be desensitized to other people's judgments and start to externalize or get rid of this deep sense of shame and secrecy. They might still feel this shame, but it's outside them now. At this point, ADD adults stop apologizing or attacking; they feel they are more in control, and state clearly what they need.

The focus shifts to their strengths. They no longer feel the need to hide, and are able to ask for more help or accommodations to get more assistance. As a result of these changes, they continue to build on their strengths. With this feeling of pro-activity comes a new sense of self-esteem, less depression and more hope. Once this line is crossed, people start exploring options and renegotiating their roles and relationships to make their lives work for them. A whole new cycle of acceptance is initiated. This really takes on a life of its own. I call it a Cycle of Success. That's when the need for self-protection diminishes and behavior towards others begins to change. This can be the beginning of more satisfying relationships.

The following combination of tools will help you as you progress through the grief cycle and manage your primary ADD symptoms. This is an effective way to get started. Restructuring, getting accommodations and validation, working through the grief cycle, identifying with others, and getting the education you need.

I use the word "mess" as a desensitizing tool, but it helps describe the kinds of interventions that are important, especially in working through this grief cycle.

Medication

Medication is really the cornerstone of treatment. Even though a Rolls Royce is a fabulous vehicle, it still needs the proper gas in order to run smoothly. It doesn't matter how expensive or beautiful the car is, or how great an engine it has. If it doesn't have fuel, it's just not going to go anywhere. In the same way, medication for people with ADD is the fuel that allows the brain to function smoothly and to its potential.

ADD is a neurobiological condition. No matter what else you do in order to make your life work, unless you have the basic fuel to run your

THE "MESST" MODEL

edication   Often the cornerstone of treatment, a beginning

ducation   Learn as much as possible; lectures, books, newsletters, organizations

upport   Emotional; identify with others
Physical; negotiate tasks

trategy   Intervention must match level of organizational deficit

herapy   Individual, couple or group
Communication skills, working through shame
Secondary effects; depression, self-esteem, relationships

brain correctly and efficiently, all the other interventions won't work nearly as well. You can't cure the neurobiology with psychology. It is important to look at the psychology as a reaction to living with your particular brain, but the medication is the foundation that will give you the energy to make the other necessary changes. Medication doesn't cure everything, but it gives you a stepping stone on which to build. It gives you the focus to be able to strategize effectively and engage support, to stay on track in order to make your life work again.

Getting Started

Stimulant medication, specifically Ritalin, is the most commonly prescribed and generally effective treatment for ADD. It might take some perseverance to find the right doctor to prescribe for you. Not all doctors want to prescribe medication for ADD. More and doctors now are aware of ADD and comfortable with it, so you might start your search with your family physician. Your child's psychiatrist might see that you have some of the same symptoms as your child, and she/he may be able to diagnose and treat you as well. Whoever diagnoses you should be able to refer you to a prescribing physician. Networking at your local ADD support group is also a good way to find an experienced general practitioner or psychiatrist who will prescribe to adults in your area.

There are two main kinds of medications used for treating ADD, stimulant and antidepressant medications. Stimulants can help increase alertness, focus, and regulate activity levels. They also can help reduce an individual's reactivity and distractibility. In addition to Ritalin, which works effectively for approximately seventy percent of people with ADD (Barkley, R.1977) Dexadrine and Cylert are also effective stimulant medications. As I said earlier in the Pocket Guide, ADD symptoms are most commonly linked to the inefficient transmission of information in the brain, through chemical brain messengers called neurotransmitters. Neurotransmitters send information between the millions of nerve cells in the brain. Medications used for ADD help the two most common neurotransmitters usually associated with ADD, Dopamine and Norepinephrine, function more effectively. Medication works on these neurotransmitters by making them more available where they are needed, thus "smoothing out" the transmission of information in the brain, and consequently "smoothing out" the ADD symptoms.

ADD medication has been proven to be very safe and effective. The side effects of Ritalin are small and mild, and the dose is variable. It is not dependent on weight. Drs. Hallowell and Ratey say that major complaints involve appetite suppression and sleep disturbances. According to them, ten percent of people complain of headaches. Sometimes people experience a "rebound effect" in between doses, in which they experience some headaches or the jitters. You can take a slow-release form of Ritalin, instead of or in addition to, to smooth out these side effects.

There are many stereotypes about the use of stimulant medication for ADD, for example, fears of abuse by doctors and pharmacists who are not experienced with ADD. While there are concerns when a person has a drug or alcohol abuse history, usually "most adults take the medication as a way of tuning in, not tuning out." (Huessey, 1985, quoted by Hallowell and Ratey, *Pharmacotherapy for ADHD in Adults*, 1991.) People do often have anxieties about starting medication and concerns about it, rather than just wanting to take it and abuse it.

Antidepressants

Some antidepressants are used alone to treat ADD, and others are used in combination with stimulants to help depression or other symptoms that often accompany ADD. An experienced doctor will know how to balance these to find the right combination for you. Many doctors prescribe tricyclic antidepressants like Norpramin (desipramine) and Tofranil (imipramine) or Wellbutrin instead of stimulants, as they affect the same neurotransmitters. They too increase attentiveness and decrease distractibility (Hallowell and Ratey, *Driven to Distraction*). They also seem to have a calming effect. Fewer people (forty percent) respond to low doses of the tricyclics, but when they do, the results are excellent (Hallowell and Ratey, *Pharmacotherapy for ADHD in Adults*, 1991).

Women often need to be treated for depression along with the ADD. Depression is usually associated with an imbalance in another chemical neurotransmitter, Serotonin. Antidepressants that affect Serotonin (SSRI antidepressants) such as Prozac, are often taken along with stimulants, and this combination seems to be effective for both the treatment of the ADD and the depression. Often though, a woman feels chronically depressed as a result of coping with undiagnosed ADD all her life. In these cases, once a woman is on the proper dose of stimulant medication, her depressive symptoms will be alleviated along with the ADD symptoms. This is when the depression has been secondary to, or a result of the ADD.

It is important to get as much information as you can about medication. I suggest that before people start on medication, they take the time to read enough about it to ask informed questions during their "meds" consultation. The more you know before you talk to the doctor, the more assertive you can be if you feel your concerns aren't being adequately addressed. Some sources are listed at the end of the book to help you explore medication for ADD in more depth.

Having medication "thrown at you" isn't going to be very helpful, and you need a doctor who can support and help you through this important process. You may have conflicts about taking medication. You definitely need to feel comfortable with the concept and the process before you start. You might want to manage on your own, without medication. Some people with ADD are very involved in holistic health and would rather try meditation, exercise, bio-feedback or just extensive support and structure

Why Do All the Experts Have Different Approaches?

Hallowell and Ratey emphasize that there is no single "cure" for ADD. As they say, there is no "Cookbook recipe" to find the exact medication for the right person at the right time. I feel that, just as great artists use different palettes that produce different combinations of colors, all resulting in unique works of art, so too, do experts with medications use different approaches and combinations of medicines for a particular individual and situation. Even though for most individuals, standard doses and trials of Ritalin will be effective, those who don't respond to Ritalin or who have more complicated conditions will find the most success with a doctor who has a wide repertoire of strategies. The important thing is to have good communication with your doctor, so that he can monitor your responses and adjust and fine-tune your medication.

Special Women's Issues and Medication

Many women throughout the country have asked me questions concerning ADD and special woman's issues, such as

PMS, menopause, pregnancy, sexual functioning, eating disorders and obsessive compulsive symptoms. There hasn't been a great deal written or researched about Women with ADD. Only very recently has it started to be accepted that adults can have ADD. Women with ADD are just beginning to get identified and treated, especially those without hyperactivity. These "women's issues" have therefore just begun to surface. My comments on these issues are based on the conversations I have had with women with ADD and professionals throughout the country; observations I have made in my clinical practice; and the small amount of literature written on the subject. The best and most inclusive chapter about these issues and the one that I will quote extensively in the following section is from Chapter Six, "Perchance to Dream," in *Answers to Distraction* by Hallowell and Ratey.

PMS

Many women who suffer from PMS as well as ADD have told me that their ADD symptoms become more severe during PMS, even when they are on stimulant medication. Typical PMS symptoms of depression, anxiety, and irritability seem to be even more intense for women with ADD. In addition, the ADD symptoms, which may have been helped other times of the month by medication, also seem to increase with PMS. It seems as if the stimulants are losing their effectiveness during this time.

What seems to be happening is that the chemicals in the brain that cause the PMS symptoms come from *another* neurotransmitter, serotonin, not the neurotransmitters that are causing the ADD. During the time of the month when the PMS hits, this neurotransmitter, while causing PMS symptoms, also throws the delicate balance between the other neurotransmitters and the medication off. That is why the stimulant medication doesn't seem like it is working. Women therefore, in addition to stimulant medication, may need *another* medication to help the "PMS" neurotransmitter. This will then allow the stimulants to do their job (Nadeau,1995, Chapter 14 in *Comprehensive Guide*). Dr. John Ratey says that Prozac and BuSpar are very effective for the PMS (*ADDendum*, Fall 1991). Zoloft has also been reported to alleviate PMS symptoms. "These medicines are used right along with the stimulants, and don't compromise cognitive functioning as other treatments have done" (Ratey, *ADDendum*, 1991).

Non-medically, it helps women with ADD and PMS to know that this time of the month is going to be challenging, despite their best efforts. As a result of understanding this they can do two things. One is to adjust their self-talk when their difficulties and ADD symptoms increase, so they don't berate themselves, worsening their feelings of depression, or increase their anxiety by fears that they are losing their ability to control their ADD. They need to say reassuring things, reminding themselves that these feelings are to be expected.

The second thing they need to do, is, wherever possible, adjust the demands of their environment during this critical period. They should reduce the amount of stimulation and stress during this time. They also need to increase the amount of support and structure, and take extra care to get an adequate amount of sleep, nutrition, exercise and relaxation.

Hallowell and Ratey, in *Answers to Distraction,* report that many of their female patients seem to feel that birth control pills have a stabilizing effect on their hormones, eliminating the problems of PMS and consequently the increased ADD symptoms.

Menopause

Many women in the age group between forty and sixty, going through menopause, are now being diagnosed with ADD for the first time. Even less has been written or discussed on ADD and menopause, because this is the first time in history that women in this age group have been diagnosed. They are confronting both the effect and the treatment of the combination of these conditions. As Hallowell and Ratey point out (*Answers to Distraction*), menopause *itself* has only recently began to receive wide attention and become openly discussed.

Women beginning menopause have voiced their concerns to me about the cumulative effect on their physical and mental health from the stress produced by these two conditions. Women with ADD already have very vulnerable and sensitive systems, and, as with PMS, the tremendous hormonal changes can throw off even their prior effective treatment for ADD. In addition, the effects of aging can also contribute to decreased cognitive abilities and memory, interfering with compensations they may have used all these years. The losses and stresses that all women face during this period, combined with the exacerbation of ADD symptoms due to hormonal changes, can create quite a crisis. Like anyone else going through menopause, becoming diagnosed with ADD for the first time, these women benefit tremendously from counseling, education, and support, as well as medical intervention.

Menopause creates some of the same symptoms of ADD, such as "increased distractibility, gloomy mood, irritability, restlessness, extreme fatigue, and even memory problems" (*Answers to Distraction*). Drs. Hallowell and Ratey say that it appears that when women are treated with traditional hormonal replacement therapy for menopause, the ADD symptoms improve.

I would encourage any ADD women experiencing menopausal symptoms to talk to their gynecologist about their ADD symptoms, and conversely talk with your prescribing ADD doctor about your menopausal symptoms.

Pregnancy

Another area of great concern to women with ADD, especially those who have experienced the benefits and relief of medication, is the prospect of undergoing the strain of pregnancy and nursing an infant without medication. Because women in any numbers have only recently been identified with ADD in adulthood, there are not yet any definitive answers yet on the effects of stimulant medication during pregnancy. As a general principle, women should avoid taking any medication during pregnancy, so this has to be carefully discussed with a doctor. Some women I have spoken to are so afraid of the exhaustion and stress of a pregnancy that they chose adoption instead. Dr. Kathleen Nadeau, at the 1995 ADDA conference, emphasized the fact that environmental changes and restructuring one's life during the period of pregnancy is essential, (especially in the absence of medication).

A woman may have to rethink her choices at this time; for instance, she may have to choose to work less. She definitely will have to make some adjustments if she continues her pregnancy without medication. On the other hand, some women report feeling so well during pregnancy and are so focused on the event that their sense of well-being carries them through (Hallowell and Ratey, 1995). I have noted that these women usually have support and are able to decrease their environmental demands to compensate for the loss of medication.

Hallowell and Ratey, in Chapter Six in *Answers to Distraction*, say that there are no studies available on the effects of taking stimulant medication during breast feeding and pregnancy, but they recommend in general that, if a woman can tolerate it, she go off the medication. They also report that women who remained on the medication by choice reported no visible harm to the baby and they felt instinctively that their increased feelings of calmness had a positive effect on the child. Hallowell and Ratey state that the risks and benefits of continuing or discontinuing medication during pregnancy need to be weighed carefully by a woman and her doctor to determine which choice carries the greatest harm.

In summary, it is generally advisable for a woman not to be on medication while she is pregnant. However, if a woman has extreme symptoms of ADD without medication, which would create tremendous stress on herself and the baby, she would need (as with any serious medical condition) to discuss the risks and benefits in depth with her doctor. But a woman should also remember that she might feel better during pregnancy even without the medication, especially if she restructures her life in a way that reduces environmental demands.

Eating Disorders

Drs. Hallowell and Ratey, in *Answers to Distraction*, report connections between ADD and eating disorders and suggest that perhaps the high stimulation provided by starvation is a form of self-medication for difficulties with focus. They say that some research indicates Ritalin can be effective in these cases if the woman with an eating disorder is actually trying to fix an underlying attention deficit disorder. Prozac has also been effective with eating disorders. Of course, anyone with the symptoms of anorexia or bulimia should see a physician or a mental health professional. These are serious conditions that need professional attention.

Obsessive Symptoms

Women with ADD can have a separate, coexisting obsessive-compulsive disorder. This anxiety disorder can also be helped by antidepressant medication such as Anafranil, Prozac or Zoloft. However, women with ADD may *seem* to have this disorder when they instead have developed compensations (that look like compulsions or obsessions) as a way of coping with their ADD. These symptoms include such behaviors as compulsive list-making, ruminating about what has to be done, or obsessive organizing in order to know where things are. These symptoms, though, even if begun as compensations, may take on a life of their own, especially before treatment for ADD, so that women hold onto them for dear life as a way to keep their world together. They feel if they let down their guard for even a moment, all will be lost. The behavior takes on a drive for anxiety-reduction to such an extent that it becomes an anxiety disorder. The compensatory behaviors originally helpful for ADD difficulties in this case eventually take up as much time and have as much negative impact in one's life as the original symptoms they are attempting to control. Often medical treatment for ADD will let them "relax their hold," as the medication will to some degree make up what they had been compensating for.

As in any differential diagnosis, OCD and ADD have to be carefully sorted out from one another and the meanings of the behavior determined. Behaviors that are referred to as compulsive, like shopping and overspending, are in ADD often (as Hallowell and Ratey say in *Driven to Distraction*) impulsive behaviors rather than true compulsions. These impulsive behaviors can cause serious problems, but might be helped more through treatment for ADD, whereas true compulsions are helped more by the medications that we talked about earlier.

Substance Abuse

In order to self-medicate, many people use excessive amounts of food, caffeine, or nicotine in an effort to help themselves focus or relax. In addition, to change their uncomfortable inner cognitive state, they often abuse substances like alcohol, cocaine or other unprescribed medication. In some cases, they become addicted to these substances and need to be treated for substance abuse and begin a program of recovery before many professionals will treat them for ADD. However, in some cases, if the excessive use of substances is primarily driven by this need to self-medicate, beginning a program of proper medication will often eliminate the craving for these substances. This needs to be assessed carefully in the context of the relationship with a mental health professional experienced in the area of substance abuse. The extent of the substance abuse will be determined and whether it is necessary to treat the abuse before treating the ADD.

It has been noted by many clinicians and most notably written about by Dr. Daniel Amen, that ADD and alcoholism often run in the same families. Dr. Amen feels that children of alcoholics, who may also then be children of parents with ADD, share many of the same traits. He says also that they may be more prone to obsessive-compulsive disorders. As we have said before, a combination of stimulants and anti-obsessive medication can be helpful to people with this combination of difficulties. He encourages people who may be afraid of medication because of a history of substance abuse in their families to consider the benefits of medication. (Amen, *Healing the Chaos Within*.)

Sexuality and Medication

Medication for ADD can help a woman who is having difficulty focusing during sexual relations, says Hallowell in his article, "Living and Loving with an Attention Deficit Disorder." He emphasizes that the knowledge that one partner has ADD can take away the sense of self-blame that can affect sexuality, thus setting up an intimate environment for maximum pleasure by permitting the ADD partner to stay focused. Medication can reduce the non-responsiveness or, conversely, the hypersexuality that some ADD people require in order to focus.

Women with ADD are often distractible during sex, thinking about what they need to do; this is not out of lack of involvement or lack of feelings toward the partner, but merely the inability to focus that much attention. Others use hypersexuality as a focusing device, since the high stimulation, the intensity of the moment and the passionate involvement (even if short-lived) can bring tremendous relief. Obviously, the first case can result in difficulties with orgasm, but stimulant medication can help focus to improve this situation. Hallowell and Ratey, in *Answers to Distraction*, say that medications like Noripramine and Tofranil can have negative effects on orgasm, and drugs that affect serotonin like Prozac can also have negative sexual effects. They suggest talking to your doctor if this happens.

Responses to Medications

People often experience a positive response to the prescribed medication that appears dramatic to them and others. Sometimes people know within a few hours that the medication is making a tremendous difference. They feel awake and alert for the first time in their lives—out of their fog.

On the other hand, you may not feel that dramatically different. You may have to look back over a course of several months to see that your life has improved in significant ways. For instance, you may have accomplished more, you may have stayed on track, or your relationships may have improved. Some people may need input from others to check on their improvement.

Try to be sensitive to when you are "coming off" the Ritalin so that you know what your cycle is. Should you take it every 3 1/2 hours? 4 1/2 hours? Are side effects from taking the medication or from coming off the medication? Does medication help in social situations? Does it help with reading? How does it help with emotions? Try to understand everything that goes on around the issue of medication. Keep a diary, observe yourself so that you can really understand how it affects you. Medication has great effects on every area of your life. It is not simply a matter of taking a pill in order to be able to study. Since medication has a brain-organizing effect, I feel that it is often important to take it all the time. It's also important to stay with a trial of medication long enough to find out what the proper optimal dose without side effects is for you.

According to Drs. Hallowell and Ratey, in *Driven to Distraction*, eighty percent of people can be helped by some kind of medication. Education about ADD medication is really important. Even if you saw a psychiatrist for medication in the beginning, it is valuable to talk to a counselor to track and work through the effects of the medication and ask questions about what's normal, what can be expected. There can be a wide range of feelings associated with medication. You may have to work out feelings of being disappointed, wondering "Is this all I can expect" or "What should I be able to expect, and what do I need to do now in addition to the medication?" Medication can later be a disappointment to some people who feel great at the beginning because it's so exciting, like a new toy. Women say they're so excited, they never thought that drawers actually worked before, but now they understand how you can fold clothes, put them in and close the drawers. One woman said, "I looked at the room and I could figure out how to go about organizing it and I did." They can go into a department store for the first time and not shut down, or to the grocery store. They can actually pick out clothes. They can block out the tremendous number of sights and sounds. It's these daily moments that are great triumphs for women.

The surprising thing is that medication helps not just with school or work or organizing, but also allows you to be able to stay with a conversation and to interact and connect with people in a new way. It helps reduce your anxiety, and helps you stop responding to each new distracting or interesting idea that appears to you. Medication does not increase your willpower, but it helps to reduce the onslaught of information coming in at you. For the first time, you can experience how other people aren't as bombarded or overloaded. It can be compared to the difference between vision and seeing. You might be able to see, but it is cloudy and foggy. Medication provides real vision, long-range, seeing clearly. a system for staying on track. Medication helps to make the transmission of information through the brain messengers more efficient, to help block out some of the stimuli coming in and help you filter out the internal and external information that's bombarding you. It can give you sustained energy, help you stay awake and focused and alert and cut down on emotional reactivity. It provides a cushion so you don't feel as sensitive, open, raw. Usually it can help the primary ADD symptoms.

When you are not feeling so raw or open, you are able to concentrate better. You are able to rise to new levels of success and improve your relationships; that success then takes on a life of its own. It is not just the medication for the rest of your life that makes you continue to feel better. You are also building from the effect of the medication to get your life more under control, to understand and improve your self-esteem, and to get back on track and focus.

Changes with Medication

Successful medication does not mean that a woman will like everything she experiences. As a therapist I know that medication can prompt lots of changes in relationships. Even a positive change can be difficult. When someone stops drinking (for example), there are still wrinkles in the system and a lot of what we call "change-back" messages. People might say, "You're not yourself any more. You're always making trouble now. I thought the medication was supposed to take care of that," as if the medication was a tranquilizer. People get upset. People will tell you to "take a pill," when you might be displaying real emotion for the first time that you can focus on and express. You may stay with an argument rather than fall back and get confused, not able to keep your thoughts together. This might create a real power shift in the relationship, which is good, but may increase conflict for a while.

At this point, a woman might be confronted with all her prohibitions about this kind of power and the danger she feels about making someone angry. She can take that back and work it through in therapy. A woman might at first be afraid to understand the way she feels about her partner or to confront other issues in their relationship. She may not have had the energy to deal with it or becoming too overloaded to face things before. She might see a lot of things in her life that she doesn't like any more, that she's not happy with. Medication can give her both the wherewithal to take action and also give her the power to stick with her feelings and express them, even though they might not all be positive. Because of this she might appear very different to significant people in her life. For a man, medication might be a relief to those around him; for a woman, people often experience her as changing in an assertive way. That might be uncomfortable for others if a woman has been hypoactive and suddenly she is more of a force to contend with.

It's clear from this long discussion that medication is often essential and extremely helpful for the symptoms of ADD as well as other associated conditions that women struggle with. Let's go back to the metaphor that we used at the beginning of this section: once you have the proper medication (fuel), you still need to keep your vehicle oiled, tuned up, and drive it properly.

CHAPTER THIRTEEN

Treatment Continued: The Rest of the MESST

Education, Support, Strategies and Therapy

Education

THE NEXT ELEMENT, the next stepping stone in the MESST Model, is education. I always view education as just as much emotional education as informational. The whole purpose is to help you manage your ADD and move you through the grief cycle, to be able to integrate ADD as deeply as you can into your self-image. Education provides the opportunity to learn about structures, strategies and medication, and it also helps you internalize the ADD. I would recommend you take advantage of whatever is available in your area as well as the list of resources at the end of the book. Attend lectures, conferences, hear the wide variety of information available on ADD: medication, neuropsychology, the grief cycle, emotions, relationship issues, strategies, and coping techniques.

Join organizations such as CHADD (Children and Adults with ADD), support networks that deal with adults, and subscribe to newsletters (especially if you don't attend a group). It would be helpful to associate with other adults with ADD, either in person or through reading their stories. A wide variety of newsletters are listed in the resource section, ranging from those that are research-oriented to those that are chatty. Here you will read about other people's experiences and all the latest news about ADD workshops and conferences. Getting hooked up on the Internet is also a useful outlet, for people who are so disposed. They can make wonderful connections and can even meet at national conferences after getting to know each other on the Internet. There are also good books available now on adult ADD, reaching a wide range of audiences.

Just a few months after I was diagnosed, I subscribed to the newsletter *Addendum*. After a while I got a notice that it was time to renew my subscription. It read: "Now I know how hard it is to find a stamp, and it might take hours to find an envelope, put it together and mail it, but it's very important to re-subscribe." That made a deep impression on me. I "got it"—these people really knew who I was and understood the difficulty of something like that.

Education goes a long way toward breaking the isolation. You're not just getting information, you're learning about other people's experiences. This has a soothing, healing effect, knowing that others have gone through similar experiences. People with ADD can be very isolated. They have no idea that their symptoms are a real condition. When they find out that they have it, they don't know that others also do. After they learn there are others with ADD, they don't realize that they're also experiencing the same things on a daily level. Education also goes a long way toward relieving the anxiety and self-doubt, because as I said before, it takes a long time for people to really believe that they have ADD all the time. It is good to get this idea reinforced from those who are positive about it—coping and living with it well. Education will give you the advantage of hearing these subjects talked about for the first time.

There are some wonderful conferences through CHADD (which deals with children and adults), and now there are some natoinal specific conferences just for adults. These include ADDA (Attention Deficit Disorder Association), the one held at the University of Michigan (Adult Information Exchange Network) and the Rebus Institute, in the San Francisco Bay Area. A conference is a tremendous experience for people with ADD who might only have read about it before or attended some local groups. To see a thousand or more people in the same place for several days who are not hiding any more, who are not in the closet any more, who are talking about all the things that they have experienced, meeting them live, getting to like them, getting to know them, is very exciting. You will see people at all levels of integration; from those who are very successful now, people who have been dealing with this for a long time, to people who are just starting out. This can be a good way to take the first step in alleviating some of the old feelings of shame and guilt and isolation.

Support

The next area in the MESST Model, the next stepping stone, is support. There are two components, emotional and physical, closely related to what we just said about education. Support is the next step of actually getting involved with other adults who have ADD, so support will be both emotional and physical. We'll talk about both these areas. Especially at this first stage of ADD, it's often difficult for your family and friends (who haven't been educated as you have, haven't been working at this). It is hard for them to understand your ADD, hard for them to accept it. They have their own set of emotions around ADD that they need to work through, so you can't always get the support you need right away from people close to you. That is a isolating, upsetting, and frustrating situation.

As you work through that, it's essential that you start to have support from other people who can provide a positive environment. Counseling is one place to get that, but in addition, it's important to break the isolation that you feel, develop strategies, gain understanding and take the risks that you are capable of with other people in a support group. There are large support groups (through CHADD and other national networks), where you hear other people's stories and share in a supportive atmosphere, and smaller support groups where you get education, work on communication skills and confront other kinds of interpersonal issues that might be related to the ADD. Hearing other people's stories, who are at different places in their diagnosis and treatment brings you hope, reduces your isolation, and helps you understand the process to get a better idea of where you're actually headed. Ideally, you want to be moving in the direction of eventually getting support from people in your personal circle of relationships. Until that is possible, though, it's important to start finding outside support for yourself. The better you feel about your ADD, the more you will be able to talk to people close to you about it, and be able to begin to work on that area as well.

Physical Support

Physical support means arranging to have people around you to help with the physical details of life that are hard for you. It means that you do not attempt to cope with this alone. Newly diagnosed ADD people often say, "Now that I know about this, I'm going to go home and I'm going to try harder." Doing the same thing they have always done, but "trying harder," just sets them up for frustration. Women, especially, might experiment with a better calendar or new system, one after another. This is admirable and it's helpful, but it's not the whole picture. The whole picture includes getting support from other people, support to the level needed. With each new success, you might need to go to a new level of physical support. Each new success, unfortunately, creates a new level of organizational demands which causes people to get even more frustrated. It's necessary to continually keep pace with success.

Unless women understand this concept, and are willing and open to confront their barriers to getting the kind of support they need, they're going to be lost. You're going to say, "I'm going to wait until it gets under control, until everybody's okay. Maybe I'll wait until I move to a new house, and that will solve the problem. Or I'll wait until the kids are in school and that will solve the problem. Or I'll just wait..." And it doesn't happen. What needs to happen first is a shift in women themselves. You only can focus successfully on yourself. To focus on other people, trying to get them to change and to get them to help is great, but if you shift yourself, if you yourself make one small change, while it may not seem like very much, everything else begins to shift around you. Things begin to organize around you instead of you trying to get everything else under control. This is a powerful dynamic.

We will talk more about physical support later in more detail, but it is enough to understand now that you need to receive not just emotional support, but that you actually need to rethink how you're going to set up your life. You will actually negotiate with partners, you will trade tasks with friends or consider hiring help in the specific areas you need. ADD is a disorder that causes great disorganization for many people; it does not just require ordinary help with domestic chores, and it can't be considered in the same ballpark. Many women feel barriers against getting the kind of help they need. They feel a loss of self-esteem, and more guilt and shame when they think about simplifying their lives, changing the way they've always done things. It takes time for them to add a cushion of support under them for the organizational level that they're not good at, so they can move ahead to use those special abilities they have in extra supply.

Strategies

Physical assistance

Strategies are closely related to physical support, but they are more about thinking through how to set up your environment in a way that works for you. This includes the use of technological and other physical and planning devices. Strategies include such things as putting large, clear labels on storage areas. One woman decided to line her wall with hooks for her clothes instead of using hangers and drawers. Another woman decided to create a huge wall of corkboard so she could keep notes or instructions right by the phone. This way she could remember the questions she wanted to ask or the procedures to go through.

Strategizing effectively means taking into account your real difficulties and setting things up so that you have a better chance to succeed. For example, don't shop on the days when you have extra stress. Plan enough time between activities to give yourself down-time. Try to prepare in detail the night before what you will need the next morning, when it will be harder for you to think. Allow a lot more time to process information in between activities. When you are in college, this means trying to determine a balanced course load in terms of hours and work required in various classes. At work, this means considering the use of sound blocks to create a non-distracting environment for yourself. Consider the use of voice mail instead of being disturbed by the phone. One woman figured out that she had to put her children in daycare if she were ever peacefully and successfully going to clean up her house and make dinner.

"Post-its thinking" will not be sufficient if you have serious organizational deficits. You might wind up looking like the woman in the POST-IT-HELL illustration.

Later we will go into more depth on the necessity to rethink and reorganize your life beyond the use of these strategies. These will include eliminating and reconsidering things that you have been doing automatically for years. For instance, you might now decide to go out for dinner on holidays or actually go on vacation if holiday seasons are a time of overwhelming stress for you.

Strategy Questions to Ask Yourself to Make Your Home and Life Work for You:

• Do you need background noise when other people are in the house?
• Do you need to move that TV out of the middle of your living room even though everyone else wants it there?
• Do you need to get someone to coach you at home three days a week, or to call every day?

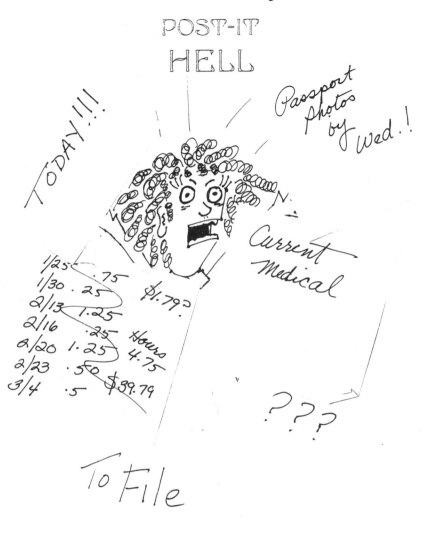

- Do you need someone to clean your house a couple times a week or straighten or re-arrange your house every day for a short period of time?
- Do you need to have someone check in with you to help you set limits on activities or tasks before you create too much?

Or Consider Options Like These:

• Trade tasks with a buddy.
• Use physical help such as noise blockers, or moving the TV out of the living room if it's driving you crazy.
• Put your children in daycare while you're trying to cook or clean.
• Put big labels all over your kitchen.
• Even if people think you're weird, don't plan too many different stressful activities on the same day if possible.
• You can set up quiet areas that are just your own. Even a little area,where you can put up a sign and no one comes in, can be your own.
• Try to focus on one thing in a day, if that's what you need.
• Use the right strategy for the right level of difficulty. Go beyond Post-its if you have a severe organizational deficit.
• If you hire a professional organizer to create great systems for you make sure you create a structure for someone to help you maintain the system.
• Experiment with physical aids like computers, spell-checks, organizers, beepers, car phones, electronic memo pads. (For some people, it's good to eliminate as much paper as possible in their lives so they don't end up looking for twenty calendars buried under other papers.)
• Consider hiring or (trading) personal help for specific jobs or areas of your life. A bookkeeper, a person to sit with you one hour a day or a few hours a week to get through paper work or to plan for the week and prioritize your tasks. Talk through things you need to do or decisions you must make out loud with a non-judgmental person.
• Many ADD people have to *hear* things beccause this allows them to process through an extra step. In order to internalize information many ADD people have to write it or say it out loud.
• Ask someone to help you with the route you have to take for the day.
• Ask someone to help you pick out three of the many projects that you want to do, and to write them down.
• Do you need a partner for projects who is good with details, so that you can contribute your complementary strengths?
• Whoever you get to help, don't let the help turn into a critical, judgmental, homework, scolding setup. You stay in control.

For other great tips and discussions of strategies look at this resources listed at the end of the book. In strategizing, if something isn't working, do it differently. Whether you live or work alone or with other people, don't keep on doing it the same old way, only trying harder. If you're always trying to go to New York but keep winding up in California, then get on a different bus! Do it differently. Don't try to do it by willpower alone. Expand your idea of help to include other people. ADD can be handled all alone only for a short time. Many situations might call for a partner or assistant to fill in the gaps and do the detail work, or someone to help you stay on track. These strategies can mean the difference between success and failure.

You need support, both emotional and physical. Someone to help you stay on track will make the big difference. It could be with your goals, with time, paper, stuff, career, projects, both long-term and short-term. This helper serves as a guide by providing a structure and a roadmap. Your helper can, in a gentle non-judgmental way, help support you. Someone can reassure you, help you regain perspective when you lose it, and put some boundaries on your often limitless ability to see and follow possibilities and connections. If directed, this particular ability can become very strong. If left unattended it will create overwhelming amounts of unfinished piles of hopes and dreams, and often debt and shame as well.

Therapy

This last part of the MESST Model stands for therapy, or counseling. As we saw on the path to success in the beginning of the last chapter, some people with ADD have an easier time getting to where they want to go after diagnosis. Others have more secondary effects as a result of living for many years with undiagnosed ADD—their road will be a little more complex. We have looked at the effects on self-concept and the pain of underachievement. There is often depression to cope with and many effects in their relationships. Overwhelmed by daily life, these women often feel isolated. These are all common themes in those seeking counseling for ADD. Often these issues can be effectively addressed in a combination of couples, group or individual counseling. Active, interactive, educational, supportive counseling is appropriate. Ideally it strikes a balance between coaching on real-life matters and exploring feelings that prevent an individual from taking the steps she desires to meet her goals.

If a woman were able to employ the strategies suggested earlier to make her life work or to find the right niche, that would be ideal, and she probably would not need much additional counseling. However, many

women are either driven to pursue an image that they are not con-
structed to achieve or else they have blocks in communication or assertiveness. Consequently, strategies that seem to the outside observer quite
easy to employ are often the most complex for women to adopt. These
feelings can become so fixed by the time of diagnosis that education is
not enough—individual, couples or group counseling to facilitate change
is needed.

What often happens for women is that these seemingly concrete
tasks bring them up against such strong internal barriers (such as
shame and guilt) that they often stop cold. When they hit a wall when
they try to restructure their lives, both they and their partners or
counselors are often baffled as to why they don't take the needed and
desired steps. This can be about seemingly simple things like asking for
more time on a test or getting help in the house. Without understanding
the depth of the problems as well as the depth of the barriers, both the
counselor and the woman will be stuck. This interaction might re-create
an experience in which the woman feels she is disappointing a significant person in her life. The point at which her neurology meets her
psychology is the point at which counseling for an ADD woman often
takes place. These feelings must be worked through before a woman can
proceed.

As we saw earlier, the woman with ADD instinctively expects to
elicit "maligning messages" with her behavior. Because of this she often
acts to self-protect and in this effort she avoids the very requests for
assistance that could help her. The drive to keep up a "mask of competency" at all costs in order to avoid the re-emergence of early painful
feelings of "not getting it right" keeps her from the assistance she needs.

Group counseling is often very effective for a woman to begin to
redefine herself and accept herself in spite of her difficulties. Meeting
and coming to respect other women with the same difficulties and
strengths as she has, helps her become desensitized to those early issues
and to put them in perspective. In addition to an individual's patterns, if
she is in a relationship (at the time of diagnosis) a couple's interaction
has also become organized around the undiagnosed difficulties. At that
point, the partner might have a backlog of resentment and anger, and so
his own feelings of grief and loss might have to be addressed before the
couple can move forward.

Pitfalls in Counseling

Often what happens in counseling ADD women is that a therapist
can get "stuck" in the organizational strategy part of the treatment,

Identifying Barriers to Behavioral Help

Shame

Cultural message

Communications Problems

Guilt

Family of origin messages

Lack of knowledge of legal rights

Mask of competency

without understanding the complexity of these issues. Because ADD counseling calls for a much more directive approach than traditional psychotherapy, a counselor may fall into a pattern of over-suggesting, and over-advising, focusing too much on behavior modification. When this happens, ADD women can feel they are being treated like naughty children instead of intelligent adults.

One therapist very experienced in working with children with ADD is now treating adults with ADD and trying to apply the same methods—with charts and stars and structure. For example, in an effort to motivate a mature, creative, vibrant woman, she said "If you keep your desk clean eighty percent of the time this week, I'll have a chocolate-chip cookie waiting for you." The client felt demeaned, to say the least. Obviously the complexity of her life went beyond this simple, condescending sort of attitude that she perceived as unempathetic. What is also perceived by clients as a lack of counselor empathy is when the depth of her difficulty is misunderstood. A woman attemmpting to communicate a feeling of drowning in backlogs of unattended business and disorganization feels invalidated when told to try simply harder to get organized, to make lists, to get a new Franklin planner. The layers of emotions around these issues are often completely missed.

The frustration that a therapist can feel when an agreed-upon plan is not carried through can replicate the shameful feelings of a woman with ADD in these kinds of situations. Giving assignments and agreeing on strategies are helpful when done in a non-judgmental way and when the client is the one who ultimately decides what is important for her. The counselor is most helpful when she can pull out from what seems like hundreds of possibilities (to the client) and help to organize and prioritize those with the client. This reduces feelings of free-floating ideas and anxiety in the client, helping her walk away with a clear idea of what she wants to do and how she's going to proceed. Even carrying three ideas on a piece of paper with her when she leaves the counseling office gives her something concrete to refer back to when she gets off track and starts to feel overwhelmed.

The focus needs to be on what the woman wants to do and what small steps she can take to move toward that goal. If there seems to be a barrier that prevents her from taking that step, it needs to be examined. Often at the root of these are shame or guilt, difficulty with communicating, or setting limits. Until and unless these are addressed, all the strategies in the world won't work because she won't be able to take the next step. What's important to remember in counseling is to strike a balance between coaching, helping someone stay on track, and exploring emotions when they get in the way of these goals. Extremes of either overcontrolling, oversuggesting, or overdirecting should be avoided. Encouraging overemoting or continually exploring the early psychological roots of behavior are both unhelpful.

Counseling Goals

When a woman gets stuck in the grief cycle and has a tremendous backlog of anger, or gets stuck in depression, and has too many complicating factors to want to move ahead, it's as if she's between two worlds. She hasn't integrated a new identity yet, but has outgrown the old one. Perhaps she is in the process of redefining her image, but the people around her resist that and she feels alone or stuck. This is one good reason to start individual or couples counseling. The process of redefining can create difficulties in communicating with other people. ADD individuals find themselves expecting the worst, misinterpreting, even sometimes creating a self-fulfilling prophecy in relationships, by employing a lot of defensive protection.

We've seen that ADD people need to protect themselves. A therapist needs to validate their difficulties and work with them to mold their lives in healthy ways. Learning new, effective strategies, rethinking self-image, often going back and examining a woman's shame and guilt are vitally important. Groups are ideally suited for this kind of learning and therapists can either provide these small support/therapy groups or refer for larger support groups or meetings.

Small Groups

Many of the issues that people talk about in a support group after the initial sessions of discussing ADD might be the same things that people talk about in any group, regardless of focus: relationships, jobs, self-esteem, problems with other people. But when ADD people get together, they talk to people who understand, speak the same language. What is apparent to me from observing groups is that the same experiences are described as in non-ADD related groups, but come from a different inner experience that only people with ADD can understand. ADD individuals have this feeling of chaos within which other every-day experiences are played out. For instance, one woman said, "Even though I'm on medication and being treated, it still feels like I'm hanging on by a thread." Other people won't understand that. They think, well, you're on medication, why are you still acting like this? Why are you still late? People with

ADD can understand from experience what it's like to take medication, what problems are still left, how difficult their situation still is.

In support groups people with ADD talk about their problematic relationships; not merely to bad-mouth, but to suggest and understand what their partners might be going through, to find helpful ways of approaching these problems, and get understanding from individuals like themselves. A group can give you hope, can give you validation that what you're feeling is real. When you try to talk to other people who don't have ADD, you might get a lot of denial. They might say: "Oh, that was my case, too. Don't be silly! What's the matter? You're smart. Don't be ridiculous! Why are you acting so weird? Why did you go off and not stay with the family during the holiday? What do you mean, you had to get away? What happened to you?" Other ADD people can give you validation that, yes, it's real, they experienced those things too and they understand what you're going through. Newly-diagnosed people can hold onto the objective reality of their situation for a while, but not all day, every day, until much later. When they start to fall back into old patterns of thinking—"I'm just a jerk, what's the matter with me?"—they can get understanding and support from their peers. Others with similar experiences will reinforce that their problems are real and difficult but there definitely is hope. They can help you hold on to your successes, to focus on them long enough to eventually shift your image.

A woman in a group who had never thought of herself as creative got encouraging feedback week after week about her interesting ideas, the enthusiasm with which she presented them and the connections that she made. She had thought of these as useless meanderings, but with this kind of enthusiastic feedback, she integrated this into her belief system about herself and started to make choices based on this new self-identity. People so easily gloss over their accomplishments, small and large—a group can freeze-frame on them so that a member of the group can pause to really take notice of their success. Later that will become a more natural part of their process.

It is also good to get support at first from other people, rather than expecting it from your partner or family. It will take your partner and family longer to work through their own grief cycle. It will be easier on both (or all) of you and more effective, if you obtain support partly from other people. Your partner has a backlog of anger or resentment to work through, so the more support and understanding you can bring to his process the easier the whole thing will be for both of you. In time, you will hopefully be able to get support from intimate relationships as well as from the ADD community. The more support you have at this time, the more you will integrate ADD and feel less defensive about it; you'll feel less misunderstood and will be able to back off and talk more calmly with your partner.

ADD is a chronic stressor, as I have said before; each new level of success can sometimes break down a coping strategy that doesn't apply to that new level of success. Once you start treatment, perhaps you will need to periodically return to group. Depending on your situation, you might need weekly, bi-weekly, monthly or more occasional "tune-ups", to get supportive help. In the next section we'll look at counseling in more depth, which is especially helpful when an individual gets stuck in the 3 R's (*Re-structuring*, *Re-negotiating* and *Re-defining*).

Summary

To summarize, these two chapters were an overview of treatment for ADD. We stressed the importance of medication, especially in the early stages. You don't know (until the medication starts working and you start working on these issues) what kinds of feelings are going to come up as you start to employ strategies. It's important for the therapist, the woman, and her family and her friends to know that sometimes irrational difficulties in employing strategies are deeply embedded. You probably need some kind of coaching or group support as you work your way through the Medication, Education, Support and Strategies and deal with primary ADD symptom management. When you get stuck because you're hiding, due to your fears of other people's perceptions of you, or out of a "crisis of confidence" as one client of mine put it, there are a lot of reasons why it's not so simple to employ medication, education, support and strategies. Adding some kind of counseling is very important so that you, your spouse, your whole family can move together as a unit as you begin to make your life work.

For a **single** person, you and your friends and family can help establish relationships and trust other people more. Legal accommodations, counseling, coaching in groups, couples, and individual sessions regularly or periodically can be very helpful in dealing with this chronic stressor. Because of its chronic nature, you may need some kind of anchoring relationship, an outside support group or coach or counselor. You might not need weekly therapy after some of these central issues are resolved, but you may later need other kinds of support as you hit different blocks in your challenges. Your ADD may come into play in more demanding situations or old emotional triggers may be aroused through specific life situations. The goal of ADD treatment is not only to become more organized, it's also to move through the grief cycle in order eventually to begin a new cycle of success. You will then be able to focus on your strengths, harness your creativity and work toward your goals with an increased sense of vibrancy and self-esteem. As you work through some of these issues, you are able to distance yourself from some of that shame or guilt about your symptoms in order to ask for help to restructure your life. You are able to keep the focus on managing your difficulties in order to mobilize and direct your strengths, not just so that you can turn into an orderly, calm, different kind of person.

Counseling can help a woman work through the process until this strange new identity of ADD is more firmly rooted. When the woman slips into feelings of, "I'm really just lazy or immature or irresponsible," even long after she gets diagnosed, the therapist can hold onto a more positive image—reinforce the idea of what ADD is all about until she herself is able to. The therapist needs to be steadfast until the woman comes to integrate the idea that she has both great strengths and great difficulties. If her therapist sees her client clearly, sorting out the ADD from the psychology, the woman will absorb this new positive reflection and internalizes this new self-view. She will let go of some of her negative expectations and replace them with more positive expectations and new images of herself.

PART IV

EMBRACING

DIAMONDS IN THE ROUGH

I view women with ADD as "diamonds in the rough"—their disorganization on the surface can hide the beauty underneath, even from themselves, and keep them locked away from people and from their own potential.

The point of diagnosis and treatment is to unearth those special qualities hidden deeply below the surface, like uncut diamonds. It is to recognize the brilliance waiting to shine beneath the rough exterior and to make the beautiful facets visible so that they can be seen and treasured.

The encyclopedia says that "with skilled cutters and polishers, these rough diamonds can be transformed into brilliant jewels." This signifies how those working with ADD women can play a role in their revelation. It also mirrors the important fact that ADD women must accept the idea that they need help from other people in order to restructure their lives to reach their full potential. This need for help does not diminish their worth. As with the diamonds, the help (mining, cutting, polishing) allows them to achieve their full worth and value.

Diamonds, despite their great strength, also have great vulnerability. With the wrong kind of blow, they can split and fragment in many directions. They can even be destroyed with intense heat. So, too, with these women who must understand what they need to do in order to live in a healthy way that protects them. As the encyclopedia says, "Even in the richest ground, many tons of earth must be taken from deep in the earth and sorted out to obtain one small diamond." The potential is locked away, but definitely worth the search.

It has become clear to me from my talks with women with ADD all across the country, that what is valuable to disorganized women (and is often overlooked) is this kind of validation and hope. What happens for an woman in a successful course of treatment is an internal shift in one's sense of self; this ultimately affects one's patterns of relationships, mood and success from that point on. I have seen many ADD women fruitlessly and obsessively search for what I believe to be a false, dead-end goal. Or they set themselves up for failure, waiting to be non-ADD-like as a measure of whether or not they are succeeding. While it is critical to focus on organizing one's life, I have come to understand that the real goal is not about becoming "cured," but about using this re-organizing not as an end in itself but as a vehicle to develop uniqueness and strengths. The point is not to become a different kind of woman, but to become more of who you really are, to make more of your own beautiful facets visible.

Ultimately, women with ADD must begin to see themselves from a different perspective. As one young ADD woman said, after eight weeks in a group where she got to know other women like herself for the first time, "I used to think of ADD women [especially herself] as bumbling and embarrassing. Now I see them as warm, exciting, interesting, and compassionate."

CHAPTER FOURTEEN

Embracing Disorganization

Embrace Disorganization?

YOU MIGHT THINK that I'm crazy to tell you to embrace disorganization. Well, I could tell you to fight it. I could tell you to overcome it. I could tell you to ignore it, to hate it, to hide it. But none of those things will work because you still would be keeping a big part of you split off from the rest of yourself. That takes a tremendous toll in terms of time and energy spent hiding, and in emotional distress. *It's both unhealthy and counterproductive to hate and hide a big part of yourself.*

The truth is, you are *all* of your strengths and *all* of your difficulties. You have some great abilities and you have some great difficulties, and all of that is you. It is not that some parts are of you are acceptable and some parts are not. Embracing all of what you are is one of the important keys to heal self-esteem wounds, to improve your mood by improving your self-talk, and to give you a strong sense of an inner core that doesn't reel from shame when ADD symptoms still inevitably occur. Embracing helps you move through the "grief cycle" to a deep sense of acceptance and *beyond*, to actual *enjoyment* of your ADD and your creativity. I'm not talking about a "Pollyanna" sort of acceptance—because without real acceptance and understanding of your true level of difficulties, you won't begin to approach getting enough structure or help to support your considerable strengths. It's only when you are able to reach out and embrace both your strengths and your difficulties that you will be able to move ahead with your life and begin what I call a "Cycle of Success."

Disorganizationally Gifted

I want to emphasize that people with ADD have great abilities to disorganize, in fact, I think they are *"disorganizationally gifted."* While I do say that "tongue in cheek," any artist knows that an essential step in creativity is the ability to dis-organize.

It is this same ability, this giftedness at disorganizing, that you can use to break down your systems and dismantle your life the "way it's always been."

In this book, I have emphasized the need to restructure your life in order to live successfully with ADD. When I say the goal is to restructure your life, I mean that you won't just cope and get by like you always have. I mean that you will completely rethink the way you live and work. It doesn't happen overnight and it doesn't happen without difficulty.

To help you achieve this, you'll use your ability to "disorganize" in order to generate fresh ways of working out new solutions. You can create many options. You might not follow them all, but in that hyperactive mind of yours you have great ability to think of ways to make things work. You will often run into barriers and have to break through them in order to make things happen in a new way. But if you start to think of embracing this disorganization, if you think of yourself as having great abilities for disorganizing the status quo, then you don't have to walk around saying, "What a mess! What a disorganized mess I am!" all the time. You can say "How can I use my creativity in thinking of new ways to help solve these problems?"

The reason that common ADD strategies alone don't always work is because they usually focus on merely controlling the negative and difficult part of the ADD. What you want to focus on is not just to take care of the difficulties, but to support the new growth. As you grow, becoming more and more successful, you'll constantly think of new ways to form cushions of support and structure underneath you. *The emphasis should be on just not managing your deficits, but on managing your successes.*

What I'm talking about is breaking up the old order. It means challenging and changing traditions held sacred in your house for years. It means challenging roles and rituals. It means figuring out where the limits are in the system, *really* talking to your partner, and challenging the way you've worked things out in the past. It's going to mean shaking up the balance of control and power in your household. You will have the wherewithal now that you're on medication. You will be able to stay in the argument and confront the issues, not ignore the way you feel or the way you want things to be. It isn't going to be easy. It would be easier *not* to act. It will cause anxiety to make these changes, to change *the way it's always been.*

You may have to enlist professional facilitation at some point because embracing disorganization means letting go of some of those cherished ideal images, and that is difficult. Embracing disorganization means working through the grief cycle *deeply*, until you are able to embrace the whole idea of ADD, and all the parts of yourself. Only then will you be able to move on.

Embracing has a positive image: it means not pretending that these difficulties don't exist and it means acknowledging that your strengths do exist. It means to reach out and hold on to both sides of yourself. Embracing actually means "to hold, to surround, to contain." When creative energy is harnessed and directed, it can grow much stronger. You can wrap yourself up into one cohesive self-image, not just scatter parts of yourself that you or others find unacceptable.

What I am suggesting is similar to the way stimulant medication helps ADD. It is paradoxical. Instead of fighting disorganization, embracing it calms you down. You relax into it. It brings a certain order, not more disorder, when you embrace it. Embracing disorganization means not just controlling it. Try all of the strategies that you can to stay organized, of course. The irony is that until you feel a bit better about your ADD, you're not going to be able to get the help you need. If you don't center your entire life around becoming perfectly organized or becoming a perfect woman, you'll develop more fully and have more time and energy to enjoy your life.

At a certain point, when you have truly integrated these disparate ideas about yourself, you will begin to create successful experiences for yourself. The success will take on a life of its own. You will start to hold on to your successes and build on them as they compound rapidly.

At some point you will cross a line after you've embraced all of yourself and embraced the ADD. You will understand that it is a necessity and not a luxury to get the help you need, freeing up your time and emotional resources, allowing you to focus on your strengths. You will understand the need to break down barriers, and find healthy ways to protect yourself. You will understand that you truly can start pursuing goals that really suit you. When you embrace yourself, your ADD, your strengths, and your difficulties, it won't hurt as much when other people don't accept it or understand you. You won't have to apologize or over-explain. You'll then be able to talk to others about what you need and set limits without putting yourself down. This validates other people as well as shows respect for yourself, even when your ADD symptoms appear.

What we're talking about ultimately, is not trying to get rid of the ADD, or waiting to get over it, but to direct it and control it. *I'm talking about living with controlled disorder,* not denying it, but recognizing it, working with it to make your life work. It is not done in a day, and it is not done with medication alone (although it is usually not done without it). You need to ask yourself, "How can I make my life work? How can I make my relationships work? How can I make my work meaningful?"

If it means doing things a bit differently than other people, then be different; it takes courage to break through the barriers of shame and guilt to ask for support. If it means breaking the mold, then break it; it takes courage to accept that you can't do what other people can do. If it means challenging the "way it's always been," then challenge it; for it takes courage to celebrate that you can often do what other people can't.

You will have to ask yourself, "How can I make life work for me even if it upsets other people in my family? How can I change the rules and roles that haven't been working? How can I tolerate the anxiety of making others uncomfortable, in a way that doesn't disregard their needs but doesn't trample mine?" Many times this will take professional facilitation.

When I say *embrace disorganization,* I am not saying *don't* get organized, or *don't* focus your attention on the creation of organizational systems, or give up on being organized. I *am* saying *don't keep trying the same things that haven't worked before, and don't keep coping alone.* Expand your idea of organizational help to include other people to help you, other people to coach you. You need to get over the obsession with being an organized person or trying to "keep it together" in the same way that non-ADD people do. Don't just try harder. Don't just get another organizational system on your own. What you need to *get is* that you must change the system. You can't compare your life to what other people can handle, because you have a disorder. A disorder means that something is not of average difficulty. It's not productive to compare yourself to others and how they live their lives. What is productive is to talk to people who have the same kind of difficulties and abilities that you do. What is productive is to really *understand* that you might need a much higher level of organizational support than other people.

Embracing disorganization means taking things apart and putting them back together in a new way. It means taking your ADD seriously. Don't wait until you're over your ADD to start your life, because you never will be over your ADD. Don't measure your success in terms of how un-ADD-like you have become, because you never will be completely un-ADD like. Know that your ADD symptoms will appear from time to time. What you do about it, what you say about it, and how you feel about it is going to influence whether things get better or worse. I've come to understand that the ultimate goal is not about becoming cured or becoming more organized as an end in itself. Organizational strategies should only be used as a vehicle for your talents, your uniqueness, your strengths.

The goal for women with ADD is to begin to see themselves from a different perspective. I encourage you, then, to stop chasing an impossible, culturally-approved dream. Step off the perpetual treadmill, embrace all the parts of yourself, and begin to take back your life.

The Three R's to Successful Living with ADD

This section is about the need to go beyond strategies, and support. It is about the need to go beyond medication, education, and even therapy. It's about Embracing Disorganization. The goal of all that we have talked about, is ultimately to *make your life work*. This means *restructuring* your life to such an extent that it now really works for you. It involves completely rethinking the way you are living your life—in your tasks and your time, at home and at work. It involves overcoming internal barriers of shame and guilt. As you see in the **3 R's chart** to accomplish this you often need additional tools. These include *renegotiating your relationships* at home and in your personal life, as well as *redefining the image* of yourself, of your work, and of your partner. You'll do this in order to more closely align with your real strengths and to deal more effectively with your real difficulties.

The strategies we talked about earlier often employ paper aids and technological tools that address the primary symptoms of ADD. They are helpful and necessary. But these strategies and support systems often fall short of helping you live successfully with ADD, because *they don't go deep enough, they don't go on long enough, they don't continuously keep pace with your growth*. And they usually don't involve the other people in your life in a meaningful way or to the extent necessary. They usually help you cope with your ADD on your own without involving your mate, your family, or your friends. But this will not be enough.

Living Successfully with ADD Is Not Something You Can Do In Your Spare Time or Fit In Around Other People's Schedules

As you begin to restructure your life, using the tools of renegotiating your relationships and redefining your self-image, you may begin to hit a barrier. At this point professional counseling may be helpful to facilitate these changes. Change means that you will need to shake up the system to some extent. This is often uncomfortable and the reason why women stop themselves.

The 3 R's

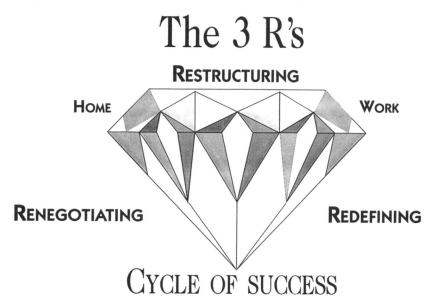

RESTRUCTURING

HOME   **WORK**

RENEGOTIATING   **REDEFINING**

CYCLE OF SUCCESS

Restructuring also includes rebalancing the family system, and with it, three primary areas of focus in your life: the focus on your strengths, the focus on your own needs and the needs of others, and the time you allow yourself for fun or recreation. For women, the way these three areas usually get divided up leaves them off-balance and on a treadmill. Restructuring helps you regain your balance.

At a certain point, you may need to rethink your life at a deeper level in order to make real and lasting differences in your personal life, and to reach other long-term, meaningful goals. In other words, in addition to dividing up the tasks in your life in new ways, you will most likely have to make other *substantial* changes in the way you live and work. This does not mean just re-arranging the different things you do, but actually cutting areas that don't work for you, and adding new areas that do work, that more clearly represent who you are. This may involve completely rethinking, reconsidering and re-evaluating those personal traditions you have always held sacred, as well as what business ideal images you have always held for yourself.

This process of personally rethinking the way you live will mean significant changes for those people around you. Things get "tricky" here—the other two "R" will be needed in order to actually restructure your life. **Renegotiating relationships** is challenging but essential, because changes in one member of a system, at home or at work, will cause changes in the entire system. Other members often will resist *even when the changes are positive.* Renegotiating at home and at work involves setting limits and protecting yourself, while at the same time moving toward relationships, instead of backing away from them. It also involves learning how to get help without sacrificing your self-respect.

Even after you have learned how to renegotiate your relationships with improved communication skills, you may still keep getting stuck. At that point, to clear that barrier, you will need to take a serious look at **Redefining your self-image.** We will look at what you are saying to yourself, and the negative messages you unconsciously deliver to yourself if you're not meeting the cultural ideal you may have internalized. This idealized image may miss your essential strong qualities as well as the difficulties that need to be adjusted to and accommodated for.

At home, your partner or family may be still holding on to certain kinds of cultural images, and stuck in their own grief cycle(s). Redefining is also about their working through *their* issues. At work, you may have to revisit your entire concept about what kind of work is appropriate for you, replacing some old dreams with new ones.

Both at work and at home, working through the 3 R's will ultimately help to define what it means to be a mature, competent, woman of value, even if you have ADD.

CHAPTER FIFTEEN

The Three R's at Work
Restructuring, Renegotiating, Redefining

L ET'S GO BACK and revisit Lucy, whom we met earlier.
When Lucy was thirty, she went to community college where she studied fashion design and art. It was there that an alert teacher noticed her difficulties and suggested that she get tested for learning disabilities. In the process, she was diagnosed instead with ADD and began to take Ritalin. She got accommodations such as extra time for tests, and eventually she earned an Associate degree. Lucy got a job in a nice department store as a window dresser, designing the windows and dressing the mannequins. She loved this job because she could be active and she got to use her creative abilities. Even though she loved the designs, Lucy had trouble with other parts of the job. She was a little clumsy; she knocked over the mannequins and dropped the pins. There were a lot of required reports and paperwork. Lucy also had trouble with the other women in the department because she spread her stuff all over the work room. They were getting a little annoyed with her, she thought.

Though she was on medication and could concentrate better, she started to feel she was bothering people and getting in the way. She began to think they didn't like her, and even started not to enjoy work. Lucy felt the other designers were laughing at her when she dropped things, and she felt bad about the little jokes they made about how much space she was taking up. She began to forget about all the great, creative, beautiful things that she was doing and started focusing on her anxieties instead. She thought that perhaps this job was too big for her, that she

212

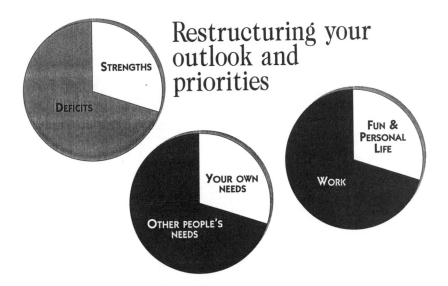

Restructuring your outlook and priorities

just wasn't smart enough. Perhaps she should transfer out of this department and get a job that didn't have so many responsibilities.

The danger was that Lucy would decide she wasn't talented enough, when in reality, she probably would do better at a higher level of design, rather than at the lower level that pulled on her weaknesses. Accommodations that would have given her more space, a different work area or an assistant for an hour a day to help with some of the detail work would have made a huge difference. For this to happen, though, Lucy would have to be willing to risk some acknowledgement of her needs. Unfortunately, this was the very thing that she tried to hide because she felt it too embarrassing to stand out from the other women in that way. In order to show her true strengths and continue to rise to her proper level, this is the kind of barrier she'd eventually have to overcome.

Getting through these lower levels of achievement, the entry and mid-level jobs are usually the downfall for ADD women, even with medication. A woman needs to work toward asking for accommodations, or at least be able to state her needs. She needs to understand herself, know what her strengths are, and value herself sufficiently to present the idea that she and her boss both have the same goal: for her to do her best work. Presenting this in a way that preserves her self-respect and focuses on her strengths is quite a challenge for women who are especially sensitive to these issues.

In this chapter, we are now going to see how to apply the three R's at work: restructuring your environment, renegotiating relationships, and redefining your self-image.

Restructuring

The Restructuring Priorities Pie Chart illustrates an example of the balance of time and focus a woman spends in three different areas:

1. The amount of time focused on your strengths (as opposed to just coping with your deficits).

2. The time spent focusing on your own needs and those of others.

3. The time you spend on fun or personal life as opposed to work of one kind or another.

First let's look at the balance between **strengths and deficits** as it applies to the area of achievement and work for a woman. It's essential for a woman not to confuse her strengths and abilities with her difficulties.

It's very common for an ADD woman to hold a job that is considered simple (because the tasks involved are simple for most people), and when she can't do that job successfully, she assumes it must mean that she needs to do even simpler work. Another common scenario occurs if she has a very demanding job that suits her abilities, but can't handle all the organizational tasks needed to support the job. She naturally assumes that she is no good at this kind of work. Eventually, she works her way down the scale until she finds a job in which she can meet the organizational demands. In other words, she is constantly trying to match and meet the requirements of her level of difficulty rather than her strengths.

It's not hard to see that a sense of underachievement would result. If she doesn't have the organizational abilities to back up her conceptual ideas and doesn't realize that she needs assistance and support for those ideas, she would be severely underachieving; constantly working in the areas of her greatest disability. The resulting frustration can affect her self-esteem and mood to a great extent.

Sometimes what holds women back at work are the internal barriers such as shame or guilt that they face when they consider asking for accommodations. Sometimes they lack the communication skills necessary to state needs in an assertive but non-defensive, non-blaming way. At other times, it's just not knowing what is reasonable to ask for, what your rights are or even feeling deserving of them. Often it is just the overriding feeling that you are not being fair to other people. Instead, the ADD woman needs to be aware that she is requesting an even playing field, a way to make the best contribution she can to the organization.

Until a woman is presented with new ways of thinking, she has absolutely no understanding of the differences that we all have in the way our brains work, our own unique "brainprints" that make some of us good at some things and others good at different things. We grow up in this culture thinking that intelligence is identified with quickness of presentation. Because people often confuse processing speed or organizational skill with intelligence, it's essential for a woman to begin to separate her intelligence and abilities from her organizational difficulties. Then she can say to herself, "This is my organizational difficulty. This is my ADD. This is not my intelligence." Only when she does this can she understand and continue to pursue her areas of strength. She will need to work continually to build a cushion of support under herself, support from other people. As she becomes more successful, her demands are going to increase. The coping and compensating strategies that she used in college, for example, are not going to work for her any more as she rises to her full capabilities.

In college, she might have had a great deal of trouble organizing ideas and putting them on paper. She might have "pulled it off" by staying up all night, spending fifty hours on a project that might take others only five hours. Even though she is just as smart, the structure that comes more or less automatically to others is not there. It takes enormous amounts of processing for her to pull it all together. This may have exhausted her in college, but she was able to survive. As she moves from college to graduate school or into a career, or when she tries to combine schooling or work with a relationship, social life or family, she will find that her compensations do not work any more. It becomes mathematically impossible to accommodate all the demands and spend all the hours with her old system of overworking. Something has to give. She either stops herself from going further in her career, or gives up the idea of a family or social life.

Eventually the kind of woman who has been "getting by" by overworking hits a wall. She feels she has to quit a job or school that she likes and has the ability to handle. If she quits she takes with her the self-image that she couldn't "cut it." A woman who's having difficulty needs to figure out that she and a particular job are often simply a bad match. She may need to walk away, or perhaps there is a way for her to keep the good parts and create a better match for the difficult parts. In that way, she doesn't have to throw away the whole job. Most likely, she won't easily find a job that is a perfect match for her, with such big gaps between her abilities and difficulties.

If she does decide to leave the school or job, it is critical that she leave with the understanding that her problem is not a matter of intelligence or ability. The job might just have too many organizational details attached to it, with little support available. When she thinks about rebalancing her strengths and deficits, she must remember that she has gaps in her abilities. I think of ability as a very tall ladder. Her ladder might be taller than most people's. It might, in fact, reach to the top of the Empire State Building, but with gaps between the rungs, or even missing rungs. If she doesn't find a way to fill in those gaps, to get to the next rung, she's not going to go anywhere, no matter how great her ability. To be successful at work, she must find the balance between strengths and deficits. She can't ignore the fact that she has deficits, but at the same time, she mustn't ignore the fact that she has strengths. She must honor both of these so that she can make both of them work for her. The point is to thrive and be successful, not become overloaded or depleted—not to stay up all night, but to make the process of your life work.

Rebalancing: Focusing On Your Needs and Other People's Needs at Work

Another area of rebalancing lies between your needs and other people's needs. At work, this often means learning to say no and set limits, both to your direct supervisors as well as to coworkers. This applies both to actual work assignments as well as to those other unwritten expectations that exist for women at work. It's difficult to learn to say no and (as we explored) to protect and project that sense of competence so very important to you at the same time. A woman who has coped with ADD all her life often feels that if she says "no" to a request, this will wipe out other people's good opinion of her. Sometimes, however, by saying "yes" to everything, you create the very situation that you have been trying to prevent. If you keep saying yes and not setting limits (in order to look like you can take on all that is asked of you) you will eventually start to make mistakes and not be able to keep up.

If a woman does a good job and continues to be successful, people will ask her to take on more. They won't say "Janis, you are doing such a great job that we aren't going to ask you to take on more work." Customers won't say, "Linda, you did such a wonderful job on this deal for me that I'm not going to recommend you to my friends." Instead, the more she succeeds, the more opportunities will arise. In some sense, it feels heady and great (after medication and treatment) to finally be successful and recognized. But there comes a point of diminishing returns as she tries to keep up the pace. She must figure out how to structure her life to make it work.

Sometimes this will mean getting more assistance; sometimes it will mean actually having to say no, learning to set limits with people in a way that doesn't reject others but that doesn't put herself down either. This happens by validating the importance of wanting to do a good job, something she and her boss can agree on as a common goal. A woman must figure out (and find a way to tell people) what will work best for both of them.

You may have to shut your door or put a "do not disturb" sign up for a certain amount of time per day. It's all right not to answer your phone every time it rings. You do not have to respond to everyone else's needs, even for charitable or good causes. It will be easier to say no when you learn to validate the importance of another person's request. You can learn to say to people, "I wish I could participate in this project for you but I'm working on something I'm very involved in right now. I'm very excited about this project, it's taking all my time. Perhaps we could schedule an hour next week to sit down and talk." In that way, you validate the importance both of the person making the request and your own needs. Once you have defined your needs and set your limits, you are free to suggest alternatives that may be beneficial to both of you.

Setting circumscribed times to deal with the requests of others is especially important for people with ADD so that their flow is uninterrupted. You might not have the time to talk to other people on an as-needed basis, so it might work to create a non-distracting, non-interrupting environment. Whether your strategy is to move away from distractions, to set up a later time to handle requests, or ask for more time or assistance, remember that the question always is: How can I make my job work for me?

Personal Life and Work

Setting limits in order to get your work done is fine, but that doesn't mean that you now have a reason to block out people and fun, even at work. Setting limits means that you can get your work done without feeling guilty or pushing people away. What you also need to figure into the equation, though, is when to stop working, to let things go a little. Recognize that with ADD, you will never really feel that everything is organized and done. Just as importantly, you must set limits with yourself about how much time you are going to spend on a project. Once you have fulfilled your own expectations for work, it is then important to interact with others in ways that are truly enjoyable, replenishing, interesting or just a pleasant diversion. In other words, lighten up and shift some of the focus to other people and causes.

You may feel overloaded at first, but if you do this on your own terms, choose carefully the things that really interest you, and take the proper amount of time to spend with the people you really care about, then giving to others will nourish you and replenish you. Giving that really comes from the heart and from your genuine interest is stress reducing and healthy. It is very different from giving out of exhaustion and guilt, saying yes to everything at your own expense. You must constantly balance these areas of your life. Check in about them with yourself or a coach frequently.

If You're Not Already Working Outside the Home or Thinking about Going to School

Sometimes it's even harder to balance these factors or get organizational help to allow you to focus on yourself, if you're not working outside the home. A woman I know had a coach come to her house once a week to help her stay organized. She wound up using that coaching time to focus on her children's schoolwork and household details rather than move toward her goal of going back to graduate school. She had to learn to carve out a part of each coaching session to focus on herself. The messages that you're going to get from others around you might be difficult to cope with. For instance, you might realize you need a house-keeper once week, or someone to watch your children after school or day care for your younger children. You might get negative comments about this from your husband, family or friends, as if these things were luxuries for someone not working outside the home. The woman with ADD has to become desensitized to these comments, to realize that these are not luxuries for her. She has a disorder for which she is being treated, and if she ever wants to enter a venue where she can use her abilities, she must find a way to plan and strategize.

Because of her difficulties, she, more than anyone, needs to have a distraction-free place and space sometime each day. It is a necessity in order for her to be able to figure out what she wants to do, to have help in moving ahead with her plans. She needs to strategize, spend time on the phone to gather information and set aside time, just as she would if she already had a job. It is essential for her to do something every day (even if only for ten minutes) relative to her plan for her life, even if she is not actively involved in a job search.

Start to carve out time and space for yourself. If you don't know what your abilities are, then take a little time each day or week to explore possibilities. Take a class, or meet a friend to talk about your plans. Go to the book store alone and look for what interests you. Take any small step in relation to your interests, strengths and abilities, anything to increase the time that you spend focusing on your strengths or discovering what those strengths are. Remember, you're trying to break a cycle, a system, get off a treadmill. You have to do something different. You don't have to do big things, you don't have to do dramatic things, you don't even have to do them for a long period of time. Even a small step makes everything around you shift. The system shifts, people shift, you become the person that people work around, rather than you working around everybody else's needs.

Make some "sacred" time every day, every week. This might mean writing something down on a calendar. It might mean having a friend come over and sit with you while you do information processing about schools or jobs. It may mean having someone call you at the beginning and end of your personal time to provide some external structure that you'll be unable to break. This might mean signing up for a class and paying in advance so that you will attend. Sometimes it's useful to get involved in an activity with another person, so then you won't feel that you can put it aside. These small steps are very important in starting to carve out that space for yourself.

A physical place for yourself at home is a must. Even if it's just a corner of a room, where you can keep your stuff, it will be a place that represents you, your strengths, your hopes, your future. You've got to have some breathing room. Imagine yourself in a collapsed building; you'd need to find an air pocket to start breathing again. That's what you're trying to do; create more air pockets so that your creative force, your strengths, your abilities aren't snuffed out. No one else is going to do this for you. No one else is going to say, "Okay, I won't ask you for anything anymore." You're going to have to find a way to say no, or say. "Not right now. I'm sorry, I'd like to help you, but this is my private time." Turn off the phones, do whatever you have to do. Don't respond to other people's needs for as long as you can manage. Fifteen minutes a day at first is fine. If you have to get out of the house to do it, do it! This can be nerve-racking at first. You may be anxious, but as you get used to it, your anxiety will be reduced when people see that you mean it, that you take yourself seriously. If you can't afford child care and your children aren't in school, trade time with a friend. Find every way to seize time for yourself.

Starting to explore what kind of work, school, or interests you're going to pursue, often requires a search for information. Because information processing is often a problem for women with ADD, a great deal of anxiety and fear can arise at this point. This can result in a response to internal barriers that prevents women from moving forward. They're afraid they might not know what to say on the phone, or that they might go blank. They may be afraid they won't remember the information or that they'll lose it and, if they lose it, they're afraid to ask for it again. These situations trigger all the old feelings of being thought weird, stupid, asking the wrong questions, losing things, being irresponsible. Find strategies for dealing with this: write down instructions to yourself before you make a call, write down information as soon as you get it, possibly keeping a bulletin board by the phone as a place to put this information. To break through your initial fears, you might call during "off" hours and leave a request for information on an answering machine. With today's technology, you can even e-mail or fax people, to get through that initial period of anxiety.

Women also resist at this point in the information-gathering stage because of fears that they ultimately wouldn't be able to succeed at a new job or school. They feel they would be unable to meet the demands of these situations. Because of their over-creative ADD minds, they sometimes think through their entire future course and see before them every possible obstacle that they might encounter. This kind of thinking can be counterproductive. What they need to do is to take the first, small step. You don't want to think too far in the future. Just take the first step, because things unfold in ways you never expect them to.

Rethinking Your Job

Ask yourself these questions:

> Is your work life working for you?
>
> If not, what changes would it take to make it work?
>
> Are these changes possible and reasonable?
>
> What steps could you take to make these changes happen?

If you find you're unable to take these steps, ask yourself what might prevent you from doing this.

Are you aware of any internal barriers such as embarrassment, or the need to protect your sense of competency, that might contribute to your difficulties in making these changes?

If not, ask yourself: is there something in this job environment that's too resistant or too toxic to accommodate what I need?

After you have explored these options thoroughly, you have to ask yourself the following questions. You should really only consider two choices.

Do I want to stay there, at this job, and make it work?

or

Do I not want to stay here and instead find another workplace that works for me?

What you're trying to figure out is whether your job has an environment that is just too toxic, no matter what you do. Is this a place where people are so non-accepting of you or your ADD or so inflexible that even if you were legally able to get accommodations, it wouldn't be worth it? The co-founders of the National Coaching Network, Nancy Ratey and Susan Sussman, in their presentation at the 1995 ADDA Conference on ADD in the workplace, emphasized that accommodations are worth asking for if the work situation in general is good and if your relationship with your employer or supervisor is productive. Otherwise, if you and the job are a bad match in the first place, accommodations probably won't be effective in the long run. Again, your two best choices are either to stay and make it work or to leave and make it work. If you decide to leave you're going to want to consider the options discussed below to see what would be more beneficial to you.

If you do want to stay and try to set your present job up in a way that works for you, and if you find that you have identified what steps you need to take but are still not taking them, identify what barriers might be preventing that. As we have seen, people often confront a wall of shame or guilt that makes it difficult to ask for help. This happens not just in one's personal life, but also when considering asking for accommodations or assistance at work or at school, such as coaching, asking for extra time, or a non-distracting environment.

How and Where You Work

Working in an Office

There are two categories of accommodations or changes to consider as you create a working environment that works for you. You can try to create changes in the actual physical environment (restructuring), and you also can try to arrange help in the form of human assistance. There are also communication strategies to use in order to make each working day effective—we discussed those somewhat when we looked at setting limits.

Let's look at what strategies can help. Creating a non-distracting environment can include such simple things as shutting the door of your office, using a sound blocking device, or arranging to work at less-busy hours, if possible. Of course, as Dr. Kathleen Nadeau says in her chapter on ADD in the workplace in *A Comprehensive Guide to Attention Deficit Disorder*, it's essential to make this strategy work for your personality type as well as for your ADD. She emphasizes that introverts and extroverts with ADD are going to have to find approaches that don't ignore this important variable.

In any case, you must prevent distractions from overwhelming you. You must know how your kind of ADD affects you. Do you work better with high stimulation? Do you need a job where you shift around, move from location to location, have a lot of stimulation to keep yourself focused, or does that overwhelm you? Do you need to work in an environment that's very quiet, do you need sound blocks to block out any extraneous noises? Either way, you've got to honor and understand that you have ADD and can't spend all your time and energy fighting against noise in your environment. You can't pretend that you're going to be able to concentrate in an environment where you can't filter out the distractions. You can't spend ninety-eight percent of your day trying to block out distractions and feeling anxious from the effort. Don't be chained to a desk if you need to be moving around. Learn to know your particular balance between overstimulated and understimulated, overwhelmed and underwhelmed.

Technology can be extremely helpful in effective time-management, including computer programs, electronic beepers and reminders. A more important strategy for many women with ADD is to ask for human assistance. This kind of assistance can be invaluable and often makes the critical difference in whether a woman with ADD is going to be able to succeed at her job. This would include either assistance in typing and word processing, filing, making copies, or collating materials, for example. If these are the essential tasks of your job, and this is also your area of difficulty, this could be a situation where you might want to rethink whether this job is for you at all.

Even if you don't ask for formal accommodations, there are other ways of creating either formal or informal structures to provide the help you need. Informally, this might include setting up ways for people with whom you work to remind you of important things. For instance, this might include asking a co-worker in a positive way to stop by your office on the way to a meeting. You can request regular check-ins from a supervisor to go over the projects that you are currently working on in order to help yourself stay on track. You might request regular, short meetings that would help you be realistic about the amount of work that you agree to take on. This can be framed in a positive way with your stated intention of meeting your mutual goals, which include you doing the best work you can. In these check-ins, especially at times when you feel the work load is increasing to a point where you will be unable to manage it, you can try to reach an understanding together of what the priorities really are.

The focus of these sessions should be to generate alternatives that satisfy the goal of getting the work done well. Instead of an all-or-nothing attitude, for example, you might suggest the following: First, I can accept a lesser assignment and do high-quality work on it. Second, I can complete all this work in an expanded time frame. Or, I can do all of this work with assistance. This clearly defines your limits and also leaves the decision-making with the supervisor, instead of you trying to meet impossible demands and being unable to produce the quality of work that you want. Again, this is not a pass-fail, all-or-nothing, either-or situation. You want to focus on doing a job well rather than on what you don't do well.

Working at Home or On Your Own

If you are considering a change in how you work, or if you're already working at home or on your own, it's essential to consider the amount of structure and stimulation that you need if you're working alone. There's a narrow band where things often work very well for people with ADD. The challenge is to stay within that narrow band because once you move outside it, things can often go wrong. The paradox seems to be that people who need structure are able to have that in a large corporate organization. Working for someone else there, however, also includes more limits, rules, time frames and structure. That kind of framework also includes demands, bureaucracies, paperwork, or boredom and frustration. On the other hand, working alone (which usually suits your talents and entrepreneurial and creative abilities well) often leaves you without any structure, out there on your own, in the realm of the "underwhelmed." You can either fade away or get way off track or overwhelmed with details and paper.

Whereas you might feel suffocated in a bureaucracy or a company, when you are working alone with nothing external to come up against, you might fall into an abyss of nothingness. The essential ingredient, is to set up structure and external stimulation for yourself in advance. You can hire assistants to provide organizational support for your business or your independent work. You can get a partner who has the opposite kinds of skills from yours. Thom Hartmann, in *Attention Deficit Disorder: a Different Perception,* calls these other types of people "farmers." They can help with the daily maintenance, record-keeping and detail work that's so difficult for people with ADD and they provide a great complement to your "hunter" skills. The other human strategy that you might integrate into your independent work life would be to get a coach to check in with you every day, keep you on track and provide you with needed stimulation. Working for yourself, provides a great way to capitalize on your strengths, but it's important to understand in advance that it will pull directly on your deficits as well. You want to focus on your strengths, but you must provide and prepare for your difficulties; don't ignore or deny your weaknesses, but work with them.

No matter how you work, at home, on your own or for someone else, recognize and honor your particular activity levels. Learn to know the kinds of jobs you can't work at for a straight eight hours a day. Come to terms with variability in your energy levels, whether because you can't sit still all day or you can't stay "up" the whole day straight through. Even though medication will help tremendously in these areas, these variables might still continue to be factors in your life to consider. This might mean going through another grief cycle because women say, "I don't want to have to consider all of these things! Why do I have to be so different?" It's essential to consider not just what kind of job one is qualified for, not just what a person is good at or what her interests are, but also what the actual work environment is and what an actual work day requires.

> What does it really mean to be a lawyer?
>
> What does it mean to be a writer?
>
> What does that mean day to day?
>
> How much boring paperwork or filing, is involved?
>
> Do you work outside or inside?
>
> Do you move around a lot?
>
> Do you move from office to office, location to location, desk to desk?
>
> Do you have to move all your materials with you?
>
> Do you have to transport everything, move quickly?
>
> Do you have to go to a lot of meetings?
>
> Do you have to write a lot of reports?

It's important to think through the small details that make up a typical day at a particular job. Informational interviews or talking to people in a field you are interested in would help you gain the necessary understanding. Remember that it is not just the organization you will be evaluating, but the organizational demands as well. If you decide you do have enough interest in a field, can you design a way to work in that environment, through assistance or restructuring? If it doesn't seem as if it would be easy to restructure a traditional work setting, do you want to do the same kind of work in a way that's more independent, as a consultant or on your own? Or, do you want to take the same skills, abilities, and interests that attracted you to that field and apply them to another field that can better accommodate your organizational difficulties?

Always remember that you want to continue to move toward your strengths, not merely accommodate your difficulties. When people only consider their difficulties, they eliminate a whole range of occupational options that might allow their creative abilities to emerge. Many people with ADD have a great ability to conceptualize, see connections, see the big picture. They might be great if they were able to arrive at that level in a job or profession, but moving through that middle level is so confounding that many of these individuals automatically hold themselves back. Instead, start thinking about how to move ahead while getting support for your difficulties.

College

Much of what I have said about work also applies to college. Restructuring by asking for accommodations at school often involves overcoming the same internal barriers. Students can arrange with the student disability office for accommodations (extended time on tests or non-distracting test-taking environments). Figure out a balanced class load, and communicate these issues to your instructors. Get tutors and coaches to help you stay on track or help you in your writing assignments. What often interferes with students with ADD of all ages are the feelings of embarrassment, shame or guilt involved with asking for special accommodations. They sometimes feel that this is an admission that they are not very smart, or that they are asking for some special advantage instead of understanding they are asking for a level playing field. This often happens when people haven't sufficiently integrated and understood what ADD means in their lives.

Communicate with your teachers about your difficulties instead of hiding them, because otherwise they have no idea how hard you are working. They just know that you don't turn papers in on time, and don't know you have spent hundreds of hours on a paper because of your difficulty in pulling your ideas together. If you don't communicate with your instructors, they might have an entirely different image of you. When it comes to a point at which you might have to ask for an extension, an incomplete or extra help, you will have a much better chance of being successful your if professors know the kind of difficulties that you have as well as the kinds of effort that you make. What you don't want to do is let shame or guilt interfere to the point where you make things worse after you miss a test or deadline, by avoiding the whole subject. This just increases your anxiety as well as sabotages your chances of success. If you do work through your feelings of embarrassment and get legal accommodations at school, establish good working relationships with your professors, you increase your chances of success greatly.

Investigate the attitude and accommodations offered by a particular college that you are considering. There are some excellent guides listed in the resources section of the book to help you with this.

If you are a young woman in school, it's ideal if you can enlist the support of your parents and involve them in your ADD diagnosis and treatment. This would help them understand why you might need to or might have already changed programs, schools or directions. You'll need your family's support and your school's support if you are to succeed; to get the kind of accommodations that help you, the kind of reduced load that you might take, or the kind of balanced program that might work for you. You're going to have to cope also with trying to balance having fun, and taking time to nourish yourself. Dealing with drugs on campus and those kinds of social pressures will make your ADD focus difficult. Self-image concerns at a young age also make it especially complicated to accept the idea of having an attention deficit disorder. The whole idea of taking medication at this age is also more threatening to someone who is struggling with self-esteem and the natural insecurities of this stage of life.

A young person often sees medication for the brain as making a statement about sanity, weaknesses or intelligence. This is another reason for family and possible professional support. You're just forming your issues of independence; this might make you feel more dependent, cause anxiety about your ability to be in the world, to take care of yourself and to get the right kind of job. Since it adds a whole layer of pressures, it's very important for you to seek support and meet other young women with ADD who have become successful. They've worked through these problems of self-image, gone on medication, and made their lives work for them. The good news is that if you do it early enough you'll be likely not to develop confusion later on. You'll pick a career and an atmosphere in which to work that can support your strengths. You might need to re-shift your ideas or think of new role models when forming relationships, intimate relationships and friendships. It's important that you start to value yourself, and not hide these parts of your ADD. If you hit a wall, sometimes a counselor, can help you work through those issues.

Renegotiating Relationships

Sometimes you just need the communication skills to know how to set limits, to know how to communicate in a positive way about yourself, and know how to maintain your self-respect while getting what you need at work. This is where we move into the next R as it applies to work. If you get stuck, some kind of professional consultation or counseling for communication skills can help you rethink this. It's going to help if you've worked through your grief cycle; the deeper you do that, the less shame you have attached to this whole thing. You'll be effective in getting what you need by communicating in an assertive way without over-defending and explaining, convincing others or moving into a position of self-deprecation to get what you want.

> *A young woman, Bridget, had spent more time than expected on a project that she didn't have ready for the meeting the next day. She started acting defensive and separating herself, creating an aura of doing something wrong, when actually what she needed was a positive way to state the truth: that she had created something very special, but to get it done on time, she would need an assistant to help her with the details, making copies and collating it. All that she could focus on at the time was that her ADD difficulty in completing projects on time was going to bring her negative responses. In actuality it was her behavior that brought the negative feelings from people, rather than the ADD problem itself. She needed to learn to say: "I've done something really special and I'm excited about it. I think you're going to love it. I need some extra time or I need some assistance." The situation already existed and she needed to be able to reframe it to convey that she was sorry for any inconvenience, without putting herself down.*

When the symptoms arise in any kind of ADD problem, instead of sending the message of: "I'm really messed up, I really don't deserve to be here, I'm not doing a good job," do your best to employ strategies that are going to help you take control. When the inevitable happens, and you're late or you forgot or mislaid something, don't make it worse by avoiding the situation or putting yourself down. You want to be able to

Validation

Negotiation

Appreciation

Reciprocation

communicate that you are sorry for any bad effect that you have created, that this person or the project is important to you and that you want to be able to do the best job you can under present circumstances. "Yes, I was late and I'm sorry it has had a bad effect. I think having assistance would help avoid that in the future. Right now what we can do to make this work is ... ," emphasizing the positive nature of what you have accomplished.

When you need help with something and you're looking for informal coaches, say something like, "I get so involved in my work, I'm so interested in the project that I lose track of the hours, but it's very important for me to be on time for this meeting. So could you do me a favor? I'm going to put the meeting time down in my book, but just as a backup, I'd really appreciate it if you could stop by on your way to the meeting." Then you might offer to reciprocate something that this person could appreciate. You always want to reciprocate when someone helps you. Positive communications to other people also involves setting limits. Women are afraid to set limits, to say no, because they think it's going to mean criticism, rejection, a bad message to the other person. It's going to have to be validating that this is important to you, that you wish you could accommodate them, but right now it's not going to work. You may suggest another way to make it work—for example, if it's a big lunch that you don't want to go to, you might ask the person to meet alone with you. Let them know it's important for you to talk, but you find it difficult in a distracting environment.

As you see in the Four Step Validation chart, there are four essential ingredients when approaching these kinds of situations: Validation, Negotiation, Appreciation, and Reciprocation. What's important is for you to describe what you need, what works for you, what people can do to help you be effective and what you can do to meet their needs. You don't have to go around telling everybody you have ADD. It's very off-putting. You only need to go to that length if you need some legal accommodation or if there is someone that you want to inform about your ADD for some particular reason. Describe what you need, validate that you and the other person both have the goal of doing a good job. You can say something like, "When you explain this to me, it's very important for me to get it. What really works better for me is if I could have it written down so I can refer to it. I sometimes have difficulty with remembering these kinds of verbal lists. I don't want to have to interrupt you all the time, so perhaps you could leave the instructions typed up next to the computer." If you need to be alone and you're afraid of appearing rude to people, of shutting them out or saying no, it's always better to try to state it first, tell them how you're feeling, that you don't intend to be rude. With ADD often your attempts at self-protection can look as if you're shutting people out. It's important to find a way to make it work for you, but you don't want to do it in a way that they can misinterpret or react negatively. You might say:

"I don't mean to be rude but I'm really going to be buried in work for a couple of hours so I'm going to shut my door. I'll open it when I'm done with this report."

"When I get interrupted, everything leaves my mind. I'm going to turn my phone off for a couple of hours every day."

"I'd really like to answer those questions. How about if we schedule a time, maybe on Friday at one o'clock so that I can prepare and give you a lot of attention."

"In the middle of my day, I'm sometimes distracted and I can't give you the kind of attention that I'd like to."

"It's really important for me to do a good job, so I need you to write down the instructions."

"I know I'm hard to follow sometimes. I get so carried away with enthusiasm for this subject. Let me know if I lose you. Please interrupt."

"I have trouble keeping track of time because I get so involved in my work."

"This discussion with you is so important to me, but I have difficulty blocking out the noise in here. Let's find a quieter spot so I can really concentrate and give enough attention to what you're saying."

If someone is trying to explain something to you and you're not getting it, you might say, "Thank you for being so patient, instead of Sorry I'm so dumb."

If you bump into something, say, "I'm sorry I messed up your books instead of, I'm sorry I'm so clumsy."

Instead of saying, "I can't or I won't do that, you might say: This kind of task is very difficult for me to do." Then make a suggestion as to how to proceed, either with other kinds of instructions, or more time or with assistance.

Always validate the other person, validate yourself, and then suggest another situation instead of feeling that you have to be available on demand. If it's a boss that's asking you for more and more work, you can say that you feel good that they're asking you to do this work and you really enjoy it, but you feel that to do the best job you either need an assistant, or a different time frame. Even though you hate to give this project to someone else, it might be the best for the company to do at that time.

What you don't want to do is hide and pretend that everything's okay—overworking, taking things home and not doing a good job. Things will slip by and you will get more and more anxious about it. This buildup of anxiety underneath anything good that you have done either feeds the feelings of being an impostor or the feelings that things are going to fall apart. That's going to affect your behavior and your relationships.

Redefining

Sometimes even if you renegotiate and you're able to say what you might want and your communication is good, things still don't always work. You might really want to change jobs or change niches but you might be holding onto a corporate image. Perhaps you've been taught a certain way of working is appropriate for someone of your education, or your intelligence or your abilities. It might take a while to find new role models, of a way to work independently or else in different ways. Also what does it mean to be a mature, successful, competent woman in the workplace? Does that mean you can't stay home part-time if you want to? Must you work full-time, even if you don't need the money? Would that mean being a failure, if you found yourself exhausted by working five days a week? Perhaps you should try to work ten hours a day even a couple of days a week. Or sometimes it's better, instead of having to work two jobs, work one job on one day, splitting your week. Sometimes it's better for people who are able to focus all their energies in just one area completely for a few days at a time to then take time to relax.

You might also be getting messages from husband, family or

SELF-TALK

ADD Happens	When ADD is more Accepted
BLUNDER	ACCEPTED
DISORGANIZE	ADD Happens
SHUT DOWN	
Negative Self-Talk	**Positive Self-Talk**
"I'm so stupid!"	"It's that ADD again"
"Forget all this garbage"	"I'm mad at the ADD"
"It's just an excuse"	"It's just an ADD attack, ride it out!"
"What's the matter with me?"	"I give myself permission to relax?"
"What a jerk!"	"It's a signal that too much is going on!"
"I'm a mess"	"Take time to think it through"
"It's hopeless"	"Box it up, Put it on hold, Get help!"
DEPRESSION	You are able to separate from the ADD

friends, who don't understand you get more exhausted than other people from a certain kind of pace, especially if you have a home life. Accept the fact that you might work in different ways, with different spurts or different kinds of energy levels, even after medication, that bombardment or overstimulation might be too much for you. Through counseling or support groups, you might find incredible talents, strengths and creative abilities that you might not have ever decided to use. It might be just the right thing for you to explore. Professional counseling can help get that support for you, while you work through these issues with your mate or your family.

Two essential things can happen in counseling when you redefine who you are in a positive way. When you understand your ADD you are able to sort out your primary symptoms, your neurology, from your psychology and your core self-image.

Previously we discussed negative self-talk. The illustration, Self-Talk, shows the effect of both negative and positive self-talk. When ADD symptoms emerge—and they will continue to emerge—you have to expect them, and understand that's going to happen. Your occasional ADD symptoms after you're working out, organizing, taking medication is not what's going to cause the problems. At that point, you have to make a decision not to make it worse. What you do to make it worse degrades your mood as well as affects your relationships. You see in the left half, where ADD happened, where you might blunder, disorganize, shut down—you would go into negative self-talk such as "I'm stupid, forget all this garbage, what they're saying about ADD is just an excuse. What's the matter with me? I'm such a jerk."

This leads to depression, especially at work when these things happen. But at that point, you're able to separate out and say to yourself, "I don't fall all the way down now" when that happens. You're able to separate out your strengths from your deficits and see that they're separate. You might say, as we see on the right hand side of the chart, "Oh, it's that ADD again! I'm mad at the ADD." It's just an ADD attack, ride it out. They're going to use those as signals. "I give myself permission to relax." This is a signal that too much is going on, I'm not having enough help. Or you might use strategies like, box it up, put it on hold, get help. But you know that it's a signal that you need to take action. It's not a disaster. When you're able to calm yourself down, talk to yourself, the episodes go away, like an anxiety attack.

Summary

As long as you keep in mind your overriding goal of making your life work, you'll continue to figure out how to support yourself enough to keep going. It may mean a lot of renegotiation with your partner, your family. When this happens, you might need to creatively rethink your whole image. Many women don't even think they're creative. It doesn't seem like creativity to them before treatment; it seems like confusion and chaos, which it is, but the trick is to now rein those in and direct them into creative pursuits.

After they see new possibilities, meet with other people and get feedback on their ideas, their self-image will change. They can see new options, new opportunities open up. They might have to rethink the way that they want to work. Maybe going back to corporate America and having a three-piece suit and a briefcase isn't something that's going to work for you, but perhaps your entrepreneurial talents are great and perhaps you just need to find a partner to help support you, or an assistant. So if you're not working presently or you're not in school presently, you want to slowly start carving out time and space for yourself. Do it one step at a time and restructure your life to make it work for you. If that takes renegotiating and redefining, if that takes professional help, then go ahead and do it!

CHAPTER SIXTEEN

Restructuring: at Home and in Your Personal Life

L ET'S GO BACK and visit Jodi and see what has happened to her since
she was diagnosed and began medication.

*Jodi has been diagnosed with ADD and has started taking the
medication, Ritalin. She finds that this gives her much more energy
for her daily tasks, and she feels calmer when all the typical daily
frustrations arise. She has even begun to read again, starting with
several of the latest books on ADD. She has a good "feel" for what
ADD is about and what she needs to do to make her life work better.
Her husband thinks that this is great, and is happy that she's feeling
better. He's especially glad that Jodi doesn't seem to cry so easily any
more.*

*Once a month, he baby-sits while she attends CHADD meet-
ings, where she hears speakers on ADD in adults. Jodi sometimes
notices now, however, how little help her husband actually gives her
around the house and with their daughter. They're beginning to fight
about this issue, whereas before they never did.*

*Jodi now has a housekeeper who comes in once a week to do
the major cleaning. She feels hopeful because she has a new organizational system installed in her computer to help her with bill-paying and time management. In addition, her mother now comes over*

*once a week to help her organize her papers piled up in the house
and also to arrange some of the backlog of clutter accumulated over
the years.*

   *Three months after being diagnosed and starting medication,
Jodi goes back to her therapist, whom she hasn't seen since just after
she began medication. Jodi is upset and confused because she's still
not organized, and on top of that, she's feeling angry and lonely.
She wants to know why the medication isn't working better.*

RESTRUCTURING YOUR ENVIRONMENT

TASK DIVISION
ADD Partner · Non-ADD Partner Together
Outside person

Changing, Eliminating & Simplifying
Roles, Rituals and Traditions

Throughout the rest of the book we will look at what a woman like
Jodi may need to do and think about in terms of restructuring her
environment.

   Restructuring involves making deeper changes in the way you live
your life. I have seen this happen most successfully as a result of ongoing
changes in **three important areas**. The first, as we've seen when we
looked at *Restructuring at Work*, is to **rebalance** those parts of one's life
that aren't working anymore.

   As the diagram Restructuring your Environment indicates, in addition, you must rethink **the division of tasks in your household,** finding
ways that work for you. Beyond that change means often **going to a
deeper level,** where you actually alter or eliminate the way you have
always done things.

Rebalancing

The balance in ADD families, partnerships and in an ADD woman's life
very often needs readjustment. The diagram ADD in the Family System

ADD IN THE FAMILY SYSTEM

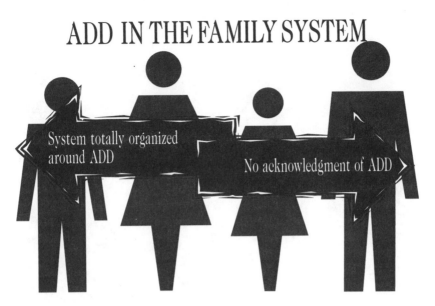

System totally organized around ADD

No acknowledgment of ADD

shows different ways that ADD is handled in the system. When a person has ADD, either before or after diagnosis, one of two things usually happens. The system can become totally organized around the ADD; in other words, everybody is somewhat of a slave to it. Everything else stops as people become servants, overwhelmed by the disorganization, impulsivity, or activity of the ADD person. Family members spend their energies trying to solve the ADD individual's problems, taking over all the tasks. Eventually they begin to feel lost and resentful.

At the other extreme, what often happens is little or no acknowledgment of the ADD. There is superficial recognition by the family after the diagnosis, as well as superficial support, but no real willingness to change the way the system operates. This often happens to women, especially to those without hyperactivity, who haven't had the energy or power to assert themselves. Through the years, because of her failure to meet "the woman job expectations" we talked about earlier, a woman may have lost self-esteem and been identified as the problem in the immediate as well as the extended family.

The picture on the following page of a man and a woman by Degas expresses the loneliness that a woman can feel in a marriage or a partnership when she is diagnosed with ADD, and then continues to cope on her own at home. She is trying to "fit" her ADD in around everything and everyone else. Even though she feels better as a result of

the medication, and may employ some new strategies (as Jodi did), she still may have a sense of loneliness, and even resentment. She has started to go through her grief cycle, and is beginning to understand her ADD. Her partner, however, (understandably, because this is not happening to him) has not spent the same time and energy becoming educated and working through his own process. The situation is different now because the medication gives the woman the energy not only to feel these new feelings, but to express and stay with them.

Making changes in a family system can arouse anxiety and often elicits "change-back" messages. For instance, a woman might hear, "I liked you the old way." This happens more in systems where women get treated for ADD rather than men. For men, medication can often work to make them more open and receptive to their partners. For women, medication helps them to become more assertive and more likely to engage in conflict than they would have before treatment.

In order to rebalance the family system a woman must think through three important areas of focus in her life. If you have had severe problems related to ADD, these areas probably have become out of balance. As we noted earlier, women often balance the overwhelming demands of their environments on their own backs, cutting what they can out of their own needs, contributing further to their depletion. A woman can mentally check these areas periodically when things seem overwhelming, to see if any of them need readjusting.

Previously, when we talked about restructuring at work we saw the three pie charts that represent the imbalance in an ADD woman's life. Now we will look at how the balance of these three areas affect a woman's life at home.

1. *The time spent focusing on yourself vs. the time spent on other people's needs.*

Setting limits on the kind of time you expend on other people's needs doesn't include the kind of giving that nourishes you and others. The setting of healthy limits on your time and energy, instead, will allow you to have more time and energy to connect and engage in real relationships. This "true" giving of yourself is different from giving because of the difficulty of "saying no." Healthy self-protection and the healthy setting of limits will allow you to feel safe enough to venture into a close relationship. Learn to set limits, not as a defensive way of pushing people away, but as a way of enriching yourself, and keeping yourself focused on moving toward your own goals.

Remember, you can set limits even when others keep asking you for help. You can set limits even when people are nice to you or ask you to help a good cause.

A woman needs to carve out a place and a time for herself. Don't wait until you have a month, a year, the perfect environment, or other people's cooperation before you focus on yourself. If you just start to make one small change where you focus on yourself, eventually other parts of the system begin to shift around you.

2. *The balance in your life between the time spent on work and play.* Work includes job-related activities, plus any tasks, routines, or other stressful personal activities. By play, I mean time spent in replenishing activities—creative, fun, recreational, relaxing, social, or spiritual arenas.

To accomplish this, you might have to make a commitment to other people or pay in advance so you actually follow through on the activity. Put a date in your appointment book, an anchor to involve another person so you can't get out of it. Women have to learn to push the envelope of work versus play, beginning to tolerate the guilt of having fun when their work is undone. You need these recharging times, but set them up in a way that won't overwhelm or drain you.

I know women with ADD can't believe this, but it's true. Even though you take time out from work, which you are already overwhelmed with, you'll find that to engage in recharging activities will give you more emotional and physical energy.

Consciously make choices to allow you to take care of your mood, knowing that you have a sensitive system and that you react easily. Even with your best efforts, if you do occasionally start to feel overloaded, keep a few ideas in mind to allow you to get back into balance. These can be simple things, such as taking a walk in the middle of a party, or finding a quiet place to be alone for a while, as you regain your balance. The point is, you don't need to reject opportunities for fun and socializing because you feel you might become overloaded.

I hear many women say, *"I'm waiting for the demands to stop,"* but the demands never stop. I've even heard them say, *"I realize that I need to sleep, I need to eat."* These are basic things. Women with ADD are desperate to find time in their schedules "to get their lives done." Rebalance your "time budget" and stop taking it out on your own emotional and physical health.

3. *The time spent on developing your strengths vs. the time and energy spent focusing on your difficulties.*

It is no secret that focusing on your strengths is a key element on the path to success. This has been validated in educational psychology, career development, or any kind of personal growth training. The focus in ADD treatment, however, often becomes "managing the ADD," which often translates to overfocusing on the deficits and not the strengths. Obviously it is critical to get help for these deficits. But it is frustrating and counterproductive to spend all your time and efforts trying to manage your weak areas. This keeps you on a treadmill where you can get weaker, with lower and lower self-esteem. As an alternative, find a way to put a little more energy each day into your areas of strength, or into your dreams. Managing your deficits can then be for the purpose of moving toward goals that reflect who you really are and your true abilities.

Carve out a little space each day and each week for the purpose of discovering what those strengths or dreams are, if you don't already know. *New ideas about yourself will emerge when you shift your focus to your strengths. It will then become much easier to figure out how to manage your difficulties, because you will have created an internal structure for yourself, and a new internal picture to move toward.*

When your time in these three areas is more in balance you will begin to feel whole. The picture of these pies can help you remember that you don't merely want a small piece of life, or just the leftovers. The choice of how much of life you want is yours.

Dividing up Tasks

The second area of restructuring involves the division of tasks in the household, according to each person's strengths and difficulties. This sounds simple, but is really quite complex, as the emotions that this restructuring brings up are more difficult to deal with than the actual tasks themselves. I talk about this division of tasks as if a person were living with a primary partner, but it is necessary for a person in any type of living situation to go through this process, even if they are living alone. *You must go through the restructuring process with another person.* By definition, restructuring means finding ways to compensate for your deficits and get the right kind of support and structure that you need. If you don't have a primary partner, find another restructuring partner to help you achieve these goals.

I now suggest a process in which to begin your restructuring. This will involve a **restructuring meeting,** ideally to take place on a weekly basis. During these dialogues, it is important that there is a spirit of team work and cooperation, rather than an adversarial position.

At the beginning of this process you and your partner will engage in determining what each of your strengths and weaknesses are, so you can make better decisions about the division of tasks.

Strengths and Weaknesses—We All Have Them

Everyone, not just those with ADD, has things that they do well and things that are difficult for them. Each individual's brain has strengths, weaknesses, and variations from some "norm." For the purpose of these meetings it's crucial not just to focus on the ADD person's difficulties, but to know both partner's strengths and difficulties in order to assign the right person to the right job. As in any well-functioning business, assigning appropriate tasks to the right person is the smart thing to do.

The first step in dividing tasks up in an effective and less stressful way, is to realistically assess and discuss each partner's strengths and areas of difficulty. This is both in terms of the tasks themselves, and the qualities they bring to the partnership.

Use the common strengths and difficulties listed below as a starting point for your own discussion. The purpose is to increase the communication of the partnership, not just to mechanically divide up tasks, like dealing out cards. It may take several conversations to come up with some workable ideas.

1. Begin by discussing the strengths of the partner with ADD. (For instance: creativity, spontaneity, enthusiasm, conceptual abilities, brain-storming abilities ...). Think about using these abilities as you divide up your daily tasks.

2. Discuss the strengths of the partner without ADD. (Possibly organizational abilities, dependablitity, planning skills, follow through ...). Obviously these can be a great complement in an ADD partnership.

3. Discuss the difficulties of the partner with ADD. (For example: time, money or clutter management; paperwork; prioritizing, getting started, distractibility ...). Again, you wouldn't want to put someone with these difficulties in charge of tasks that require slow routine work.

4. Discuss the difficulties of the partner without ADD. (Do they take on too much responsibility; are they too controlling; do they lack spontaneity; do they get lost in details ... ?) These qualities won't be the same for every non-ADD partner. In fact, the non-ADD partner may have some of the same problem areas as the ADD partner, even if less severe. This is when a partnership would have to turn to outside help, as we will see later.

Try to be as specific as possible when discussing strengths and difficulties. For example, a person can have great organizational skills in some ways and poor ones in other ways. A woman with ADD may have great planning and conceptual ability, mentally planning a complete trip from start to finish, deciding each step that needs to be taken. But she might not be able to manage the details of putting that plan into action. So when you are specifying your area of difficulty for this exercise, don't just say "poor organizational skills," but specify difficulty in carrying out many small details.

Next pick the three areas of your life together in terms of tasks that most impact either the individual or the partnership. If something is extremely difficult the way it is presently structured for the ADD partner, or if an aspect of the household's functioning is stressful for the non-ADD partner, address these areas first.

Below are a few typical areas you may want to start your discussion with. The important thing is to find out what the critical areas are for you.

Grocery shopping

Financial management

School and child-related schedules, activities

Clothes shopping

Social obligations

Household maintenance

Food preparation and clean-up

Try brainstorming together as you would in a business, figuring out what makes more sense for one partner to handle. Especially try to think what part of a task one partner should handle. Determine the level of difficulty as well, whether it is mild, moderate or severe. In this next phase of task division you will use this information about level, severity and specificity to decide the different ways a task can be accomplished. For each task you address, use the list below as a scale to determine where your level of difficulty may fall in order to generate options about how the task can be altered to fit and accommodate your particular partnership. The first question to ask: "Is this something the ADD partner realistically should handle at all?" Is this something at which she's just a disaster, that causes her such overwhelming anxiety it affects every area of her life?

It rarely needs to be "all or nothing." Use the following list to start thinking about how a task can be approached or altered to accommodate your level of difficulty.

Getting the Right Kind of Help

1. Should the partner with ADD do the task at all?

2. Do the task alone, but with paper or mechanical aids (Post-its, calendars, planners, beepers).

3. Need written guidelines set up by non-ADD partner (written instructions on how to balance your checkbook; diagrams of where the dishes go in the cupboards).

4. Need non-ADD partner in room, not doing prescribed tasks, but his presence helps her focus. The non-ADD partner can be doing his individual work in the room at the same time, just to provide enough external structure for her to stay on track.

5. Needs non-ADD partner as co-participant in activity (this must be done in non-toxic, or non-controlling way); cleaning up the kitchen or bedroom together; grocery shopping together; doing checkbook together).

6. Non-ADD partner takes over the task, but the partner with ADD is now the assistant in the activity.

7. Non-ADD partner takes over, but the partner with ADD is present in the room, a non-participant in the activity. (Cleaning up, doing checkbook etc.) This is beneficial because even though the partner with ADD is not participating, their presence gives a feeling of support, and can lessen resentment.

8. Non-ADD partner is willing and able to do the activity alone, and the partner with ADD reciprocates in some other way.

9. If the activity is something neither partner is willing or able to do, then an outside person must be brought into the system.

Together think of friends, family, or a professional, to fill in the gap, either on a "paid or trade" basis.

Nobody Wants To Do It— Let's Talk

If neither one wants to do certain tasks or neither has abilities in a certain area, what are the options? Should we think of paid help, a professional, a friend, a family member or acquaintance to fill in the gaps? Trading tasks with a friend or neighbor is always a good idea. If you're going to pay for help, what kind of adjustments in the budget or family time will this mean? Obviously, this can only be done by two people who are willing to talk and renegotiate. If they can't, they're going to have to have some help talking through these things, as we'll see in the next section on renegotiating.

But really think through the benefits and costs of having a paid person help you. *Isn't it possible that hiring a bookkeeper once a month may be more cost effective than couple counseling every week to argue about the bills not getting paid?*

It's smart to think about outside help in this way, especially if the strain of living without it is causing medical, psychological, marital or financial crises more costly than the help that could often alleviate these problems.

In all areas, think the process through in detail together. For instance, is cleaning the kitchen really impossible, or is prioritizing the different tasks (as other people do automatically) the real barrier? Maybe having your partner present in the kitchen while you cook or clean, or you assisting him may be the thing that works for you. Brainstorm together! Think through the process that is really causing the difficulty. In any given situation, is it cognitive processing, difficulty in sequencing, or prioritizing, or is it an attention problem, a need for stimulation or outside structure? Is it difficulty with: attention to detail, impulsivity and shifting, visual spatial planning, motor difficulties, or a need for outside structure in order to stay on track? It's necessary to identify the problem before you can find the right solution.

Simple interventions work for the least severe deficit. If there is a minor organizational difficulty, Post-its, DayRunners, or new calendars may do the trick. A moderate level of difficulty would require a person being in the room with the ADD person to guide her. The next step may be part-time help, or even full-time help, especially if your areas of difficulty overlap. Just because a partner is not ADD, it doesn't mean he may not have difficulties in certain areas himself. Just pushing tasks onto him isn't going to work either. As you proceed, you will be able to figure out exactly what intervention will be necessary to accommodate each difficulty, and who will do it. There are so many possible ways to structure this that don't involve all-or-nothing thinking like "you do the cooking and I'll do the bills."

Just being there with a person with ADD can be tremendously helpful. For instance, bill-paying is something that the ADD partner may be lost at; this may be a task that the couple can do together. Side by side, one person can be writing out the bills while the other person is putting them in the envelopes. One person could be in charge and the other one be the assistant. If roles are designated like that, there won't be too many struggles. Another solution is to have the non-ADD person do the bill paying, and have the ADD partner in the room, watching, or minimally helping out.

If you are going to do tasks together, the non-ADD partner needs to do this without putting the woman down or controlling too much. Working together side by side can be a great thing if you're not good at a task, so you can retain some sense of control. Having some understanding about your money is much better than not knowing anything at all about your finances.

Don't try to change everything at once. Your choices could include any household tasks—things you might not even think are problems, as well as those that are difficult: cooking, cleaning, dishes, grocery shopping, clothes shopping for the kids. Try to break through your ideas of roles and gender at this point. Discuss anything that seems difficult or overwhelming—household maintenance, coordinating individual schedules, buying clothes for the family, talking to teachers, maintaining the cars, making the beds, handling the bills, balancing the checkbook, making social engagements. Don't forget about all the other areas of your life: making recreational plans, paper management, fun management, intimacy, etc. Time eats away at these when you are living with ADD. And remember, there may be areas that you don't view as a problem, but your partner does.

Rewarding Yourself

You want to always reward yourself after you have one of these restructuring sessions. Decide on some kind of fun, mutually-agreed-upon activity. These meetings can also be a good way to know each other better on a deeper level. If your relationship has lost some of the communication you once had, these meetings can be a vehicle to start talking again. Don't turn these sessions into drudgery. You might want to hold them away from home in a place that you both consider fun. Have your meeting every week at the same time so that you don't get into a battle of wills over who's remembering and who's not remembering. If something happens and one of you can't make it, take the time to reschedule.

If you do this effectively with the purpose of making it work for both of you, not just for the purpose of getting chores done, you'll be surprised by the effect that it has. Your restructured life starts to feel better. You are more in control, you have less resentment. And your sex life, your romantic feelings, may even improve as well, as you will be in a better mood, and have more emotional and physical energy.

You Can't Do It All

The non-ADD partner can't help the ADD person with everything, but he can help her figure out what kind of outside help or arrangements they're going to make. In the same way, the non-ADD partner might need to have agreements to go out and have a good time by himself, or to engage in some kind of social activities that might be too overwhelming or too much for the resources of the ADD partner. You'll have to discuss all this. The point is to make life work, without draining anyone, and without building resentment.

Support is not, on one hand, co-dependency, which is taking responsibility for and being emotionally in charge of everything. The non-ADD partner doesn't have to do everything, but often helping to strategize about how to get help or thinking through plans is the greatest help. Along with reassurance, this provides the feeling that "we're in this together." Neither partner will feel as bombarded all the time with demands, and neither will feel such a need to retreat or feel frustrated by demands. If the ADD person has special needs and mini-panics during the week but knows that this will be addressed during the weekly meeting, it can help her feel more supported and calm.

There also needs to be a mechanism for daily panics and daily centering, if a coach isn't available. If this happens frequently, it would be a good idea to get a third person involved. Maybe the spouse can suggest a time, in a gentle way with a little reassurance, if that is more convenient. Or perhaps give five minutes at the beginning of the day to assist with centering and prioritizing. Often mini-panics are just a sudden loss of perspective, and a reassuring word helps enough to get a woman back on track. A coach can facilitate this process. The more you can get needs like this met outside the basic partnership, the more energy and interest remain with the spouse or partner, allowing for deeper work and help within the relationship.

Reciprocating

You might want to think about reciprocating in some way when it comes to tasks, exchanging some chore you could do, or providing some special favor to your spouse in return for assistance in your weak spots. Always remind the members of your "support team" that you really appreciate them. Actually providing or doing something for them will keep the system healthy and prevent resentment from developing.

Household Help for the Messy Internal World

It's not just external task division that needs figuring out. The ADD woman will often need help with planning, ordering her inner world, if only for a few minutes a day. She can do this with a coach, a friend, her partner, or a counselor.

Coaching

It is important for ADD individuals and couples to add something to the system to stabilize it. The non-ADD partner can't provide all the stabilizing effect, especially at first when so many feelings are activated. Having someone come in and see the whole backlog of clutter and stuff that you have can be intimidating, but I promise you it can be wonderful to find a "Coach." This can be someone trained and paid, or someone that you helped to develop, a non-judgmental friend who's organized but flexible. Especially today, people feel isolated and lack the kind of support systems they once had from friends and family. For adults with ADD who absolutely need external structure to function well, coaches can make a tremendous difference and provide a critical link on their road to success.

There are three main areas in which a coach can help in your personal life. First, she/he can **help you stay on track** and help you prioritize to meet your goals. This can involve daily, brief check-ins about your plans, how to accomplish them, making sure they are small and manageable, and help you get back on track when you get off. Women with ADD have a great deal of trouble choosing from all the myriad ideas in their heads. On top of the ADD difficulties all the social expectations present many dilemmas. All these variables can seem to be of equal weight. A coach can help a woman bring a few tasks to the forefront. This takes practice. It can be very helpful to sit down for a few minutes every day with your coach to help you pull this together.

Next, your coach can help you see your successes by being supportive, almost a **cheerleader**, helping you keep that balance. As I said, a person with ADD can have sudden losses of perspective and a coach can help her regain her balance. Thirdly, a coach can be right in your house to help you **maintain systems,** put papers away, getting to all the stuff that you hate: that boring, repetitive filing, paying bills, balancing the checkbook or going through papers.

Remember to use the coach to keep the focus on yourself, not just on household stuff or processing materials for other members of the family. Use this coach for yourself and use this opportunity to move toward your personal goals as well as take care of other obligations.

There are now organizations training and matching up people with coaches, such as the *National Coaching Association*, which publishes *Coaching Matters* (reference in back of book). Their goal is to match ADD adults who want to be coached with those wanting to coach others. There are also associations of professional organizers to help get you organized but find someone to help you maintain systems, not just set them up. Then there are informal coaches, friends, acquaintances, paid assistants—anyone who is accepting, non-judgmental, calm, and organized and can help you think through what you want to accomplish and gently keep you focused.

You may need to try a few people before you work out the process, since at first you may not know what works for you. Don't let that deter you. This is often not expensive; you may even trade services. You can do this with a buddy system, where you both decide you're going to do a task and call each other to check in at the beginning and the end of the agreed period.

It's important to understand why someone wouldn't take advantage of having a coach. The shame of having someone come in your house and see what you've been living with often can prevent a woman from taking advantage of a coach. This is true even if money is not an issue and even if someone willing to help is available. It can bring up tremendous feelings that have to be confronted.

For example, a client told me that her best friend volunteered to come over to her house to help her organize. The woman rejected this idea for months, but after counseling and working through some of these feelings she finally said yes. The embarrassment about having people see the way she lived, had greatly impacted her life and relationships for years, preventing her from having friends over as well as paid help or babysitters. This in turn had even influenced her career decisions. At first, having her friend there helping her was agonizing for her. She felt in a "one down" position. But then she started reciprocating by taking care of her friend's house while the friend was out of town. She gradually became desensitized, allowed her to help with some of the tasks that were easy for the friend and very difficult for her. The combination of reciprocation and desensitization helped this woman work through these feelings, making her feel in control by implementing these choices in her life.

In an article I wrote for *Coaching Matters* I discussed the strong feelings that often arise in coaching. Vulnerable feelings come up in the process of working with a coach because you are confronting lost dreams, lost opportunities and mistakes, with each new pile uncovered. Often an ADD person will become very emotional in a coaching session. If a coach works with a couple, their dynamics change with the addition of this neutral third person. This allows the couple to confront issues they aren't able to alone. Coaching works very well with a professional counselor in the picture so that the individuals can take the feelings that arise in coaching back to counseling sessions to work through. The coach, on the other hand, fills a need the counselor can't, by going into the home where many of these feelings are triggered and can be confronted.

Single Women

Sometimes women take a long time to let people see their lives. It's especially difficult, if you're living alone, to maintain this kind of structure for yourself. It's extremely helpful to get external stimulation and structure from a coach. Situations such as being a single mom create a special set of responsibilities even for a person without ADD. This can make it difficult to have to negotiate with a person with whom you are not intimate about these difficulties. In fact, if you have a "significant other," you can turn that negotiation into part of your courtship and your evaluation of each other, about task division and living together.

A single woman without any structure or help may have fewer responsibilities at home, but she also has no markers to stay on track or structure with. A woman with children has many responsibilities, but without children has less structure. Each situation has its own dilemmas. In each case, you need a coach or somebody to help you stay on track .

When a Professional Counselor Can Be a Coach

A professional counselor can do this kind of structuring and coaching for you, especially at the beginning, if you don't have someone else in your life who is willing to learn to do this. Even with a professional counselor, though, it's important for you to maintain control, and avoid somebody "assigning" you tasks _they_ think are important. Someone to help you pull out a few small steps to focus on, is very helpful. When you get bogged down, you can then see what you wanted to do that week, or that day.

SPRING CLEANING THE INTERNAL WORLD

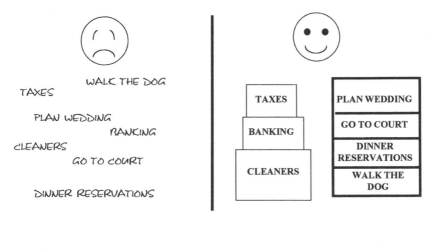

Spring Cleaning the Internal World

This picture, Spring Cleaning the Internal World, illustrates what some people have found helpful in bringing order to an internal world that often seems chaotic. They may use images such as pulling down the shades in order to block out other thoughts or wrapping up less important concerns in boxes and putting them back on the shelves. They may take these down one at time to open them up as they need them. At first all the options seem equally important and can be very confusing. A coach or counselor can help you mentally box them up and prioritize what's important. Then you can make a plan of action, always taking small steps. On the left side of the diagram everything seems of equal importance, disorganized and messy inside; on the right side, the whole picture feels much more ordered and structured, and much less overwhelming.

The Deeper Level: Changing the Tasks

Cutting, and Altering

We've looked at Rebalancing and Dividing up tasks, both internally and externally. Now the third and deepest level of restructuring is to actually cut, alter, really rethink and often let go of the way you've always done things. *This means simplifying, eliminating and redesigning the roles, rules, and traditions often held sacred in families for years without being re-examined, even though they no longer work.*

Too Many Tasks

Sometimes there are just too many chores to go around. Both people may be working outside the home. You might have children. If there are too many tasks, or those that you have are too complicated, rethink them. Is the way you do them too time-consuming? Do they use up too much emotional and physical energy? You probably don't have to do all that you're currently doing. You might be doing what's expected of you, but not having any fun or recreation. You might not be socializing enough, not having enough nourishing or romantic time with your partner. Everyone needs time for fun, for friends, for extended family—and time just to enjoy your life, doing whatever you like to do.

If there's just no way that you can meet all your obligations, you might now have to restructure your life in a deeper way. Up until now we have discussed re-ordering your life. Think now in terms of omitting tasks or changing the requirements. You may have to challenge areas in your family, religious, or cultural life that you previously thought were untouchable or unchangeable. How do you handle traditions that have never been challenged before? Sometimes they've been held sacred for many generations. These include holidays, annual rituals (such as getting the children ready for school in September), or even daily routines. What obligations in place for a long time can be rethought? Are there any obligations that you can eliminate, change, or simplify?

To achieve these changes you will have to communicate in deeper ways than you ever have before, because these alterations will affect many other people.

Rules, Roles, Rituals, Traditions

I'd suggest sitting down again with your family with a list titled Rules, Roles, Rituals, Traditions, Holidays, Structures, and Obligations. Together try to come up with what those mean in your family. We have been talking about couples, but, of course, if you don't have a partner, it's just as important for you to think about this in terms of your extended family, your friends or even just yourself. You might need to change some of the important things in your life, or those significant to someone else. Maybe you don't want to do this, or maybe you do! (Think of that yearly family vacation that might be a nightmare!) Too many rules, roles and rituals stop you from fully engaging in life. Changing the "sacred" things in life doesn't come without a price, however. Giving up traditions entails going through a grief cycle. It's upsetting to think that you can't do whatever you want because of your disorder, but you can do other things wonderfully well. You'll learn that there's another side to life, different from what you've always done.

You're really not denying your traditions or giving them up but rather supporting your strengths in freeing your energy for what you most want to do. You don't want to dissipate the newfound energy you have now that you are on medication.

Changing traditions doesn't mean giving up nourishing activities. Remember the Priority Pies. You want to restructure to meet your needs, to get the desired pieces of the pies, not to just get rid of tasks.

Rethinking How and What You Do

In terms of simplifying or eliminating tasks, consider these kind of questions and alter them to fit your own situation.

Do you always have to go to the grocery store?

Can you order or make arrangements by phone?

Can you have items delivered?

Can you hire an assistant, a college girl, perhaps, to do some errands—Pick up the cleaning, take your children after school for an hour or two? This can take a great load off you.

Must you always go the department store to buy clothes, or could you do more through catalogs and shopping networks? Can you buy more of similar items, so that when you lose your socks, you'll still have matching pairs?

There are many books with suggestions on how to eliminate clutter or eliminate junk mail. Stop subscribing to so many magazines or newsletters.

Can you have baskets with big labels for mail or keys? Put up big, brightly-colored labels in your house (if you can get over feeling self-conscious about it). Some people use only hooks in their closets and rooms instead of hangers. You can line your walls with cork boards if mere notepads are not sufficient for the number of ideas you generate.

Prepare for the fact that you have ADD. Memory devices, beepers that remind you of appointments, are strategies that can simplify life.

Do you have to do Mothers' Day exactly the same way every year? Can you take your mother to a play instead of entertaining?

Must you have in-laws over for brunch at a certain time every month? Can you take them out instead?

Can Grandma buy some of the school supplies necessary? Set up a new tradition that might be fun.

Can your husband be the one to call the school when you need information?

People who want special things at the grocery store can make their own trips if they're old enough.

Do you have to cook that big dinner on Friday night even though you've worked all day and you're overwhelmed and exhausted? (Do "take out" food on Friday night or order in.)

Do you have to give the most elaborate theme birthday party in town?

More Talking

Start out at your weekly family meetings discussing these rituals in depth. It can be fun to talk about multi-generational issues, how these traditions got started, why it's "the way it's always been done." Talking about the past takes some of the focus and blame out of the present, helping you understand what you both bring to this marriage (if you are married). What are the meanings of these traditions to each? Discuss first how you're going to maintain your new plan and write a simple one down. What's the first step you need to take as a couple? Discuss any internal barriers that keep you from making these changes. Some couples take a step forward, and then the extended family comes over and makes disparaging comments about what the man is doing for the woman. This sends the couple right back to the way things always were, even though the new way was working for them. What kind of family-of-origin messages might be interfering with your abilities.

You can use the Task Division Chart to structure the discussions I've outlined in this chapter. The best way to use this is to make copies, each of you filling it out alone and later using it as a basis for discussion and comparison. In the first column, write down a few areas you think are the most important to work on. Then just put either your initials or a check mark under the columns that apply to your willingness or ability to do these tasks, either alone or together. After all your discussions, you may decide that an outside person may be most appropriate. In the last column, indicate if you feel that the task should be eliminated, simplified, or drastically changed instead.

Taking Small Steps

We've covered a lot of ground in this restructuring discussion. But go slowly, both individually and as a couple. Don't set yourselves up for failure by taking on too much at one time.

Tasks or Areas of Conflict	Able/Willing Alone	Able/Willing To Do Together	Not Able, But Will Be There	Outside Person	Change Task

Counselors can support you, investigate with you, be curious with you if you run up against barriers. Counselors should not just deliver rewards and punishment, oversuggest or be demeaning (gold stars etc.) but examine points where ADD meets resistance and work through it. Resistance has many forms: internal pictures, relationship patterns, communication patterns, shame, self-esteem, depression, primary planning difficulties. Counseling should identify barriers that keep you from restructuring, and not set up a situation in which you disappoint another significant person, frustrating each of you. You don't want to wind up in a position of self-deprecation.

The Rest of the Story ... Jodi

At the beginning of the chapter we saw changes that Jodi made after diagnosis. Though these are good and necessary, they may not go deep enough or far enough to help her integrate all her experience. They also may not be enough to allow her family to come to a new level of reorganization to accommodate Jodi's ADD. The entire family will begin to thrive when they can break out of their old patterns of relating and thinking about Jodi.

Jodi's mom has been coming over every week to help her. It's hard for Jodi to deal with the anger she feels when her mom says things like: "I don't know how you can live like this! What kind of example is this setting for your daughter? Actually, I don't completely believe in this ADD stuff. I think you're still not trying hard enough." Both her husband and her mother say these kinds of things to her: "Why are you still like this? I thought that with the medication you wouldn't be like this any more. Now you are going to therapy, we are both helping, you have a housecleaner and it's still not enough!"

If you get stuck in the division of tasks you may need to renegotiate your relationships, often with professional counseling. You need to work with your family, your friends, to set limits in a non-defensive way, to set up an environment that works for you without pushing others away. You need to find ways to communicate with your partner that allows you to maintain your self-respect and equality in the relationship, while considering his needs as well.

In the next chapters we'll look further at how to make your communication more effective and assertive in the process of re-structuring.

CHAPTER SEVENTEEN

Renegotiating Your Relationships

I N ORDER TO go further in restructuring your life you often need the communication tool which I call renegotiating. This involves renegotiation of relationships with your family, extended family, friends; learning how to set limits in a non-defensive way. You'll learn to protect yourself in healthy ways in order to set up your environment to work for you and others.

Toxic Help

How do you get assistance from your spouse or partner, or from anyone in your life—your mother, your friend, or even a professional helper without getting what I call toxic help? The Toxic Help symbol represents

help that is harmful even when given by someone in the process of helping you. It's difficult to reject the negative words while still communicating appreciation and attempting to move toward structuring a helpful relationship. You may feel that any limits you set on negative messages from other people may be a threat to continue getting the help you need. You might think, "How could I be so ungrateful, to criticize somebody who's helping me?" It's important to separate out "help" from "not-help." The initial period after diagnosis is an especially vulnerable time because you're trying to build your self-esteem and focus on your strengths. But you must not allow yourself to be put down in order to get help. That's too high a price to pay.

You require self-respect, but that's difficult when you feel so vulnerable and part of you still believes the negative attributions are true. When helpers comment on your difficulty with tasks, you still are easily triggered into those old feelings of shame and incompetency. It is important for you to begin to change the way you measure success. You may have difficulty with tasks, but the new basis for measuring your success is not how good you are at doing those things, but how well you're getting it taken care of.

Even though friends and family members may not understand your ADD, you don't necessarily want to walk away from relationships that are potentially valuable in many ways. You may decide eventually that you have to, but through renegotiation try to keep and nurture what's good in the relationships, if there is potential there.

Toxic help can come from a parent, a partner, or a paid person in subtle, judgmental ways when you don't stay on track, if you don't meet your stated goals. Messages such as those delivered by Jodi's mother, such as, "You are living like a child," or "What a bad parent you are," or "I thought you were over this," do not contribute anything of help or value. Others may try to motivate you with behavior-modification, awards, or stars, as if you were a child or even worse, a dog. They might set up goals for you to accomplish that they've created for you, or, in other cases, might attribute psychological reasons for your difficulties in meeting these goals. All these things don't work for adults with ADD, instead making them feel diminished and misunderstood, and feeling as if they have disappointed somebody important to them.

Setting Limits

It is important to learn to communicate that what someone is doing is not helpful. Learn how to tell them that even though you appreciate their efforts and intentions, it would be more effective not to spice up the help with these kinds of comments. Be specific about the kind of the communication you'd like, with examples.

The "I-messages," basic building blocks of communication, are essential here. You can say, for example, "I appreciate that you're helping me. It's a great relief to have you sweating through these things with me.

But at the same time, I find myself becoming somewhat depressed and anxious and even angry sometimes when I hear myself being put down like that." If you're close to the person, you might go on to say that it brings back a lot of bad feelings. "Since I know you want to be helpful, it would be great for you to encourage me and focus on how well I'm doing in general, or on some of my positive attributes. Because I'm not always sure how to get what I need it would be helpful if I were more control of the way we're going about this, or at the least, to work as a team."

This kind of working relationship is not always possible with a family member who brings a lot of resentment from the past. In that case, it's better not to have that person with you, especially at the beginning. Perhaps later, when they better understand the ADD and what's helpful, they will be able to work collaboratively with you in more effective ways. After you feel more comfortable in your new skin and are better able to communicate in a non-defensive way, you will be able to say things in a less reactive and clear way.

What you don't want is to be in a situation of supposed help with either a professional or a family member that recreates old feelings of frustration, of disappointing people, or that you're doing something wrong. You don't want to feel that you're lazy if you haven't stayed on track that week, or that you are deliberately sabotaging these efforts, or that you're somehow still a child. You need someone helpful and encouraging, who notices your successes until you are able to hold onto them yourself.

When people get diagnosed with ADD, sometimes it takes a long time before they can hold on to the idea of themselves as having strengths. When they make mistakes or are confronted with their difficulties, it's easy for them to fall back into a "bad me" position. Even after diagnosis, people sometimes still feel they have a character defect, put themselves down and attribute it to a lack of motivation. Often professional facilitation is very helpful at this point. Eventually, when you have had enough positive reflections and enough successes and experiences, you'll be able to remember them yourself and build on them. It will then be much easier to attract and construct *helpful* help for yourself.

Globally Dismissed

When someone knows you have ADD, you might find yourself being treated more like a child or being overprotected. More importantly, you may be thought of subtly as less-competent in a global way, instead of having some specific areas of weakness. I call this being "globally dismissed." Many clients have reported over-solicitousness by other people who know they have ADD or not being referred certain tasks because the ADD is misunderstood.

For example, an ADD woman had trouble in prioritizing. Her husband sat down and helped her each morning to pull out the few things she wanted to do and prioritize them into a schedule. Other than this difficulty and other kinds of organizational difficulties, she was competent and intelligent and could plan very well.

(A lot of people think that ADD people don't plan. Many can plan very well; they can have great organizational abilities in terms of seeing the whole picture. They can plan a grand scheme out to minute details; it's just the carrying-out of those details that's difficult for them).

This couple was preparing to make a cross-country move that required much planning and coordinating. The woman had her responsibilities and the man had his, but without even realizing it (until it was discussed in counseling) he was taking over more and more decisions. He made decisions in her area of the division of tasks, and he didn't consult her. He undid her decisions. He realized he was dismissing her unconsciously, feeling she was incompetent across the boards because she had specific areas of difficulty.

When dividing up tasks, it is important to keep a sense of self-respect, and not to insist on dividing things up 50/50 in terms of sheer numbers. There might be a lot of qualitative help that an ADD person can give back in terms of emotional support, creative help, conceptual help, or other areas beside the actual task division.

"I Can Only Do Two Things Well"

As you see in the Monet's picture of a woman surrounded by her beautiful garden, Monet said, "I can only do two things well—garden and paint." This point so strongly expresses the narrow band of abilities that people with ADD have. They might not do a wide range of things as well as another, but do have a few areas in which they do wonderfully well.

Domination, Dependency and Other Fears

In dividing up tasks, as we have discussed, renegotiation often brings up a lot of issues around power and control that are present to some extent in every relationship. With ADD this can sneak in and have a strong effect, play an important role without you recognizing it. This might happen where the spouse or partner who is able to do daily tasks in a more-organized fashion starts to feel dominant in the relationship, exert-

"I only know how to do two things.
Garden and paint."

Claude Monet

ing more and more control. Slowly power can slip away from the ADD partner. The woman with ADD can start to feel less and less self-esteem, and move into feelings of:

"I'd better not rock the boat."

"He's doing all these things for me."

"I'd better keep my mouth shut."

"I'd better not express my feelings."

"How can I tell him I'm angry when he's helped for me so much?"

"If I don't watch it, I can turn him away."

"How far can I push this whole thing?"

"Eventually, he'll get sick of me and leave me."

"I'm not a good partner anyway."

Many women have these kinds of fears of being alone or being abandoned, that turn into dependency and push away feelings of anger or setting healthy limits in order to get the kind of help and support that they need. I've seen women stay in emotionally-abusive relationships because they feel they can't be completely independent and take care of everything that they need to on a daily level. Of course, many women feel this kind of strain, but ADD women with these kinds of daily problems experience this to a greater extent and that impacts their decisions to stay in a relationship. Because these women know how easily they get overwhelmed and exhausted, they might not be able to work a nine-to-five job in a traditional way. Like all women, but to a greater extent, ADD women express fears about being old and alone, or have more bag-lady fantasies, it seems.

What they need is learn to say is, "I'm really appreciative of everything that you're doing, and you're really helping me, but I still find I am angry about this other issue." To do this often takes professional facilitation.

The Four Steps to Renegotiating Relationships

As you saw in the Four Step Validation chart that we looked at when we discussed the workplace, the four main things to remember when renegotiating your relationships are: validation, negotiation, appreciation and reciprocation. When someone is helping you, first validate the importance to you of that person's feelings, that person's needs, of the relationship, and the importance of the issue for the other person. For instance, you might say to your partner, "I understand your need to have people over to the house. I know it's important for you that I come out with you and socialize. But that's difficult for me for these reasons. We need to find a way for you to be able to socialize without me sometimes, or, if you want people over, for you to take charge and make more of the arrangements." Or you could say, "We can socialize together outside the home." Trying to find a way to look for common ground is what negotiation is all about.

The focus is on problem-solving, not on you as the "problem" to be solved. In every relationship, both partners have different needs, but with ADD it's often more extreme. Find a healthy way to protect yourself and validate and honor your own ADD but also to legitimize and validate the needs of your partner, so neither one is sacrificed. This involves a real understanding and acceptance of ADD by both you and your partner. Each partner understands their own strengths and weaknesses as well as their partner's and tries to make this combination work. They have to come up with solutions that are not like other people's solutions, but that doesn't matter as long as they work on them as a team. This can't involve black-and-white thinking, but rather becoming solution-oriented and generating lots of options. Again, this can require professional facilitation, especially at first, to be able to maintain a non-blaming stance as you're trying to problem-solve and beginning to really listen to each other.

The next thing after negotiation, when someone helps you with actual tasks is, obviously, to appreciate them verbally. After that, reciprocation can keep the balance so that the ADD person is not just a recipient of help, or becoming identified as the person who is causing the problems in the family. Reciprocation can take into account all of a woman's strengths. These might not be in the same areas as the original task that was done, but she can reciprocate in other areas.

Looking for Common Ground

We'll now go into a little more depth on the subject of negotiation. I offer a script that I wrote for practicing negotiation that can be very useful.

When Jimmy Carter mediates internationally he looks for common ground between two countries. He wants to find what they have in common in terms of goals. He isn't looking for their differences, or for someone to blame. This is not easy. It takes a lot of practice, so I've given you a fictional scenario that might happen with an ADD couple sitting down to one of these negotiation sessions. I suggest you do it for fun with your partner. Read through the script together and then substitute your own area that you need to work out. You can do this time and time again with different issues that arise. Eventually, you won't need the script, but it's an easy model to follow when you are trying to problem-solve a specific area. Start with something fairly concrete at first and then move into more difficult areas later.

These are the negotiating steps: 1) Really hear what the other person wants, 2) Say that back to them, and then 3) Take in what you like about that suggestion, but also what doesn't work for you; then suggest your own solution. 4) Repeat the process with the first person, moving through to some kind of workable solution that, at least on a trial basis, is acceptable. Realize that it might not work but that you will come back to the negotiating table without blaming each other.

First decide what issue you'd like to work on. After that, if you feel stuck or if you need more information before coming to a decision, decide what the next step should be. Who is going to be responsible for it? Mark it down in your calendars and how it will be followed through. After every session, follow with verbal appreciation and offers of reciprocation. Set this up so that you have fun with it. Do it over a glass of wine or over ice cream, or with a walk afterwards, or in the bathtub, or when the kids aren't there.

The Script

Non-ADD: This is what I propose. How does this work for you?

Since this is my area of strength and not yours, why don't I just take over the checkbook for you?

ADD: I like the part of not having to deal with this since it's so difficult for me, but what doesn't work is the feeling that you will have all the control. I will feel like a little kid and may get resentful. How about if we do it together?

Non-ADD: That may work, but it sounds a little vague for me. I feel more comfortable when things are clearer. How about since I have an ability to do things regularly, I will set up a schedule; for instance, to look at finances every Sunday night. You will be able to depend on that and since structure is important for you, this may be helpful for you as well. You could come into my office at that time and sit with me as I do this so you will feel more in control and won't be in the dark.

ADD: That sounds good. How about if you remind me, though, since I'll probably be so caught up in something else. Since it bores me, even though I definitely want to do it, I have a feeling it's going to be hard for me to get there.

Non-ADD: I don't mind reminding you, but I don't want this to turn into nagging and resentment.

ADD: OK. How about if you remind me just once or twice, even with a Post-it or a message on the phone a day or two before. Then if I don't come, the consequence is that I won't know what's going on but at least it will get done.

Non-ADD: And then I won't have to feel as though I have to make you come to this meeting. It's all agreed to in advance.

ADD: Sounds good. Thanks for trying this out and working this out. Why don't we see if there's something I can do that's difficult for you?

Non-ADD: Let's both get out our appointment books and write this in. I'll even pencil it in two days before to remind you. I'm really glad we sat down and discussed this. It's really been bothering me. Let's see if this works.

Friends, Families and Social Obligations

In addition to renegotiating at work, and with your partner, when you eliminate or change rituals, it also has a great effect on friendships and extended family. The way you set even healthy limits affects other people, and you'll find they have reactions. It will be important to learn how to communicate these things in a way that validates the importance of your relationship and also tells others what you need to have a good relationship without moving away from them. When asked by others for a contribution, you might take a few minutes to say, "Let me think about it. I'll call you back tomorrow." Don't feel you have to make a decision right then, because that's when you're going to feel more pressure. Give yourself time to say, "I need to think about the best way to handle this. I do want to contribute, but I don't know if I would be effective at this time because of my other commitments." Stating your dilemma at this point is very effective. Then get back to them. Write things down so that you will be able to remember them in your next conversation. You might try to come up with solutions that aren't all-or-nothing. You might offer to donate money or clothes, or ask them to call you next year. You could say, "I can't donate time to go on a campaign around the neighborhood, but if you give me flyers, for example, I'll hand them out at work." Or, "I'm really not good at doing these mailings, but I wouldn't mind making ten calls."

The next area in which women get in trouble in relationships is a result of feeling bombarded by too much stimulation. People without hyperactivity especially feel that they have to get away from family gatherings or parties. They feel overloaded or exhausted and they can't keep up. They might have difficulty carrying on a good conversation, trying to think of what to say in the middle of so much activity. What many people do in this situation, as we talked about before, is to mysteriously walk away. They retreat to another room or just not show up for these kinds of events, or become quiet or upset or withdrawn. All these responses give signals to other people that you don't care about them. They don't know that you're having such a hard time or why. You don't have to go around screaming ADD all the time, but you can just explain you get overwhelmed and overloaded, that you need some down time and you'll be back in a little while. You'd like to take a walk by yourself.

If you do want to talk to somebody, you might say, "I really do want to talk to you, but I find that I can't block out the noise here. Why don't we find a quiet space?" In response to a party invitation, you might say, "I get overwhelmed by parties, but I really would like to talk to you in more depth. Why don't we make a date on Friday?" If you go to an event, give yourself permission to leave early when you're worn down, knowing that you want to go and connect to people, but that you want to leave before you stop enjoying the situation. Set it up, think it through in advance, so you don't feel anxious. Plan for your ADD.

Women with ADD sometimes have a difficult situation when they are in the position of staying in the homes of friends or relatives or people they don't know well. Because they don't have their own place to stay organized they are unable to arrange and maintain their things. They are self-conscious about their disorganization, they feel bombarded, they don't have enough down time, and they get overwhelmed.

An ADD woman needs to be able to make other arrangements that will work for her, if she can. Either don't stay as long, or stay at a hotel if you can afford it, but make sure to set it up in advance. Don't put yourself constantly into situations that are working counter to your ADD because it does affect your relationships with other people.

That requires saying no, setting limits, and describing your needs.

But I'm No Good in the Kitchen

An ADD woman will be in a group situation where she's just not comfortable. This could be a social event involving a lot of domestic, routine tasks, and might involve food preparation, setting the table, washing dishes or participating in other domestic activities. In addition to having difficulty with the distraction and bombardment inherent in these group activities, women have difficulty figuring out how to stay focused and what to do in these unstructured, unclear situations. These can bring up a great deal of anxiety because the woman with these problems feels great shame when these so-called failures at the basic job for women are made public for all to see. This often leads to avoidance of these gatherings, unfortunately causing the loss of important relationships and opportunities.

Instead, these women may have to learn to ask for directions, or to find informal coaches for situations where everybody else seems to know what to do. They need to state clearly what they would be able to do. "If you tell me exactly how you'd like me to help you, give me the instructions, I'd be happy to help. I know everybody has their own way of doing this." Ask for specifics and say what's difficult for you. Always try to focus on positives and what you can do well, instead of putting yourself down and highlighting your insecurities. Validate the other person's importance to you. Always keep your own sense of what your corresponding strengths are. "I'm not good at chopping vegetables, but I'm great at organizing games for the kids."

Disconnecting

Learn how to touch base with people that you're disconnecting from. One woman said that she sat in her room, falling more and more into a depression, counting the number of invitations and notes that she hadn't responded to, all the people who had fallen through the cracks. It's important to find a way to touch base, even if you only have a few minutes. You can find ways that don't take a lot of time. Fax or e-mail these days, or a message on the answering machine, will let someone know you are thinking of them, that you can't follow up on everything right now, but it's a way to not disconnect. Many women, after a long disconnection never see the person again. They avoid them and let them go because it's too painful to face what they fear will be reprimands or critical statements, bringing back memories of these difficulties.

Earlier in the book we looked at the chart called Secondary Effects that showed the kind of misinterpretation cycle that can happen in these kinds of situations. We see a better outcome in the bottom half of this chart. When her ADD symptoms emerge at this later point, when she has more self-acceptance and understanding of herself, and her ADD, a woman doesn't compound her ADD problems by how she behaves in reaction. Instead of avoiding people because she fears they will think she's weird or stupid, or because she fears a reprimand, she may talk about it in a simple way or talk to herself in a supportive way that allows her to continue to stay in relationships. At this point she no longer adds to the ADD complications with these extra layers of emotionally distressing relationship difficulties.

SECONDARY EFFECTS

REPEAT THE CYCLE   SYMPTOMS OCCUR   SHAME, EMBARRASSMENT

PERCEIVE ADD AS SHAMEFUL   PROTECTIVE MANEUVERS

WITHDRAWAL

BLAME THE SYMPTOMS RATHER THAN BEHAVIOR   WITHDRAWAL BY OTHERS

WHEN THE FEELING OF SHAME DIMINISHES, THE CYCLE IS BROKEN

LAUGH   EXPLAIN

STOP BEING LONELY   MOVE TOWARD PEOPLE

©Sari Solden, 1994

Emotional Support

You might not be able to get through all these issues without professional facilitation at first, especially if either partner has a backlog of interpersonal patterns that are hard to break, a history of resentment, or a background of communication patterns that are not working.

How will the non-ADD partner get extra emotional support so he won't get burned out and resentful? How will the ADD partner get support from others so she doesn't always have to depend on the non-ADD partner, especially so she won't feel so lonely? Broadening out her base of support will help her feel more understood while she's going through the period right after diagnosis. She doesn't want to burn out her partner on one hand, and she doesn't want to feel so alone on the other hand.

There might be a lot of hurt and resentment on both sides of the partnership, strong triggers beyond the ADD difficulties. Professional facilitation might highlight certain ADD behaviors more clearly and the non-ADD corresponding reactions. What is the meaning of caretaking to the non-ADD person, especially if he can't get over some of the resentful feelings? For the ADD individual, what does it mean to have to be taken care of? For the non-ADD partner, what does it mean to be ignored sometimes, or feeling that promises are sometimes broken? For both of them, what abandonment issues are being triggered? You'll see whether some of these are really symbolic of other, earlier issues for you. Professional facilitation can be helpful for getting a handle on this and working through it.

As we go to the last chapter, we'll see that even though a woman may have worked through many of these communication patterns, divided up the household tasks, she may still feel stuck. This might necessitate a serious look at what image you and your partner may be holding on to. Are either one of you insisting on a culturally approved ideal image of what a mature, successful, competent woman should looks like, waiting for that time to arrive before you begin to enjoy yourself or your partnership?

CHAPTER EIGHTEEN

Redefining Your Self-Image

A T SOME POINT in the process of restructuring and renegotiating, you will have to redefine your image of yourself, and both you and your partner will ultimately have to redefine your image of your partnership. Your family is not going to look like everyone else's; your partnership is not going to be like everybody else's. No matter how good you feel about yourself, even if you've worked through a lot of these issues, if you're still waiting for the day when you're going to look like a non-ADD person, you will constantly be set up for failure. This is what can stall your progress and prevent you from taking that last step toward an exciting, fulfilling life together as a couple or as an individual—a creative, interesting, satisfying life.

The Partnership

If the non-ADD partner finds he's stuck, it might be because he is not moving through his own grief cycle. We talked about the grief cycle for the ADD partner, but I've also written one for the non-ADD partner because they're often the lost person in this system. They are not moving through the grief cycle as rapidly, they're not getting help for this from support groups, and often they're not as involved because it's not happening to them. Being stuck in this grief cycle is about more than grief. It is about working through your feelings of loss and anger, toward acceptance. But it's also ultimately to accept and value your partner and not merely to accept, but to celebrate them. Non-ADD partners often object to this phrase, "celebrating your partner." You are celebrating the person, not celebrating the difficulties. You're accepting the person, not necessarily liking or enjoying the difficulties. In the end, though, you must on some level celebrate the person that you're with to make your life work.

Once non-ADD partners works through this, they realize that the ADD is not being done to them; they understand this isn't a passive-aggressive act or a failing as a mature person. Additionally, they realize that they don't have total responsibility for the other person and that it's not necessary to sacrifice their own needs. They're able to let go of a lot of frustrating and angry feelings when they work through this grief cycle.

As an ADD woman you are going to have to work through this to understand that you can be a wonderful, contributing member of a partnership. Even if you already accept yourself as a mature and whole woman, sometimes it's still a struggle to accept yourself as a good partner. In addition to being a successful, mature, competent woman you are also a loving, exciting, interesting contributing partner, even if you don't fit the cultural mold. This means both you and your partner seeing you as a whole woman.

The subject of your brain and its particular strengths and weaknesses is something you and your partner have to become comfortable and familiar with. Understanding that each of our personal biochemical makeups influence our behaviors can provide an additional "lens" through which to view our relationships. Validating each person's individual variations, strengths, and weakness would be helpful for any couple, ADD or not. Because people involved in ADD partnerships have to squarely face these issues, though, they have an opportunity to reach a higher level of marital communication, acceptance, and understanding.

Going through a cycle of grief allows the Non-ADD partner to appreciate and embrace the ADD partner as a whole human being and to cherish the unusual mix she is.

Grief Cycle for the Non-ADD partner

It's important to know these stages in order to understand it's natural to feel these feelings. Even more, it's essential to go through them in order to work through your feelings so your relationship can begin to work for both of you.

Denial

Even if you accept the ADD diagnosis, you still have difficulty accepting the neurobiological explanation for behaviors. You deny the degree of impact this will continue to have in your life. You deny the kind of change the whole family will need to make, both physically and emotionally, to live successfully with ADD

Anger

You personalize the ADD behavior as directed at you. At some level, you still feel it's "being done to you." Even if you get past this, you feel anger that this is happening and anger at the impact it is having on all parts of your life. You feel resentment and begin to blame and devalue your partner. You can have feelings of betrayal; this was not the life you envisioned. You may feel embarrassment around other people, become focused on changing her/his behavior and feel everything revolves around her/him.

Bargaining

She/he will take the medication and go to group and things will be more normal. You will read some books and attend some meetings and figure out how to help her/him change; or you will just take over to get some sense of control.

Depression

This situation doesn't appear to be as easily controlled as you had hoped. You feel overwhelmed, depleted, used, out of control. The demands and pressures increase and you feel hopeless. You even start to consider the viability of staying in this relationship. You have forgotten all the strengths and value of your partner and feel great loss over what you had expected in this marriage. You become overfocused on her/his problems. You feel no partnership, no way to work things out together. You feel responsible for everything. You are isolated as a couple from friends and family who don't have these kinds of problems. You are embarrassed and feel increasingly isolated from your spouse.

Acceptance

As you work through these emotions, there comes a shift in outlook. Expectations become more realistic; areas of deficit become more circumscribed so they don't affect the good areas of the relationship.

Together you learn to control areas of problems. The ADD is external-
ized, it does not define the ADD partner. You still get frustrated and
angry at times but the symptoms do not feel directed at you. Positions
become less polarized as you and your partner become more solution-
oriented. You begin to relate again as peers with areas of strengths and
difficulties. Expectations of both partners become more realistic. When
you have worked through grief and loss and accept that you are different
from non-ADD families you form a different concept of what a mature,
loving, valuable partner can be. You combine areas of strength to form a
partnership, finding solutions, minimizing effects and accessing
strengths. To do this, both partners must agree to that common goal.

Your Core Self-Concept

As you see in the Self-Concept illustration, what happens at a certain
point in redefining is that the ADD woman embraces or incorporates
into her idea of herself all her strengths and difficulties, even though
none of them completely define her. Through professional facilitation
and after a long period of support from other people, a woman begins to
integrate these ideas as she works through the grief cycle. The picture on
the left shows all the difficulties and strengths, all the feelings, clumped
together with the sense that "this is all I am." After a long, positive
process, the core feeling about herself starts to separate from the feelings
about the ADD—the sense of self becomes more cohesive and stable. An
individual is able to reach out and say, "Boy, I have a lot of big gaps here.
It's a long stretch, but I can now hold onto the idea that I have great
abilities as well as difficulties that are way out of line with my strengths,
and they are all part of me. I must remember both sides and not deny or
minimize my difficulties or deny or minimize my strengths. I need to
figure out how to "work both sides of the room."

"That shame that I used to feel when something ADD-like happens,
doesn't completely disappear but it doesn't define me any longer. I'm
sensitive to it, but I know why I'm being triggered. I've planned for it. I
know how to work with it. It's external to me now." Professional facilitation can with this because, as I've said before, it takes a long time before
an individual gets to this point. The therapist can hold onto this idea of
the integrated woman until it can be incorporated into the way the
woman sees herself. When this happens it will color all her choices and
decisions from then on—what jobs she's going to apply for, what relationships she will pursue. Before that time, her self-image did not allow
her to see opportunities or to see that she had choices.

When her ADD symptoms used to emerge she used to panic and

REPAIR OF SELF-CONCEPT IN TREATMENT OF ADD

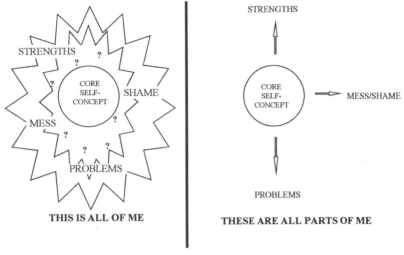

THIS IS ALL OF ME   THESE ARE ALL PARTS OF ME

berate herself, become depressed or withdraw. Now when her ADD symptoms emerge, because of her improved self-image, understanding, and improved communication skills, she no longer initiates a negative downward cycle. Even when her ADD symptoms emerge, she is able to stay on course because she's not saying bad things to herself, she's not moving away from other people, and she's not closing her eyes to opportunities. She is moving toward her abilities because she knows how to build support and structure for herself to keep pace with her success. She's increasing her sense of control and choices. Most of all, she's not trying to be someone else. At the end of the road, it's not going to be a different person there. It will be her, but more revealed in her totality.

The Cycle of Success

The journey really ends, or a new dream begins, really, with a point that people get to that I call a new "Cycle of Success." A woman crosses a mysterious invisible line at some point and becomes proactive, having integrated the idea of ADD deeply into her identity. She is able without the same level of self-consciousness or shame to ask for necessary accommodations or personal help. Because she feels more secure, she is able to reveal more vulnerability. The shame doesn't disappear completely but she is able to take the necessary action in spite of these feelings. She then understands and can communicate that what she is asking for is not a luxury, or a special favor, not something she is trying to "get away with," but something she needs to make her life work.

Your life is now restructured, your communication is more effective, and you have redefined your self-image. After you have worked with these three R's, you balance your life more effectively. You have embraced this idea of ADD, taken it into your identity and have redefined what it means to be a successful woman in our society.

The goal of all ADD treatment, then, is to move through the grief cycle and then beyond it to a new cycle with a life of its own. After you've reached a stable level of acceptance, as a result of all the changes you've integrated into your life, a new momentum takes over. After you have crossed this line, you arrive at a new level of confidence. A new sense of strength there allows you to feel less vulnerable, less threatened, less endangered when ADD symptoms appear. Things don't always go well, of course, people don't always give you the help you ask for. Things don't always work out or happen magically, but there's a whole new mind-set of possibilities and hope, a new self-view. For the first time, there's an idea of, "Yes, I have these difficulties, but I'm also all these other things too. They're all part of me. Even though I do all I can to minimize the negative effects to other people, I'm through apologizing for who I am."

SUCCESS

The illustration "Success" shows what happens beyond the grief cycle, as you begin a new Cycle of Success.

Shame separates from your core feelings about yourself. You still sometimes feel shame, but it doesn't color your feelings about yourself, even when your ADD symptoms arise.

Unusual rather than defective. You now see yourself as unusual rather than defective. You have the same symptoms, but you almost (believe it or not!) start to enjoy them to a certain extent. You start to see yourself as an interesting sort of person with originality.

Creativity harnessed out of chaos. Instead of creativity gone wild, you start to direct and harness your creativity and turn it into productivity. You can imagine the possibilities that could result from directing and putting boundaries around all that strong creative energy. When this creative force is harnessed and directed, it feels exciting and satisfying instead of chaotic.

Communication becomes assertive. You've learned to state your needs

Shame separates from core

Unusual rather than defective

Creativity harnessed out of chaos

Communication becomes assertive

Energy returns

Self-talk changes, mood improves

Support easier to get

in a non-defensive, non-aggressive way. As your self-image changes and you lose the shame, you are able to set limits. When you're able to set limits, you're able to bring success to you. You understand that setting limits does not mean admitting you can't do something. You realize that a limit is a boundary, a way to increase your success. You're able to start protecting yourself in healthy ways, stating your needs, becoming solution-focused with other people through an increased sense of communication options.

Energy returns. You can just imagine, when you start to ask for help, your time and energy return. As a combined result of the needed help, the medication, and because the depletion and overload are under control you don't have the overwhelming sense of burden any more. You don't spending so much time hiding. When you have more help and a feeling of control the rest of your life becomes more regulated. You're sleeping, you're eating, and exercising more. You're more able to make time for entertainment or recreation and nourishing relationships. You're taking in energy from the work that you're doing or the activities you're involved in bring out more of your creativity and your strengths.

Self-talk changes, mood improves. Depression and anxiety aren't pulling you down. You don't go into a downward spiral when you make a mistake, making the situation worse. You recover your balance much

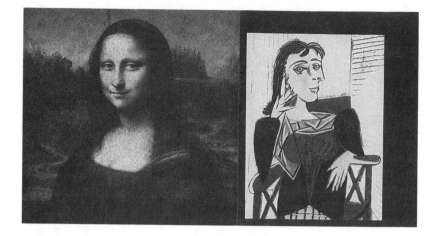

faster. You can separate out your neurological difficulties from your character, and you can figure out what you can control and what you can't.

Support is easier to get. When you can't get your work done because you're creating more than you can control you're going to find assistance. You know that you don't have a character defect. You have an image of yourself as a creative person who needs help to fill in some of the gaps. You know that you need coaching or structure or support. You know you need people to speak to you in a helpful way. You know you need to demand self-respect.

At some point it all crystallizes. You see yourself as a person with great creativity and ability who has organizational problems. That's all. You lose the shame; or if you don't lose it, you are able to act anyway.

I'd like to end by contrasting the Picasso portrait of a woman with the Mona Lisa. The Picasso presents a new image of what beauty is, one the woman with ADD can hold onto. This image can be a symbol to contrast with and to replace the image of a traditional model, portrayed by the Mona Lisa. You can see that they are both wonderful works of art, but they represent very different kinds of women. The calm, serene look of Mona Lisa is a beautiful, organized, stable kind of figure. But it's certainly different from this exciting, vibrant picture of Picasso's image of a woman, who portrays the ADD woman. Both are beautiful images, but very different. You can see that if the Picasso woman spent her life trying to be the Mona Lisa, it would be a setup for failure. That's why I describe the Picasso as a multifaceted woman, reflecting the concept of a diamond in the rough. It all comes together.

A woman of depth, of vision, moving and changing, surprising,
A woman of many facets, exciting, engrossing, engaging,
impossible to predict.
One of a kind, doesn't quite fit the mold, but definitely priceless,
and a treasure, if she could only see it.

About the Author

Sari Solden, MS, MFCC, is a psychotherapist in private practice, who specializes in individual, couple and group work with ADD adults and their partners. She trains and serves as a consultant to mental health professionals in the diagnosis and treatment of adult ADD. She is a frequent presenter in local, regional, and national conferences and has contributed to national ADD publications. A graduate of the University of Michigan, she moved to the San Francisco Bay Area where she obtained a Masters Degree in clinical counseling at California State University. She holds a marriage and family counseling license (MFCC) in California. She recently returned to Michigan, where she is licensed as a professional counselor.

In addition, Ms. Solden has received several awards for her "creative writing". She also plays drums and keyboard in an amateur jazz/rock band.

Ms. Solden's son, Evan, is a college music student. She currently resides in Ann Arbor, Michigan with her husband, Dean.

ACKNOWLEDGMENTS

I want to acknowledge a long list of people who have supported me through the years, both personally and professionally.

First, I want to thank the group of people who specifically helped give shape to my ideas in order to see this project through. It was in large part the encouragement of my publisher, Tim Underwood, that gave me the impetus to undertake this project. He recognized that what I had been observing and discussing with him was important and worth writing about. I am extremely grateful to have such a wonderful executive assistant, Susan Berneis. She has been incredibly patient during the course of this project, and extremely skillful at being able to sort out my "over-creations" to turn them into understandable form. Great appreciation goes to Carol LaRusso, for her skillful and sensitive editing, through which she brought calm and order to my manuscript. It was a wonderful experience to work collaboratively with someone whose abilities and judgement I value so much. I want to acknowledge and thank Howard Morris of Frontier Productions for many of the beautiful graphics in the book. And special gratitude to Kris Vaneck, whose organizational skills I admire, and whose friendship I value. As part of the "team," I am incredibly grateful to my husband, Dean, who worked many long hours on this project and did a tremendous amount of editing and synthesizing, patiently helping to sort out and pull together my ideas. He has made an enormous contribution to this book.

I want to express deep appreciation to Dr. John Ratey, Kate Kelly, and Peggy Ramundo for their support, not just in this project, but for their warmth and encouragement in the course of our personal and professional association. Kate Kelly and Peggy Ramundo's book *You Mean I'm Not Lazy, Stupid or Crazy?!* was an important turning point for me both personally and professionally because it was the first time I read in so much depth about the real life experience of women with ADD. Dr. John Ratey's contribution to the understanding of adult ADD is immense. His two books on ADD, written with Dr. Edward Hallowell, *Driven to Distraction* and *Answers to Distraction,* have opened up worlds of understanding to countless adults who had been struggling to understand their confusing life experiences. It was a few years before I ever met Dr. Ratey that I discovered a phrase he coined that I have frequently quoted ever since when emphasizing the importance of viewing adults through . . . "The Lens of Attention."

In addition to those people I just mentioned who helped me with this current project, this book owes its culmination to experiences that started several years ago. I am well aware that I wouldn't be at this point without the support, encouragement and belief of many people along the way. I take this opportunity to express to them my sincere gratitude.

I will always appreciate the opportunity Caroline Summer gave me to enter and explore this world of invisible disorders. I thank the entire staff at Family Service Agency in San Rafael, California, for creating such a supportive and accepting environment which allowed me to grow and develop my ideas. Eternal gratitude and love to Darlene Klaif who is always with me, guiding all my work; she gave me enough room and respect to develop who I am as a therapist. Dr. Beatrice Pressley encouraged me in a quiet but powerful way to develop the creativity she saw and appreciated in me. Dr. Geraldine Alpert supported and guided me as I tried to understand my confusing set of life experiences. It was her openness to new possibilities and explanations that ultimately led me to discover the answers I needed.

When I relocated to Ann Arbor, Michigan, from California, I was given a chance early on to become part of the national ADD community by presenting my ideas at the annual adult ADD Conference held in Ann Arbor. I want to thank Jim Reisinger for giving me this opportunity.

During the last few years at conferences across the country I've had the chance to get to know many individuals in the ADD professional community. These are incredibly warm, accepting, and fun people with whom I quickly felt at home. I want to give special thanks to Dr. Kathleen Nadeau for graciously supporting and encouraging my ideas on Women and ADD.

On a personal level, I want to acknowledge Lisa Csaklos, who made my beginning work in this field so much fun, and who, by being a model of *organization*, allowed me to more clearly understand *disorganization*. Words cannot adequately express my feelings for my friend, Adriane Lonzarich, who has been there all along, with constant support and understanding. Her special gift of treasuring small moments of beauty and valuing differences, has been a continual inspiration for me. I want to mention a few long-time friends with love: Annie, who could fold clothes in perfect rows at an early age; Chi-Chi, with whom I had to flee our dorm room at midnight to escape the mess; and De-De, who got up at five A.M. to watch the moon and the stars with me. I want to express my love and appreciation to all my many other friends through the years, for their support and encouragement.

I was fortunate to grow up in a family that valued differences and creativity. I express my love and gratitude to them for the chance they gave me to develop and grow in my own way. My mother, Marion Shubow, gave me a unique combination of support, structure, and freedom that allowed me to be able to develop my strengths without having to struggle to conform to more traditional cultural expectations. My father, David Shubow, taught me the underlying principle of the creative process—that in order to create, one must first be able to destroy. This concept of thinking about the ability to disorganize as a way to create new structures influenced my ideas about living success-fully with ADD. My brother, Michael, taught me that even brilliant people, if they hate to wear wool pants, need to go on a less traditional route through life. And finally, Marie, gave me tremendous understand-ing and acceptance that has stayed with me even though she's been gone for many years.

I want to also thank Lucille Solden and the rest of my husband's family. Their encouragement and constant support has made a tremen-dous difference to me. I especially want to thank Jodi, who each day I know her, teaches me to respect the mysteries of the brain and the power of the human spirit.

I want to express great love and respect for my son, Evan, who has taught me every day of his life about the complexity and resiliency of human beings. His determination has filled me with wonder and has made me vigilant in both my work and personal life about noticing small successes and recognizing quiet strengths.

My husband and best friend, Dean, has given of himself in this project more than I even could imagine someone would give to another person. More important than the wonderful partner he has been in this project though, is the partnership we have in our life together. So much of what I know about living successfully with ADD has come as a result of our success together. It is with deep appreciation that I thank Dean for his unwavering support and love.

To all the women who struggle with disorganization and who have shared their stories with me so openly—I want to give special thanks. You inspire me each day to continue to break out of traditional molds, and spur me on to continue to find ways to compensate for my difficul-ties so that I can continue to pursue my strengths. Most importantly, I want to thank all the clients with "invisible disorders" with whom I've worked. In the face of confusion and pain, you have given me the privilege of witnessing remarkable portraits of perseverance, strength, and courage.

RESOURCES IN THE FIELD

Newsletters and Organizations

Special Interest Newsletters:

Adult ADD
Challenge, Inc., P.O. Box 2001
West Newbury, Massachusetts 01985

ATTENTION (The National CHADD newsletter)
499 NW 70th Avenue, Suite 101
Plantation, Florida 33317
(954) 587-3700

ADDendum
Editor: Paul Jaffe
Box 296
Scarborough, New York 10510

ADDult News
c/o Mary Jane Johnson
2620 Ivy Place
Toledo, Ohio 43613

Rebus Institute
1499 Bayshore Boulevard, Suite 146
Burlingame, California 94010

The ADHD Report
Guilford Publications, Inc.
72 Spring Street
New York, New York 10012
(800) 365-7006

ADDhoc AudioMagazine
800-975-0004
1155 Rosewood, Suite A
Ann Arbor, Michigan 48104

The ADDed Line
3790 Loch Highland Pkwy.
Roswell, GA 30075
(800) 982-4028

Catalogs

SourceADD catalog
1155 Rosewood, Suite A
Ann Arbor, Michigan 48104
800-975-0004

ADD Resources
Mail Order Material
154 Curtis
Valparaiso, Indiana 46383-9111
(219) 465-1655
Fax (219) 462-5141

A.D.D. WareHouse
1-800-233-9273 for catalog
(305) 792-8944
Fax (305) 792-8545

ADD Online

AmericaOnline
Adult ADD Support Group
ERICNJB@aol.com

Compuserve
Use "GO ADD" command
For more information, send mail to
70006.101@compuserve.com

Prodigy
Adult ADD Support Groups listed under
Support Groups Medical

Listservs
Numerous Internet discussion lists on
various topics pertaining to ADD

Organizational Help and Coaching topics

Coaching Matters
National Coaching Network
Post Office Box 353
Lafayette Hill, Pennsylvania 19444
Sandra Felton (provides organizational books and products)
5025 SW 114th Avenue
Miami, Florida 33165

National Association of Professional Organizers (NAPO)
1033 La Posada Drive
Austin, Texas 78752
(512) 454-3036
National Study Group on Chronic Disorganization
1142 Chatsworth Drive
Avondale Estates, Georgia 30002 (404) 231-6172

Organizations/Conferences on Adults

National Professional Consortium in Attention Deficit Disorders (NPC ADD/ADHD)
MCCG Institute for Developmental Medicine
771 Orange Street
Macon, Georgia 31201
ADDA (National Attention Deficit Disorder Association)
Post Office Box 972
Mentor, Ohio 44063

AIEN (Adult Information Exchange Network)
Post Office Box 1701
Ann Arbor, Michigan 48106
CHADD (Children and Adults with ADD)
1859 North Pine Island Road, Suite 1885
Plantation, Florida 33322
(305) 587-3700
LDA—Learning Disorders Association
4156 Library Road
Pittsburgh, Pennsylvania 15234

Information on Support Groups

CHADD (Children and Adults with ADD)
499 NW 70th Avenue, Suite 101
Plantation, Florida 33317
(954) 587-3700
National CHADD has listings of local support groups

Adult ADD Association
1225 E. Sunset Drive, Suite 640
Bellingham, WA 98226

ADDult News
c/o Mary Jane Johnson
2620 Ivy Place
Toledo, Ohio 43613
ADDult News offers information on starting support groups

BIBLIOGRAPHY

Sources

Books

ADD (ADHD and ADD Syndrome), Dr. Dale Jordan. Pro-Ed, Austin, Texas 1992

Attention Deficit Disorder: A Different Perception, Thom Hartmann. Underwood Books 1993

ADD in Adults, Dr. Lynn Weiss. Taylor Publishing, Dallas, Texas 1992

Answers to Distraction, Edward Hallowell, M.D. and John Ratey, M.D. Pantheon Books, New York 1995

A Comprehensive Guide to Attention Deficit Disorder in Adults, edited by Dr. Kathleen G. Nadeau. Brunner/Mazel, New York 1995

Diagnosing Learning Disorders, Bruce F. Pennington, Ph.D. The Guilford Press, New York 1991

Driven to Distraction, Hallowell and Ratey, Pantheon Books, New York 1994

Healing the Chaos Within: The Interaction Between ADD, Alcoholism and Growing up in an Alcoholic Home, Daniel G. Amen, M.D. (Audio/Workbook Program) 2220 Boynton Avenue, Suite C, Fairfield, California 94533

Medications for Attention Disorders: (ADHD/ADD) and Related Medical Problems. (Tourette's Syndrome, Sleep Apnea, Seizure Disorders). Edna D. Copeland, Ph.D. Resurgens Press, Atlanta, GA 1991, 1994

The Misunderstood Child, Larry Silver. McGraw TAB Books, Human Services Institute

Succeeding Against the Odds, Sally Smith. Jeremy P. Tarcher, Inc., Los Angeles, California 1991

Windows into the ADD Mind, Daniel G. Amen, M.D. (Video) 2220 Boynton Avenue, Suite C, Fairfield, California 94533

You Mean I'm Not Lazy, Stupid or Crazy?! Kate Kelly and Peggy Ramundo. Scribners, New York 1995

Articles, Tapes, Letters, etc.

"ADD and Women's Issues," Dr. Kathleen Nadeau with Sari Solden. Tape B-32, 1995 ADDA Conference, available from Repeat Performance, 2911 Crabapple Lane, Hobart, Indiana 463342 (219) 465-1234

"ADD: Not Just for Boys," Tara E. O'Brien, Warren H. Phillips, . Andrea Rubinoff. Reprinted in CHADDER, July/August 1994

"ADD in the Workplace: How Coaching and Simple Interventions can Increase Worker Productivity," Nancy Ratey, Ed.M. and Susan Sussman, M.Ed. Tape B-14, 1995 ADDA Conference. Repeat Performance

Reply to letter, page 14, John Ratey, M.D., in ADDendum, Issue 6, Fall, 1991

"Girls with Attention Deficit Disorder: A Silent Minority? a report on behavioral and cognitive characteristics," C.A. Berry, M.D., S.E.Shaywitz, M.D., B.A. Shaywitz, M.D., reprinted in *Pediatrics*, volume 76, number 5, November, 1985

"Attention Deficit Disorder without Hyperactivity," Thomas E. Brown, Ph.D., reprinted in *CHADDER*, Spring/Summer 1993

"Whatever Happened to ADD without Hyperactivity?" Dr. Dale Jordan, Director, Jones Learning Center, University of the Ozarks, Clarksville, Arkansas. Reprinted in *CHADDER*, 1991

"Living and Loving with Attention Deficit Disorder: Couples Where One partner has ADD," Edward D. Hallowell. M.D. Reprinted in *CHADDER*

"Medical Management of Adult ADD," Stephen Copps, M.D. Tape B-10, 1995 ADDA Conference. Repeat Performance

"Pharmacotherapy for ADHD in Adults," John J. Ratey, M.D. and Edward Hallowell, M.D. and catherine L. Leveroni. Reprinted by ADDA, 1225 East Sunset Drive #640, Bellingham, WA 98226-3529 (206) 647-6681

"Women and ADD," Dr. Kathleen G. Nadeau, reprinted in *ADDult News*

"Foibles, Frailties and Frustrations Seen Through the Lens of Attention," John Ratey, M.D. and Andrea Miller. Reprinted in *Challenge*, January/February 1992

Recommended Readings and References (By topic)

ADD and Women

You Mean I'm Not Lazy, Stupid or Crazy?! Kate Kelly and Peggy Ramundo., Scribners, 1995

"ADD: Not Just for Boys," Tara E. O'Brien, Warren H. Phillips, Andrea Rubinoff Reprinted in *CHADDER*, July/August 1994

"ADD Women: How They are Different," Sari Solden, M.S., M.F.C.C, in *Challenge*, Vol. 9, No. 2, March/April 1995

"Special Diagnostic and Treatment Considerations in Women with Attention Deficit Disorder," Chapter written by John Ratey, M.D., Andrea C. Miller and Dr. Kathleen Nadeau, in *A Comprehensive Guide to Attention Deficit Disorder in Adults*, edited by Dr. Kathleen G. Nadeau.

"Perchance to Dream," Chapter 6 on women in *Answers to Distraction* by Edward Hallowell and John Ratey

"Women and ADD," Dr. Kathleen G. Nadeau, reprinted in *ADDult News*

"ADD and Women's Issues," Dr. Kathleen Nadeau with Sari Solden. Tape B-32, 1995 ADDA Conference. Repeat Performance

"Women and ADD; Take Back your Life," Sari Solden, 1995. Tape 3-G, Repeat Performance

"Women and ADD: Coming Out of the Messy Closet," Sari Solden, Tape of Session of the AIEN 1994 Conference at The University of Michigan, Ann Arbor. Take Two Recording and Duplicating Service, 1155 Rosewood, Suite 700, Ann Arbor, Michigan 48104

"Why Housekeeping is the Worst Job in the World," Dr. Kathleen Nadeau, Tape of Session of the AIEN 1994 Conference at The University of Michigan, Ann Arbor. Take Two Recording and Duplicating Service

"Girls with Attention Deficit Disorder: A Silent Minority? a report on behavioral and cognitive characteristics," C.A. Berry, M.D., S.E.Shaywitz, M.D., B.A. Shaywitz, M.D., reprinted in *Pediatrics*, volume 76, number 5, November, 1985

ADD and Intimacy
"Living and Loving with Attention Deficit Disorder: Couples Where One partner has ADD," Edward D. Hallowell. M.D. Reprinted in *CHADDER*

"The Biology of Intimacy in ADD," John Ratey, M.D. Tape B-18, 1995 ADDA Conference. Repeat Performance

ADD in Adults, Dr. Lynn Weiss. Chapter 11. Taylor Publishing, Dallas, Texas 1992

ADD Without Hyperactivity
"Differential Diagnosis of ADD vs. ADHD" Chapter 6 in *A Comprehensive Guide to Attention Deficit Disorder in Adults*, edited by Dr. Kathleen G. Nadeau. Chapter written by Dr. Thomas Brown

"Attention Deficit Disorders: 'Without' and 'Beyond' Hyperactivity," Thomas E. Brown, Ph.D. Tape KN-2, 1995 ADDA Conference. Repeat Performance

"Attention Deficit Disorder without Hyperactivity," Thomas E. Brown, Ph.D., reprinted in *CHADDER*. Spring/Summer 1993

"Validity of the Diagnostic category of Attention Deficit Disorder without Hyperactivity: a review," B. B. Lahey, C. L. carlson, in *Journal of Learning Disabilities*, 24:110-120, 1991

"Whatever Happened to ADD without Hyperactivity?" Dr. Dale Jordan, Director, Jones Learning Center, University of the Ozarks, Clarksville, Arkansas. Reprinted in *CHADDER*, 1991

Disorganization in Adults/Coaching
"A Bridge Over Troubled Waters," By Sari Solden, M.S., M.F.C.C. Printed in *Coaching Matters*, National Coaching Network. Post Office Box 353, Lafayette Hill, Pennsylvania 1944

Organizing for the Creative Person: Right Brain Styles for Conquering Clutter, Mastering Time and Reaching your Goals, Dorothy Lehmkuhl and Dolores Cotter Lamping. Crown Publishers

You Mean I'm Not Lazy, Stupid or Crazy?! Kate Kelly and Peggy Ramundo. Scribners, 1995

"Two Heads are Better Than One: The Ins and Outs of Being an ADD Coach," Susan Sussman, M. Ed. and Nancy Ratey, Ed.M. Tape W-8, 1995 ADDA Conference. Repeat Performance

"Taming the Time Monster," Peggy Ramundo. Tape B-21, 1995 ADDA Conference. Repeat Performance

Substance Abuse and ADD
Healing the Chaos Within: The Interaction Between ADD, Alcoholism and Growing up in an Alcoholic Home, Daniel G. Amen, M.D. (Audio/Workbook Program) 2220 Boynton Avenue, Suite C, Fairfield, California94533

"Sorting Out Chemical Abuse and ADD," Dr. Lynn Weiss. Tape 5-D AIEN 1995 Conference at The University of Michigan, Ann Arbor. Repeat Performance

ADD and the Law

Attention Deficit Disorder and the Law, Peter and Patricia Latham, J.D. JKL Communications, 1016 16th Street SW, Washington, DC 20036

ADD and College

ADD and the College Student, Patricia O. Quinn, editor. Magination Press (Division of Brunner/Mazel) 1994

Survival Guide for College Students with ADD or LD, Dr. Kathleen G. Nadeau. Magination Press, 1994

"ADD and the College Student," Pat and Peter Latham, J.D. and Dr. Kathleen Nadeau, Ph.D. Tape W-5, 1995 ADDA Conference. Repeat Performance

ADD and Work

Succeeding in the Workplace, Peter and Patricia Latham, J.D. JKL Communications

Focus Your Energy, Thom Hartmann. Pocket Books, New York, 1994.

A Comprehensive Guide to Attention Deficit Disorder in Adults, Dr. Kathleen G. Nadeau, editor. Chapter 16, "ADD in the Workplace" by Dr. Kathleen Nadeau

"Don't Bite the Hand that Feeds You: or, Helping Your Employer Accommodate You," Pat Boyd, for Lisa Poast. Reprinted in *Rebus Report,* Spring 1995

"ADD in the Workplace: How Coaching and Simple Interventions can Increase Worker Productivity," Nancy Ratey, Ed.M. and Sue Sussman, M.Ed. Tape B-14, 1995 ADDA Conference. Repeat Performance

Children through Adults (LD/ADD)

ADD: Why Johnny can't Concentrate, Dr. Robert Moss. Bantam Books, 1990

The Hyperactive Child, Adolescent and Adult: ADD Through the Lifespan, Dr. Paul Wender. Oxford University Press 1987

Attention Deficit Disorder in Adults Workbook, Dr. Lynn Weiss. Taylor Publishing, Dallas, Texas 1994

Keeping a Head in School, Mel Levine, M.D. Educators Publishing Service, Inc., 1990

The Misunderstood Child, Larry Silver. McGraw TAB Books, Human Services Institute

Living with a Learning Disability, Barbara Cordoni. Southern Illinois University Press, 1987

Succeeding Against the Odds, Sally Smith. Jeremy P. Tarcher, Inc., Los Angeles, California 1991

ADD Self-Assessments

"Adult ADD Questionnaire," Dr. Kathleen G. Nadeau. Annandale, Virginia, Chesapeake Psychological Services

"Brown Attention Deficit Disorder Scales (BADD)," Thomas E. Brown, Ph.D. San Antonio, Texas, The Psychological Corporation, in publication

"Copeland Symptom Checklist for Adult Attention Deficit Disorders," Edna D. Copeland, Ph.D. MCCG Institute for Developmental Medicine, 771 Orange Street, Macon, Georgia 31201

"Jordan Diagnostic Checklist," in *ADD (ADHD and ADD Syndrome)* by Dr. Dale Jordan, Pro-Ed, Austin Texas, 1992

"20 diagnostic criteria," Edward Hallowell and John Ratey, in *Driven to Distraction*

ADD Adult Strategies and Issues

"Attention Deficit Disorder in Adults," Melissa Thomasson, Ph.D., reprinted in *Challenge*, Volume 5, number 5, September/October 1991

Attention Deficit Disorder in Adults Workbook, Dr. Lynn Weiss. Taylor Publishing, Dallas, Texas 1994

"Fifty Tips for Coping With Adult ADD," Edward Hallowell, M.D. and John Ratey, M.D. Reprinted in *CHADDER*, January 1993

"The ADD Family: Turning Chaos into Order," Kate Kelly, M.S.N., R.N. Tape B-19, 1995 ADDA Conference. Repeat Performance

ADD and Medication

Medications for Attention Disorders: (ADHD/ADD) and Related Medical Problems. (Tourette's Syndrome, Sleep Apnea, Seizure Disorders). Edna D. Copeland, Ph.D. Resurgens Press, Atlanta, Georgia, 1991, 1994

"Medical Management of Adult ADD," Stephen Copps, M.D. Tape B-10, 1995 ADDA Conference. Repeat Performance

"Pharmacotherapy for ADHD in Adults," John J. Ratey, M.D., Edward Hallowell, M.D. and catherine L. Leveroni. Reprinted by ADDA, 1225 East Sunset Drive #640, Bellingham, WA 98226-3529, (206) 647-6681

A Comprehensive Guide to Attention Deficit Disorder in Adults, Dr. Kathleen G. Nadeau, editor. Chapter 10, "Pharmacotherapy of Adult ADHD" by Timothy H. Wilens, Thomas J. Spencer and Joseph Biederman

Neurobiology of ADD

"The Neurobiology of Attention Deficit Hyperactive Disorder, From Cerebral Glucose Metabolism in Adults with Hyperactivity of Childhood Onset," Alan Zametkin, M.D. In the *New England Journal of Medicine*, 323, 1361-1366

Driven to Distraction, Hallowell and Ratey. Chapter 8, pp. 235-244. Chapter 9

A Comprehensive Guide to Attention Deficit Disorder in Adults, Dr. Kathleen G. Nadeau, editor. Chapter 2 by Patricia Quinn

You Mean I'm Not Lazy, Stupid or Crazy?!, Kate Kelly and Peggy Ramundo. pp. 17-20

Medications for Attention Disorders: (ADHD/ADD) and Related Medical Problems. (Tourette's Syndrome, Sleep Apnea, Seizure Disorders). Edna D. Copeland, Ph.D. Resurgens Press, Atlanta, Georgia, 1991, 1994

"Genetics and Neurobiology of ADD," David E. Comings, M.D. and Robert Hunt, M.D. Tape GS-3 AIEN 1995 Conference, The University of Michigan, Ann Arbor. Repeat Performance

INDEX